T0140628

The Information Retrieval Series

Volume 48

Information Retrieval (IR) deals with access to and search in mostly unstructured information, in text, audio, and/or video, either from one large file or spread over separate and diverse sources, in static storage devices as well as on streaming data. It is part of both computer and information science, and uses techniques from e.g. mathematics, statistics, machine learning, database management, or computational linguistics. Information Retrieval is often at the core of networked applications, web-based data management, or large-scale data analysis.

The Information Retrieval Series presents monographs, edited collections, and advanced text books on topics of interest for researchers in academia and industry alike. Its focus is on the timely publication of state-of-the-art results at the forefront of research and on theoretical foundations necessary to develop a deeper understanding of methods and approaches.

This series is abstracted/indexed in EI Compendex and Scopus.

Jiqun Liu

A Behavioral Economics Approach to Interactive Information Retrieval

Understanding and Supporting Boundedly Rational Users

Jiqun Liu
School of Library and Information Studies
University of Oklahoma
Norman, OK, USA

ISSN 1871-7500 ISSN 2730-6836 (electronic)
The Information Retrieval Series
ISBN 978-3-031-23231-2 ISBN 978-3-031-23229-9 (eBook)
https://doi.org/10.1007/978-3-031-23229-9

This Springer imprint is published by the registered company Springer Nature Switzerland AG
The registered company address is: Gewerbestrasse 11, 6330 Cham, Switzerland

For my wife Jixin for her unconditional love, understanding, and support that make this book project possible.

Foreword

Since the early days of computer-based information retrieval (IR), there has been a steady, although relatively small, stream of research and theory supporting the view of IR as inherently interactive, and therefore necessarily concerned with including the person as an actor in the IR system. Already in the early 1960s, various researchers, both librarians (Taylor, 1962) and IR system designers (e.g., Doyle, 1963), were pointing out the dynamic and negotiable nature of the "information need," which has brought the person to engage with the IR system. Taylor (1968) made this point succinctly: ". . . in this paper, an inquiry [to an IR system] is looked upon not as a command, as in conventional search strategy, but rather as a description of an area of doubt in which the question is open-ended, negotiable, and dynamic."

Building on this early work, and in concert with the emergence of cognitive science in the mid- to late 1970s, a "cognitive viewpoint" in information science began to take shape. As applied to IR, this view stressed that IR systems and the people using those systems needed to construct accurate and dynamic models of one another, in order to engage in interaction leading to effective information retrieval. Following the ideas of the cognitive viewpoint, in the 1990s, researchers in both information science-oriented IR and, to some extent, computer science-oriented IR began to explicitly investigate the nature of interaction in IR systems.

These lines of research, and their results, led to the emergence of a specific subfield of IR, now known as interactive information retrieval (IIR). In general, IIR considers the nature of the interaction as a cooperative and collaborative conversation among the person engaged with the system and the other actors in the system, e.g., the interface and representation and retrieval subsystems. This stance has led to a substantial body of theory and research, exemplified by two highly significant texts: Ingwersen and Järvelin's (2005) *The Turn: Integration of Information Seeking and Retrieval in Context* and Ruthven and Kelly's (2011) edited volume, *Interactive Information Seeking, Behavior and Retrieval*. A central tenet of this approach, based on both theory and experiment, has consistently remained that, for the IR interaction to be effective, the IR system must hold an accurate and dynamic model of the person interacting with it.

Despite this extensive record of theory and research supporting the necessity of understanding the person interacting with the IR system, and despite pleas to consider the user of the IR system in IR system research and design, from researchers including the ACM SIGIR Salton Award honorees Karen Spärck Jones (1988) and Tefko Saracevic (1997), mainstream computer science-oriented IR, for the most part, remained stubbornly wedded to a system-oriented paradigm, concentrating on document (information) representation, retrieval models, and ranking mechanisms, considering the person as solely a query input device.

Recently, however, some change in this attitude has become evident. The ability of systems to engage in voice conversations with people has led to substantive research in conversational IR, which requires meaningful interaction between system and person, even to the extent of some degree of understanding of the person's motivations and characteristics. As evidence mounts that people engage in search *sessions*, IR researchers have begun to develop models of searchers' behavior over the course of a search session, based on empirical observation or theoretical considerations. Simple, strictly behavioral search models are being enhanced by considering characteristics of the searcher, such as such as preferences or search intent. And it has been noted that evaluation measures of IIR system performance depend upon the model of the searcher that they imply and that, therefore, proper evaluation requires appropriate search models. Such models have been suggested as the basis for simulating searcher behavior in offline evaluation of IIR systems, as well as for the design of interaction strategies. This emerging (re)turn in mainstream computer science-oriented IR research to recognition of the importance of understanding and modeling the person who engages with the IR system, in the design and evaluation of such systems, is both welcome and highly promising. But much still needs to be done to realize this promise, in particular identification of the characteristics of the person most salient to understanding and modeling search behavior.

The book at hand presents a new and significant step in this quest. Models of search behavior to date have all made strong simplifying assumptions, in particular in assuming uniform and "rational" action on the part of the searcher. But this assumption flies in the face of what we actually know about people's decision-making. Understanding *why* people behave in the ways that they actually do, in apparent contradiction to what one would expect of economically "rational actors," is fundamental to developing models of search behavior that can be used for effective design, simulation, and evaluation.

In this book, Jiqun Liu convincingly proposes the framework of *behavioral economics* for precisely the purpose of understanding and taking account of what we know of how and why people actually behave, in order to understand and model search behavior and to appropriately design and evaluate IIR systems. He begins by providing a nice exposition of the relevant work in psychology and economics, which undergirds this approach to understanding human behavior, and demonstrates, through theoretical argument and exposition, its potential application to understanding and modeling people's search behaviors. He continues with an extensive review and critique of existing models of search behavior and of IR system evaluation, from the point of view of the behavioral economics framework. Finally, he demonstrates the practical application and promise of use of this framework, by describing and presenting results of research using it.

The framework presented in this book clearly provides the basis for a new and more realistic understanding and modeling of searcher behavior and, therefore, for more effective design and more realistic evaluation of IR systems. It is a major step toward realizing the goal, proposed in the earliest days of IR, of truly person-centered interactive information retrieval.

October 30, 2022
New Brunswick, NJ, USA

Nicholas J. Belkin
Distinguished Professor, Emeritus,
School of Communication and Information,
Rutgers University

References

Doyle, L. B. (1963). *Is relevance an adequate criterion in information retrieval evaluation?* Technical report SP-1262, System Development Corporation.

Ingwersen, P., & Järvelin, K. (2005). *The turn: Integration of information seeking and retrieval in context.* Springer.

Ruthven, I., & Kelly, D. (Eds.). (2011) *Interactive information seeking, behaviour and retrieval.* Facet Publishing.

Saracevic, T. (1997). Users lost: Reflections on the past, future, and limits of information science. *SIGIR Forum, 31*(2), 16–27.

Spärck Jones, K. (1988). A look back and a look forward. In *Proceedings of the 11th annual international ACM SIGIR conference on research and development in information retrieval* (pp. 13–29). ACM.

Taylor, R. S. (1962). The process of asking questions. *American Documentation, 13* (4), 391–396.

Taylor, R. S. (1968). Question-Negotiation and Information Seeking in Libraries. *College & Research Libraries, 29*(3), 178–194. https://doi.org/10.5860/crl_29_03_178.

Preface

Understanding how people behave and why people behave in such ways is a central topic to information seeking and retrieval as well as a variety of other scientific disciplines and areas concerning human behavior research, such as cognitive psychology and behavioral economics, learning, and education. There is substantial empirical evidence demonstrating that people are predictably irrational and usually rely on existing beliefs, heuristics, and mental shortcuts, especially when they are making decisions under uncertainty regarding available resources, situational restrictions, and possible outcomes. For example, health information searchers may easily trust online medical information that confirms their existing opinions and expectations. When learning a new topic, students often heavily rely on top-ranked search results on search engine result pages and stop at short satisficing answers rather than exploring more informative and credible information sources. Online shoppers are likely to quickly accept immediate mediocre recommendations after encountering several bad-quality products (triggering low reference levels in mind), without examining all available items.

Despite the findings on human biases and cognitive limits from multiple disciplines, many existing formal user models in information retrieval (IR) and other computing fields were built upon psychologically unrealistic assumptions about perfect user rationality. Consequently, the IR community still faces significant challenges when seeking to bridge the gap that separate users' beliefs and actual behaviors from the predictions made by rational normative models and simulation algorithms. Since decision makers are boundedly rational, they often act intuitively without conducting complex utility estimations and are subject to multiple systematic biases when making search decisions under uncertainty. Investigating users' *bounded rationality*, which are not compatible with the assumptions underpinning most IR algorithms and mechanistic analyses, would break new ground for user modeling and behavior prediction. It would also enable intelligent systems of varying modalities to better support users' decisions both within and beyond interactive information seeking, searching, and recommendation.

To achieve this goal, this book brings together the insights from three areas, *Information Seeking and Retrieval*, *Cognitive Psychology*, and *Behavioral Economics*, and shows how this new interdisciplinary approach can advance our knowledge about users interacting with diverse search systems, especially their seemingly irrational decisions and anomalies that could not be predicted by normative models. The first part of this book introduces the general notions and foundations of this new approach, as well as the main concepts, terminologies, and theories. The second part describes the systematic biases and cognitive limits confirmed by behavioral experiments of varying types and explains in detail how they contradict the assumptions and predictions of formal models in IR. The third part first synthesizes the findings from existing preliminary research on bounded rationality and behavioral economics modeling in information seeking, retrieval, and recommender system communities. Then, it discusses the implications, open questions, and methodological challenges of applying the behavioral economics framework to different sub-areas of IR research and practices, such as modeling users and search sessions, developing unbiased learning to rank algorithms and adaptive recommender systems, implementing bias-aware intelligent task support, as well as extending the conceptualization and evaluation on IR fairness, accountability, transparency, and ethics (FATE) with the knowledge regarding both human biases and algorithmic biases.

This book introduces behavioral economics framework to IR students and scientists seeking a new perspective on both fundamental and new emerging problems of IR as well as the development and evaluation of *bias-aware* intelligent information systems. This book is especially intended for researchers working on IR and human-information interaction who want to learn about the potential offered by behavioral economics in their own research areas. Overall, with the first thorough review and discussion on this new exciting research field, our work offers graduate students and researchers a comprehensive report on the interdisciplinary insights, state-of-the-art results and techniques, open questions, as well as new research opportunities on both user and system sides. We hope that this book can serve as a useful starting point for studying human-bias-aware IR and encourage students and researchers from diverse backgrounds to further advance the science and technology on supporting boundedly rational people interacting with information and AI-powered search systems.

Norman, OK, USA Jiqun Liu

Contents

Acronyms

BITS	Bias-aware intelligent task support
CACM	Context-aware click model
CBDT	Case-based decision theory
CIS	Conversational information seeking
CM	Cascade model
DCTR	Document-based clickthrough rate model
DL	Deep learning
EDT	Expectation disconfirmation theory
ERR	Expected reciprocal rank
FATE	Fairness, accountability, transparency, and ethics
FCM	Federated click model
HCI	Human-computer interaction
HMM	Hidden Markov model
IB	Information behavior
IIR	Interactive information retrieval
IR	Information retrieval
IS	Information seeking
LTR	Learning to rank
MDP	Markov decision process
ML	Machine learning
nDCG	Normalized discounted cumulative gain
NLP	Natural language processing
PBM	Position-based model
PCM	Personalized click model
PRP	Probability ranking principle
RBP	Rank-biased precision
RCM	Random click model
RCTR	Rank-based clickthrough rate model
RL	Reinforcement learning
RR	Reciprocal rank

RS	Recommender system
SERP	Search engine result page
SIGIR	Special Interest Group on Information Retrieval
TCM	Task-centric click model
TREC	Text Retrieval Conference
UBM	User browsing model
ULTR	Unbiased learning to rank
VCM	Vertical click model

Part I
Foundation

Chapter 1
Introduction

Abstract Understanding how people behave and why people behave in such ways is a central topic to information retrieval (IR) as well as a variety of other scientific disciplines concerning human behavior research. There is substantial empirical evidence demonstrating that people are predictably irrational and usually rely on existing beliefs, heuristics, and mental shortcuts, especially when they are making decisions under time pressure and uncertainty. However, features of human biases and bounded rationality are usually ignored or abstracted out from formal user models, which may lead to errors in simulating and predicting search behaviors and challenges in modeling users' in situ search experiences. In this book, we seek to synthesize the insights regarding bounded rationality from behavioral economics, cognitive psychology, and information seeking and interactive IR (IIR) research and develop, a behavioral economics approach to modeling and supporting boundedly rational users engaging in search interactions. This beginning chapter provides an overview of the background and motivations behind our research and outlines the structure of this book.

1.1 Background

Scholars in the area of information seeking and retrieval (IS&R) often seek to understand, support, and evaluate multiple aspects of people's interactions with information through varying channels and intermediaries (e.g., librarian, friends and families, information search systems). Understanding how people behave and why people behave in such ways is a central topic to IS&R as well as a variety of other scientific disciplines concerning human behavior research, such as cognitive psychology, behavioral economics, learning, and education. There is substantial evidence from cognitive psychology and behavioral economics, demonstrating that people are predictably irrational and usually rely on existing beliefs, heuristics, and mental shortcuts, especially when they are making decisions under time pressure and uncertainty regarding available options and resources, restrictions, and possible outcomes (Camerer, 1999; Conlisk, 1996; Kahneman, 2003; Thaler, 2016). These characteristics of *bounded rationality* contribute to the individual differences in

J. Liu, *A Behavioral Economics Approach to Interactive Information Retrieval*, The Information Retrieval Series 48, https://doi.org/10.1007/978-3-031-23229-9_1

human behavior and increases the challenges of predicting human activities and experience. According to Simon (1955), bounded rationality refers to a broad scope of descriptive, normative, and prescriptive explanations of effective human behavior that deviates from the assumptions and predictions of perfect rationality. Due to the boundaries and situational limits of human rationality, people cannot access or examine all possible alternatives and thus often attempt to satisfice or make *good enough* choices in decision-making, rather than to optimize (Kahneman, 2003). Also, individuals' preferences in judgments are usually determined by changes in outcomes relative to certain reference levels (e.g., pre-interaction expectations, prior outcomes from a similar scenario, existing beliefs, opinions, and experiences from other people).

Investigating, understanding, and predicting the impact of human bounded rationality is a key step toward modeling human behavior and experience across varying contexts in a more accurate manner. The impacts of bounded rationality appear to be straightforward and intuitive in real-life tasks and are often considered as part of human nature that constantly shapes and sometimes determines the choices and judgments at both individual and group levels. However, in scientific research, the impacts of bounded rationality are usually abstracted out of formal models mainly for reducing computational complexity and hidden in unobserved contextual variations and random errors behind mathematical functions and statistical models. One of the widely employed justification is that although there are individual differences and sub-optimal behaviors at local levels, people are generally rational at population level, and formal rational models are still robust in terms of capturing the majority of variances and characterizing statistically significant between-group differences in behaviors and judgments. However, in both research and real-life applications, we constantly observe systematic, ubiquitous deviations of real-life human behavior from the optimized results of rational models, significant divergences between human judgment and model predictions, as well as users' confusions and frustrations with system recommendations offered based on algorithmic simulations. To improve the performance and experience of human-information interaction, it is critical for researchers to further understand the constraints and limits around users and leverage the learned knowledge in designing adaptive and proactive system implicit nudges, interventions, and explicit recommendations.

Exploring individual user's characteristics (e.g., knowledge state, emotional state, cognitive loads, search skills) and situational factors (e.g., task facets, external search interruptions, social interactions) is not uncommon, especially in interactive information seeking and retrieval research (Belkin, 2008; Ingwersen, 1996; Liu, 2021). Going beyond system-oriented factors (e.g., textual features of documents, rank position, search result surrogate presentation), it is critical to investigate how *boundedly rational* users actually decide their search tactics (e.g., query abandonment and reformulation, continue browsing, clicking) and evaluate retrieved information (e.g., relevance, usefulness, credibility) and their overall search experience (e.g., task load, user engagement, search satisfaction) in uncertain scenarios. In addition, how system features (e.g., algorithmic biases, personalized recommendations) interact with human biases and cognitive limits still remains an open challenge. Among varying user and search context factors explored in IS&R research, factors closely related to bounded rationality (especially human cognitive and perceptual biases) have received less research attention than other factors, such as search task facets (Li & Belkin, 2008; Liu, 2021), users' knowledge regarding the search topics and domain (Liu et al., 2016; Wildemuth, 2004), and search system components (Capra et al., 2013; Kelly & Azzopardi, 2015).

While some researchers from IS&R communities have explored the role and effects of bounded rationality at different phases of information seeking (e.g., query formulation and information need expression, browsing, search stopping and abandonment, information evaluation) (e.g., Agosto, 2002; Azzopardi, 2021; Mansourian & Ford, 2007), many existing formal models and offline evaluation metrics of information retrieval (IR) were built upon psychologically unrealistic assumptions about user rationality in search interactions, such as unlimited computing capability, linear browsing style, objective and consistent evaluation criteria, and equal static sensitivity to perceived gains and losses. These (over)simplified assumptions can reduce the computational complexity in training models and fine-tuning parameters and allow researchers to bypass unknown deviations of users' actual behavioral patterns from what is normatively expected based on rational models. Nevertheless, formal models built upon these assumptions often face obstacles when seeking to characterize seemingly irrational effects and biased judgments that systematically deviate from mathematically optimal options, such as reference dependence bias, anchoring bias, decoy effect, peak-end rule in evaluation, and effects of expectation disconfirmation (Azzopardi, 2021; Kahneman, 2003; Liu & Han, 2020). A deeper issue behind the scenes is that we cannot rely on one model to accomplish two largely different, sometimes even opposite goals, namely, to depict optimal behavioral patterns derived from rational models (how users *should* behave) and to predict the search strategies, evaluation criteria, and decisions from users engaging in real-life information seeking episodes (how users *actually* behave).

In this book, we will synthesize the insights from behavioral economics, cognitive psychology, and information seeking and interactive IR (IIR) communities on bounded rationality as the foundation (see Fig. 1.1). The book will also review recent empirical and experimental research that examines varying human biases, behavioral patterns, and evaluation strategies related to different aspects of bounded rationality. Apart from IIR studies, we will also include research that demonstrates the impacts of bounded rationality on user judgments from closely related fields, such as recommender systems (RecSys) and human-computer interaction (HCI). Furthermore, we will discuss the value and implications of applying behavioral economics framework to IR problems as well as new directions for different areas of IR practices, such as user modeling, learning to rank (L2R) algorithms, bias-aware IR evaluation and meta-evaluation, user interface and search recommendation design, as well as FATE (fairness, accountability, transparency, and ethics) in IR. This book introduces behavioral economics framework to IR scientists and graduate students seeking a new perspective on fundamental and empirical problems of interactive IR as well as the development and evaluation of user-oriented intelligent information systems.

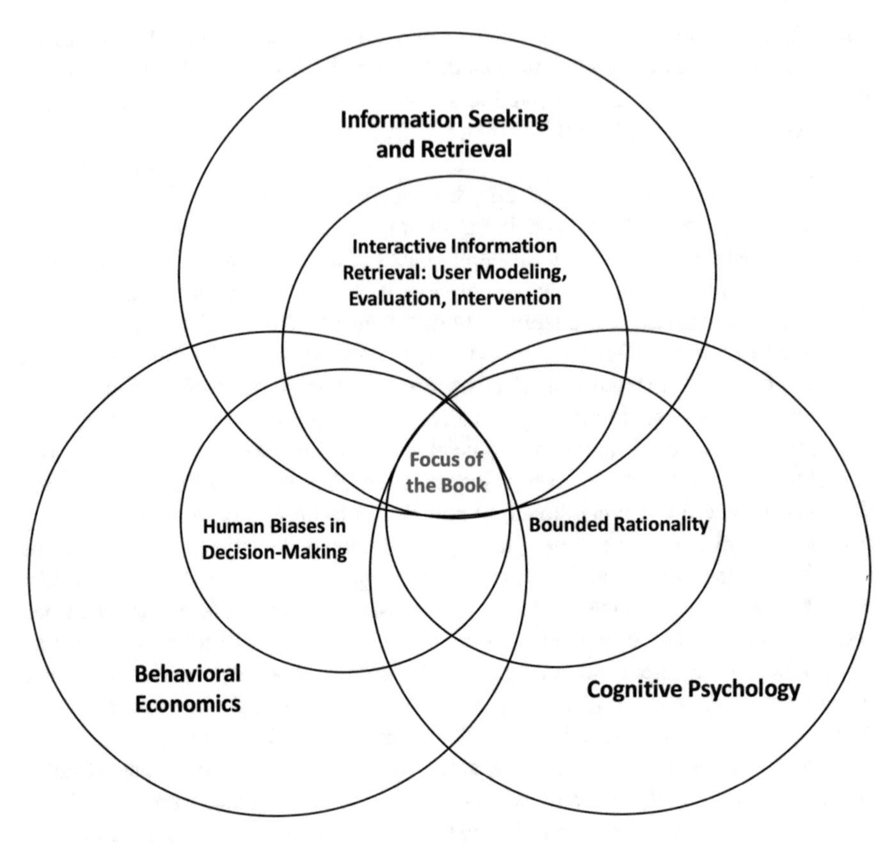

Fig. 1.1 Focus of this book

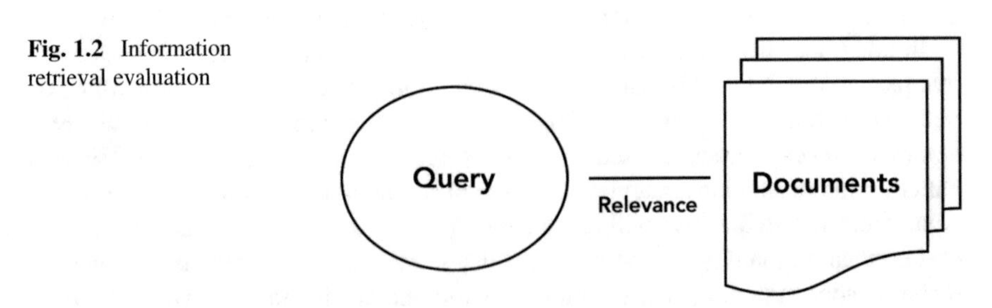

Fig. 1.2 Information retrieval evaluation

In classical IR research, a long-standing focus is to find documents that are *relevant* to a predefined information need (which is usually represented by a search *query*) and rank them higher than other less relevant documents in result lists (see Fig. 1.2). To achieve this goal, researchers have investigated different stages and components of IR processes, such as indexing and metadata, query analysis, search result and document representation, as well as ranking models. In addition, researchers have developed a variety of *relevance-based offline evaluation metrics*, such as precision, recall, reciprocal rank (RR), and discounted cumulative gain

(DCG), in order to evaluate and compare the performance of different IR systems or ranking algorithms with standard test collections (Harman, 2011). *Cranfield paradigm* as the mainstream evaluation approach has been widely applied in IR evaluation experiments. Under the standard experimental settings, researchers often run multiple candidate systems or ranking algorithms based on the same set of test collections across a wide range of predefined topics or queries (Harman, 2011; Voorhees, 2001). The performance of each system can be evaluated using the metric scores computed based on *query-document relevance* (*qrels*) (e.g., average precision or DCG scores across all topics included in the test collections).

The well-controlled settings and externally labelled relevance levels in Cranfield experiments allow researchers to test and compare systems on the same empirical basis and reuse test collections in future experiments and replication studies. Due to the strength, Cranfield experiment has been conducted through a variety of IR evaluation conferences and competitions, such as Text REtrieval Conference (TREC),[1] NII Test Collection for Information Resources (NTCIR),[2] and Conference and Labs of the Evaluation Forum (CLEF).[3] These Cranfield-based evaluation conferences have contributed to the development of many high-quality test collections. For instance, TREC-8 ad hoc collection contains high-quality manual runs included for pool construction and a large set of relevance judgments and has been reused in evaluating a series of new IR systems and ranking algorithms, which are developed after test collection itself was built (Voorhees, 2018). In recent years, this experiment paradigm goes beyond traditional document retrieval space and has been applied in new modalities of ad hoc retrieval evaluation, such as passage retrieval (Khattab & Zaharia, 2020), dataset retrieval (Kato et al., 2020), and conversational IR (Wadhwa & Zamani, 2021), and under new evaluation criteria and restrictions, such as fairness (Biega et al., 2018; Singh & Joachims, 2018), diversity (Clarke et al., 2008; Sakai & Zeng, 2019), and protection of sensitive contents and user privacy (Sayed & Oard, 2019).

Cranfield experiments and ad hoc retrieval evaluation studies enable researchers to turn complex IR problems into testable mathematical problems and to accurately compare the performances of IR systems within well-controlled, predictable settings. However, IR activities usually happen within diverse and changing contexts (e.g., tasks of varying types) and are affected by users' behavioral patterns and cognitive abilities (see Fig. 1.3). The Cranfield paradigm and associated studies do not take into account the possible impacts of user characteristics and the situations in which individuals interact with information and IR systems. One of the main reasons at the methodological level is that collecting information regarding these human and situational aspects would significantly increase the cost of labeling. Also, some of the labels heavily rely on users' own in situ perceptions and annotations (e.g., information seeking intention, emotional state, in situ usefulness judgment), which

[1] https://trec.nist.gov/

[2] http://research.nii.ac.jp/ntcir/index-en.html

[3] http://www.clef-initiative.eu/

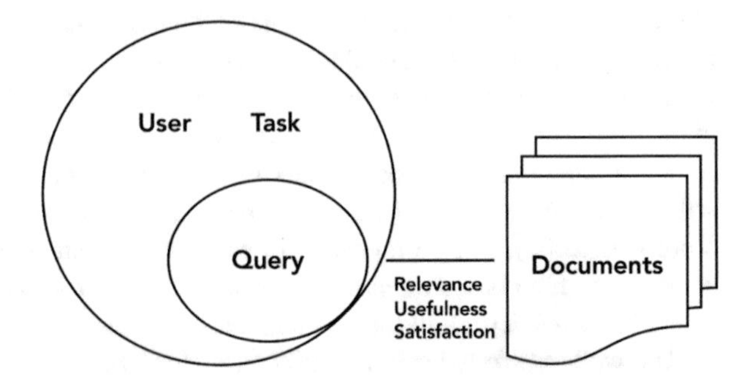

Fig. 1.3 User-centered information retrieval evaluation

may introduce new biases into data and trained models. Many of the user features and situational factors, which have received growing attention from information seeking and IIR communities and been investigated in individual user studies, may contribute to the systematic deviations of user behaviors and judgments from optimized outputs produced by "perfect" simulations.

As shown in Fig. 1.3, under a user-centered perspective, IIR researchers tend to evaluate the performance of systems over multiple dimensions, such as relevance, usefulness, and satisfaction. Differing from externally annotated relevance labels, usefulness scores measure the extent to which a document or search result item is *practically useful* for accomplishing the overarching search task or goal (Cole et al., 2009). Given this nature, usefulness labeling often relies on users' perceptions and judgments, which makes it challenging to reuse the related research resources in future evaluation experiments. Similarly, satisfaction level refers to which users are satisfied with their search outcome and experience. Recent empirical studies have shown that users' document judgments and levels of satisfaction are affected by a variety of cognitive, perceptual, and situational factors, which goes beyond explicit query-document relevance and relevance-based metric scores of SERPs (Liu & Han, 2020; Scholer et al., 2013). Apart from in situ and session-level evaluation, user and situational factors also affect other stages of IR processes and shape the way in which users decide their search tactics and query reformulation strategies (Azzopardi, 2021; Liu et al., 2019a, b). In addition, the interaction between system outputs (e.g., retrieved documents, images, knowledge cards, recommended queries) and users may also be affected and even reinforced by potential algorithmic biases (e.g., rank position bias, popularity bias, biases in learning to rank processes). This book will further analyze the impacts of users' bounded rationality on search sessions and discuss the possible interaction between user biases and algorithmic biases in later chapters.

Previous theories and research on bounded rationality encourage IS&R researchers to reconsider human-information interactions, especially those under uncertain conditions and multifaceted biases, within a decision-making framework presented in Fig. 1.4, and investigate how users' actual behaviors and judgments differ from the predictions and estimations made from formal models. In addition, the insights regarding how users behave under cognitive and contextual constraints may also help improve the transparency and explainability of user behavioral models

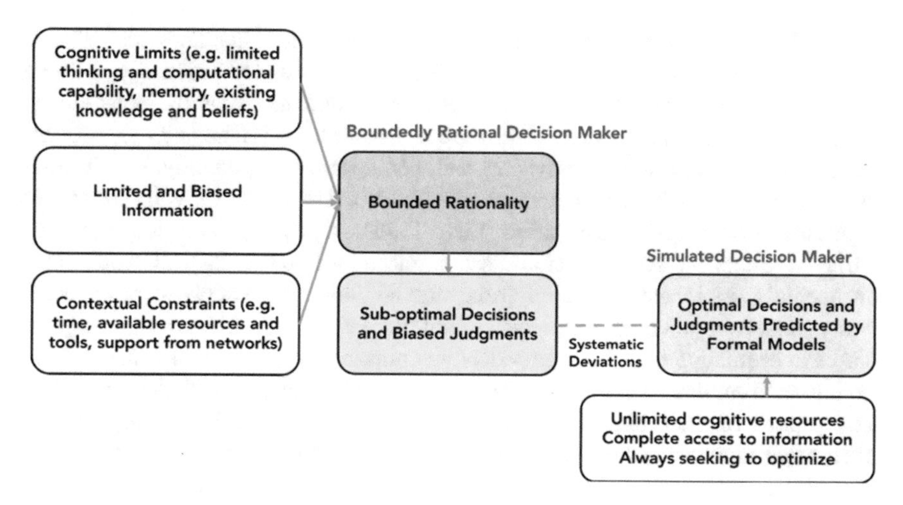

Fig. 1.4 Bounded rationality

trained based on interaction log data. Within the area of IR, the knowledge learned about user characteristics, particularly bounded rationality, and contexts of search call for a deep reflection and re-examination on the formal user models (e.g., click models, browsing models, models of search result evaluation), evaluation metrics and meta-evaluation strategies, as well as evaluation experiment design established in various experiments. Among different facets and components of bounded rationality, *human biases* at multiple levels (e.g., behavioral, cognitive, perceptual) have received a majority of attention in behavioral science areas (e.g., behavioral economics, cognitive psychology) (Kahneman, 2003). This may be because compared to other less salient boundaries of human rationality (e.g., limited memory and computing capability; restrictions in varying resources that lead to satisficing instead of optimized decisions), human biases often lead to significant, observable differences and changes in critical decision-making scenarios and outcomes. However, it is often challenging to measure and compare the impacts of human biases, especially when it is outside the classical behavioral economics experimental design where individuals' behaviors are observed in simplified and straightforward decision-making situations (e.g., choose between two different hypothetical lottery tickets; decide a journal subscription plan). To fully understand the role of human biases and bounded rationality in general at different stages and levels of IS&R, it is important to investigate the interaction between bounded rationality and other factors affecting users' information seeking strategies, perceptions in search sessions, and result judgment criteria. Methodologically, this research direction requires researchers to go beyond simplified assumptions and overcontrolled standard experimental environments and carefully examine the combination of different user study components and procedures according to the nature of specific research questions (Liu & Shah, 2019).

Our book will synthesize the insights from multiple disciplines and discuss theories and empirical findings about the impacts of bounded rationality, with an emphasis on the effects of human biases on decision-making scenarios, including the decisions at different levels of IS&R, such as search initiation and stopping, query term selection, search results browsing, and, perhaps most importantly, search result evaluation (e.g., usefulness, relevance, credibility). The recent growing interest in exploring how users' biases affect their IS&R, especially their judgments of retrieved results and search sessions, can be traced back to the classical experiments on people's significant deviations from rational economic models (e.g., expected utility model) in judgment and decision-making. People's cognitive and perceptual biases in evaluation have been empirically confirmed by a variety of controlled lab experiments conducted in behavioral economics and cognitive psychology research. The impacts of these biases involve both quantitative and qualitative aspects and often occur in multiple dimensions. To offer a general idea regarding the impacts of user biases and bounded rationality, we listed some major systematic biases with examples (empirical studies and findings) about their impacts on evaluation and judgments (see Table 1.1).

Table 1.1 summarizes a set of empirically confirmed major biases affecting users' behavior and evaluation strategies both within and beyond IS&R research. Many of these biases were observed and tested quantitatively in controlled behavioral experiments. For instance, when a user is evaluating a recommended item, they usually compare the rating and price with that of previously viewed items or a pre-existing level of expectation (reference dependence). Also, a user's rating of an entire season of a TV series could be significantly affected by the rating of the best episode (peak experience) and the last episode (recent experience). In IR contexts, users tend to spend more time on and assign more credits to top-ranked results (order effect and position bias). Also, their relevance thresholds in assessing current documents are subjective and are affected by the relevance level of the documents presented earlier (priming effects). With respect to post-search experiences, Liu and Han (2020) found that a user's evaluation of a search session is significantly affected by the peak satisfaction level and the user's experience in the last search iteration. Also, their results showed that classifiers built on delta-based (i.e., losses and gains) features could achieve better performance in predicting search behaviors than traditional models. The findings from Liu and Han (2020) are also confirmed by other empirical research on cognitive effects in satisfaction evaluation (e.g., Liu et al., 2019a, b). In classical experiments, the impacts of these biases are often measured and operationalized through monetary values assigned to different objects in simulated decision-making scenarios (Kahneman, 2003). To develop more accurate representations, recent experiments also leverage neurophysiological techniques in obtaining fine-grained measures on user biases in simple evaluation tasks (e.g., Sokol-Hessner & Rutledge, 2019).

Some of the user biases and heuristics presented above were studied on a qualitative manner as it is difficult to quantitively differentiate or manipulate them. For example, a medical information searcher tends to easily accept retrieved information that is consistent with their existing beliefs and expectations (confirmation

Table 1.1 Major systematic biases in evaluation and judgment

User bias	Definition, explanation, and references
Reference dependence	People evaluate outcomes associated with decisions based on gains and losses with respect to a reference point or expectation, rather than the absolute final assets (Tversky & Kahneman, 1991). Recent empirical studies in economics (e.g., Martin, 2017), psychology (e.g., Bhatia, 2017; Markle et al., 2018), and IS&R (e.g. Liu & Han, 2020)
Loss aversion	People prefer avoiding losses to acquiring equivalent amount of gains. In other words, it is better to not lose $5 than to obtain $5 (Tversky & Kahneman, 1992). Recent empirical studies in economics (e.g., Füllbrunn & Luhan, 2017), psychology (e.g., Yechiam, 2019), and IS&R (e.g., Liu & Han, 2020)
Framing effects	People's reactions or decisions on options depend on whether the options are presented as a loss or a gain (Kahneman, 2003; Malenka et al., 1993). Recent empirical studies in economics (e.g., He, 2020), psychology (e.g., Cao et al., 2017), and IS&R (e.g., Novin & Meyers, 2017)
Salience bias	When reviewing different options or reviewing multiple information objects, people tend to focus on the items that are especially remarkable or prominent and pay less attention to those that lack prominence (Mullen et al., 1992)
Peak-end rule; position bias; order effects: Primacy and recency	An individual's evaluation of a session or sequence of options, decisions, and/or interactions is often significantly affected by several key reference points within the session, such as the initial points, peak points, and end points. There is no significant association between whole-session evaluation and the totality of local experiences within the session (Kahneman, 2003). Recent empirical studies in psychology (e.g., Sels et al., 2019) and IS&R (e.g., Clemmensen & Borlund, 2016; Liu & Han, 2020; Liu et al., 2019a, b)
Decoy effect/asymmetric dominance effect	People (usually customers) change their preference between two options when presented with a third option (i.e., the decoy) that is asymmetrically dominated (Zhang & Zhang, 2007). Recent empirical studies in psychology, marketing science (e.g., Stoffel et al., 2019; Wu & Cosguner, 2020), and IS&R (Eickhoff, 2018)
Priming effect	Priming effects happen when an individual's exposure to a stimulus subconsciously affects their response to a subsequent stimulus (Tipper, 1985). For instance, when a user encounters a bad quality item first, they tend to rate the subsequent items more highly, than if they were presented high-quality products at the beginning. Recent empirical studies in economics (e.g., Lodder et al., 2019), psychology (Szabo & Kocsis, 2017), and IS&R (e.g., Novin & Meyers, 2017; Scholer et al., 2013)

(continued)

Table 1.1 (continued)

User bias	Definition, explanation, and references
Confirmation bias; anchoring bias	People are more likely to accept the information that is consistent with their prior belief and/or the information they initially encountered (Klayman, 1995). Recent empirical studies in economics (e.g., Charness & Dave, 2017), psychology (e.g., Kappes et al., 2020), and IS&R (e.g., Shokouhi et al., 2015; White, 2013)
Ambiguity effects; risk aversion	People prefer options and outcomes with low uncertainty or ambiguity to the ones with high uncertainty, even if the latter has higher expected utility value (Rabin & Thaler, 2001). Recent empirical studies in economics (e.g., O'Donoghue & Somerville, 2018), psychology (cf. Lilleholt, 2019), and IS&R (e.g., Eickhoff, 2018; Kazai et al., 2012)
Theory of satisficing	Satisficing is a cognitive heuristic that entails exploring the available options until an acceptable or "good enough" option (instead of the best possible option) is found (Simon, 1955). Recent empirical studies in psychology (e.g., Luan & Li, 2017), information systems (e.g., Brunswicker et al., 2019), and IS&R (e.g. Agosto, 2002; Warwick et al., 2009)
Bandwagon effect	In decision-making contexts, people tend to choose an option or make certain decisions simply because other people do so. This bandwagon effect not only affects tangible decisions but also shapes the implicit opinion formation process (Murphy et al., 2003; Nadeau et al., 1993)

bias) (White, 2013). Also, the information and opinion that an individual initially encountered can significantly affect their reaction to subsequent information (anchoring bias) (Kazai et al., 2012). In Web searching, researchers found that users often stop at seemingly satisficing results in everyday-life search tasks, instead of continuing exploring potentially more useful sources and search queries (theory of satisficing) (Agosto, 2002). Recent studies have explored possible ways in which these qualitatively characterized impacts of biases can be at least partially represented and parameterized in formal user models and offline evaluation metrics. Research progresses on this problem will be further discussed in the following chapters.

In addition, researchers have also examined the impact of some user biases with both quantitative and qualitative methods. For instance, the satisficing options identified in a sequence of decision-making can be operationalized by both quantitative measures (e.g., monetary utility values, relevance rating) and qualitative evidences (e.g., individuals' self-reported satisficing choice). Regarding ambiguity and risk aversion, decision-makers' levels of uncertainty have been manipulated both quantitatively (e.g., assigning predefined probability values to individual outcomes) and qualitatively (e.g., extracting options from an unknown domain) in experiments.

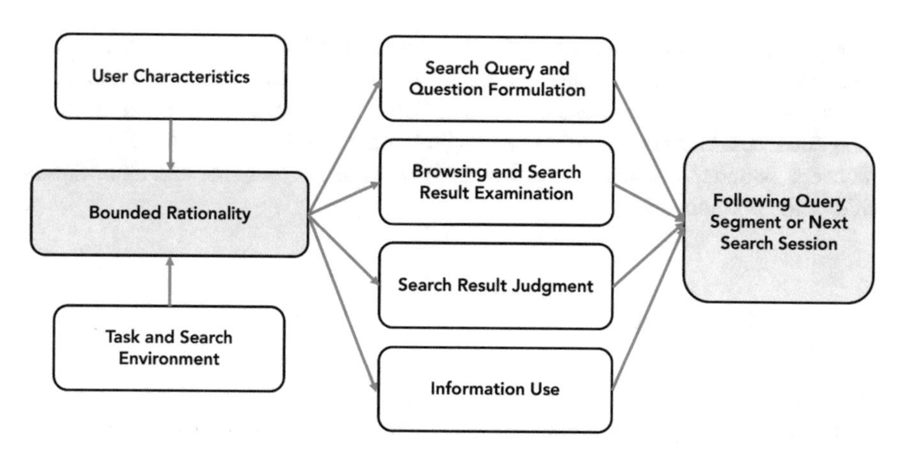

Fig. 1.5 Bounded rationality in interactive information retrieval

The findings discussed above contradict many rational assumptions behind IR experiments and call for a deep rethinking of the fundamentals of user models and the associated evaluation metrics. Also, in future studies, with reasonable assumptions and analytical tools, researchers might be able to further deconstruct the qualitative aspects of systematic biases (e.g., existing beliefs, user perceptions) and represent them with more fine-grained quantifiable measures (e.g., word embeddings, neurophysiological behavioral signals) and scalable computational models. In addition, it is worth noting that users' bounded rationality, especially cognitive biases, could go beyond the explicit evaluation and judgment phase and affect the entire information seeking episode. Different phases of IS&R, such as information need formation, query formulation, search result browsing and examination, as well as information use, could be affected by different aspects of bounded rationality and also interact with each other, especially in prolonged information seeking and search sessions (see Fig. 1.5). In the following chapters, this book will discuss the aforementioned human biases in detail and further explain how they affect the way in which users behave in their interactions with IR systems and how we can and should represent the impacts of human biases in formulating user models and developing customized search recommendations.

Recent IR studies have explored a wide range of search algorithms, complex search tasks, user populations, and search interfaces, and some of these studies connect search interactions to the factors of users' bounded rationality. Many research publications describe their algorithms, search interface components (e.g., query or question input, search result presentation, search assistance tools), user study procedures, and evaluation strategies in detail, but they are spread across numerous journals, conference proceedings, and workshops and presented in varying lengths and styles. Also, research articles from different venues and communities (e.g., user-centered IS&R communities, system-oriented IR experiment communities) have largely different expectations of their reader's background knowledge. As a result, it is challenging to synthesize existing research progresses and clear the path toward future directions, especially for IR researchers who work on interdisciplinary research problems like the ones presented in this book and need to combine and apply the knowledge accumulated through both user-centered and system-centered IR approaches. Our book provides a relatively brief but sufficiently detailed review on users' bounded rationality in IIR and covers both the user-side and algorithmic-side of the problem space.

1.2 Book Structure

We believe that our book is useful to a variety of reader groups. Readers who are from the core areas of computer science and familiar with system-oriented IR evaluation may benefit from the introductions and discussions on the simulations of bias-aware ranking algorithms, evaluation metrics, and associated experiments in controlled settings. Readers from information seeking and other user-centered research areas may find new ways in which the knowledge learned from small-scale user experiments and qualitative studies can inform the design of bias-aware search systems and provide a more psychologically realistic foundation for IR models of varying types. By discussing the origins, progresses, and future direction on bounded rationality research in IR and other closely related fields, this book aims to not only present a clearer broad picture of this interdisciplinary area to the IR community but also highlight the value of connecting the knowledge and methods developed in user studies with the algorithms and experimental techniques built in system-oriented research.

Figure 1.6 presents the basic structure of our book consisting of three related parts. To guide the reader through the key issues in understanding and modeling bounded rationality in IR and related fields, we segmented this book into several separate but interrelated parts and chapters. The first part, "Foundation," covers Chaps. 1–3. This part will introduce the fundamentals for investigating bounded rationality in IR, such as related cognitive psychology and behavioral economics

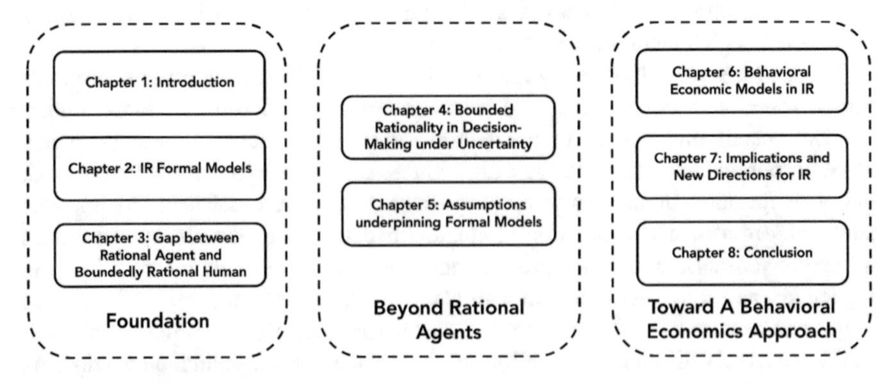

Fig. 1.6 Book structure

theories, formal user models and related implicit assumptions, and limitations of existing user models and evaluation metrics in terms of capturing users' actual search activities, perceptions, and decision-making and evaluation strategies.

Specifically, Chap. 2 will introduce a variety of classical and state-of-the-art formal models of interactive IR, including classical and enhanced versions of click models (e.g., Borisov et al., 2016; Chuklin et al., 2015; Liu et al., 2016; Mao et al., 2018), probability ranking principle (PRP) of IIR (Fuhr, 2008), hidden Markov model (HMM) of search phases and search states (e.g., Dungs & Fuhr, 2017), cooperative game framework of text retrieval (Zhai, 2016), economic IR models (e.g., Azzopardi, 2014; Azzopardi & Zuccon, 2016; Liu, 2017), dynamic models of IR (e.g., dual-agent stochastic game model) (Luo et al., 2014), as well as the hidden assumptions and user models behind IR evaluation metrics. This chapter will explain the goals of these models (e.g., predicting search actions and user satisfaction, optimizing users' search paths, improving ranking and IR interfaces), simulated situations or problems, algorithms and parameters, contributions, as well as the limitations.

The third chapter will first discuss the common assumptions of rational agent models and explain why they are psychologically unrealistic by comparing them to a series of widely studied bias-aware user models. By identifying the salient gaps between formal models and human biases, this chapter offers a starting point toward extending IR formal models and the associated metrics. In particular, this chapter will also introduce the classical rational agent models from microeconomics research (e.g., Cobb-Douglas production function, preferences, and indifference curves), which underpin various economic IR and recommendation models (e.g., Azzopardi, 2014; Zhang et al., 2016). To clarify the origin of the ideas regarding bounded rationality and research on systematic biases, this chapter also briefly introduces related theories and models from cognitive psychology and behavioral economics and explains how they are relevant to the problem space of interactive IR. These preliminary discussions on common human biases, bounded rationality, and behavioral economics theories will be further extended in Chap. 4, where we will provide more details regarding specific concepts, theories, operationalizations, and behavioral experiments design.

Part 2, "Beyond Rational Agents," will focus on the multidimensional conflicts between existing formal models of user search interactions (e.g., click and browsing models, simulated behaviors behind individual offline evaluation metrics) and the insights about bounded rationality in decision-making under uncertainty. The common, long-standing research problem of economic studies is how people allocate available, limited resources when trying to accomplish some goals. Differing from classical economic theories, behavioral economics research seeks to (1) build the analysis of the rules in resource allocation and decision-making on a more realistic psychological basis and (2) to differentiate rational man's optimal behavior from people's behavior under various biases and constraints (Thaler, 2016).

In Chap. 4, the book explains the theories and empirical evidences regarding bounded rationality and systematic biases, with the ultimate goal of applying them to a variety of IR problems and offering IR models a more realistic behavioral and psychological foundation. Specifically, this chapter reviews the basic elements of bounded rationality (Simon, 1955) as well as six widely confirmed biases in judgment and decision-making (Kahneman, 2003). Then, we introduce the Noble-award winning prospect theory (Kahneman & Tversky, 2013) and discuss how it could help explain the biases and anomalies in search behaviors. Also, this chapter will cover the peak-end rule and its impacts on people' session-based evaluations. It will conclude with a summary of the major biases and cognitive limitations in decision-making and their implications for interactive IR modeling.

With the knowledge about human biases and bounded rationality accumulated in behavioral economics and cognitive psychology research (see Chap. 4), Chap. 5 will go back to the fundamentals and seek to revise the simplification assumptions behind the formal IR models and evaluation metrics discussed in the second chapter. Specifically, taking a step forward from the preliminary introductions and discussions developed in Chap. 3 on gaps between formal models and human biases, we will first revisit and further re-organize the assumptions by model type and contrast these assumptions with the specific characteristics of people's systematic biases, heuristics, and limits that have been empirically confirmed in behavioral economics experiments (discussed in the Chap. 4). In particular, we will highlight the cognitive biases (e.g., user expectations, reference point, risk aversion) that have been missed out in most formal models and IIR research.

In addition, based on the knowledge of human biases, bounded rationality and associated evidences introduced in Chap. 4, this chapter will suggest reasonable and potentially actionable ways to revise existing assumptions underpinning formal models. Based on existing empirical findings and experimental results, we will also introduce possible boundaries, practical restrictions, and theoretical limitations of revised bias-aware assumptions. Also, with the knowledge learned about human biases, we will discuss how we can revise and extend formal user models to better represent and estimate the impacts of boundedly rational decisions in search interaction and user evaluation.

Part 3, "Toward A Behavioral Economics Approach," will synthesize the insights from both theories and experiments on related research problems and propose a novel behavioral economics approach to characterizing, understanding/predicting, and evaluating IIR and related activities (e.g., interactions with recommendations). Our hope is that the proposed bias-aware/behavioral economics approach can be established based on the solid empirical basis on bounded rationality, human biases and heuristics, and formal modeling discussed in above chapters and also provide a new perspective and actionable research agenda for identifying critical research gaps between users and systems, advancing the knowledge in human-bias-aware IR modeling and encouraging students and young researchers to further explore this field.

Chapter 6 discusses the existing preliminary research that have applied bounded rationality and behavioral economic theories in addressing IR-related problems, particularly in predicting users' interactions with search systems. These studies can characterize the boundaries of user rationality in the context of online information seeking, search, and evaluation (e.g., Agosto, 2002; Warwick et al., 2009). We will also briefly discuss potential research paths and programs on applying behavioral economics theories in addressing specific critical problems, such as predicting users' state of expectation disconfirmation, modeling search behavior, and understanding session-level satisfaction (Liu & Shah, 2019; Liu & Han, 2020).

Next, to bring in relevant findings and insights from related disciplines, this chapter will briefly introduce applications of behavioral economics theories in information seeking and recommender systems research and discuss their implications for some foundational IR problems, such as learning to rank and session-wise evaluation (e.g., Ge et al., 2020). More details regarding the specific research questions, open gaps, and methodological challenges will be discussed in the following chapters.

Built upon the discussions from previous chapters, Chap. 7 will focus on the implications, new directions, and perspectives opened by the behavioral economics approach for different areas of IR research and practices. This chapter will be connected to existing and emerging challenges in IR and offer new ways through which users and their search strategies can be represented and modeled. Some of the main themes or specific problems include:

- Modeling and predicting different aspects of users' bounded rationality from features of varying types (e.g., search behavioral features, features of the query recommendations, surrogates and documents that users interact with, eye movement features, neurophysiological features)
- Modeling whole session interactive IR processes and identifying key features and parameters that could approximate different biases and cognitive limits in formal models
- Leveraging the knowledge about users' systematic biases in constructing online learning to rank (LTR) algorithms; reducing the potential negative impacts of user cognitive biases through adaptive re-ranking and intervention; and developing multivariate scoring functions (which take into consideration users' biases and heuristics) to reduce noises and biases in click data and to improve existing unbiased learning to rank (ULTR) algorithms
- Designing, implementing, and evaluating bias-aware IR evaluation measures in sessions
- Applying behavioral economics insights in designing bias-aware intelligent task support (BITS) and improving IR interface and developing adaptive state-based algorithms to automatically learn users' bias states and provide adaptive and even proactive recommendations for addressing potential problems and helping struggling users
- Building intelligent systems that address not only system and algorithmic biases but also human biases, especially in decision-making activities under uncertainty and re-framing *Fairness, Accountability, Transparency, and Ethics* (FATE) challenges in light of behavioral economics framework and knowledge about human biases and heuristics

In the conclusion chapter, this book will summarize the main content of previous seven chapters and re-emphasizes the value of understanding users' bounded rationality and the implications of behavioral economics theories for different areas of IR practices.

We believe that this book will offer readers a valuable conceptual and empirical leap in user modeling and IIR evaluation and will become even more relevant as we move forward toward AI-assisted information interaction and human-AI collaboration in decision-making. In particular, for graduate students and early researchers in IR and interactive system fields, this book can provide a broad overview of both the existing challenges and new directions in user-centered IR and inform them about the possible problem space, new methods, and techniques for further exploration. The bibliography of this book can also serve as a good starting reading list for readers who plan to develop research proposals and conduct scientific studies in this interdisciplinary field.

We hope that our book can encourage readers to further investigate the phenomenon of bounded rationality in users' interactions with interactive information systems and explore the research challenges of developing and evaluating bias-aware search and recommendation systems that address *both* algorithmic biases and human biases. We hope to see more contributions in this area from readers of varying backgrounds in the future.

References

Agosto, D. E. (2002). Bounded rationality and satisficing in young people's web-based decision making. *Journal of the American Society for Information Science and Technology, 53*(1), 16–27. https://doi.org/10.1002/asi.10024

Azzopardi, L. (2014). Modelling interaction with economic models of search. In *Proceedings of the 37th ACM SIGIR Conference on Research & Development in Information Retrieval* (pp. 3–12). ACM.

Azzopardi, L. (2021). Cognitive biases in search: A review and reflection of cognitive biases in information retrieval. In *Proceedings of the 2021 ACM SIGIR conference on human information interaction and retrieval* (pp. 27–37). https://doi.org/10.1145/3406522.3446023

Azzopardi, L., & Zuccon, G. (2016). An analysis of the cost and benefit of search interactions. In *Proceedings of the 2016 ACM international conference on the theory of information retrieval* (pp. 59–68). https://doi.org/10.1145/2970398.2970412

Belkin, N. J. (2008). Some (what) grand challenges for information retrieval. In *ACM SIGIR forum* (Vol. 42, pp. 47–54). ACM. https://doi.org/10.1145/1394251.1394261

Bhatia, S. (2017). Comparing theories of reference-dependent choice. *Journal of Experimental Psychology: Learning, Memory, and Cognition, 43*(9), 1490–1507. https://doi.org/10.1037/xlm0000384

Biega, A. J., Gummadi, K. P., & Weikum, G. (2018). Equity of attention: Amortizing individual fairness in rankings. In *Proceedings of the 41st international ACM SIGIR conference on research & development in information retrieval* (pp. 405–414). https://doi.org/10.1145/3209978.3210063

Borisov, A., Markov, I., de Rijke, M., & Serdyukov, P. (2016). A neural click model for web search. In *Proceedings of the 25th international conference on world wide web* (pp. 531–541). https://doi.org/10.1145/2872427.2883033

Brunswicker, S., Almirall, E., & Majchrzak, A. (2019). Optimizing and satisficing: The interplay between platform architecture and producers' design strategies for platform performance. *MIS Quarterly, 43*(4), 1249–1277. https://doi.org/10.25300/MISQ/2019/13561

Camerer, C. (1999). Behavioral economics: Reunifying psychology and economics. *Proceedings of the National Academy of Sciences, 96*(19), 10575–10577. https://www.pnas.org/doi/pdf/10.1073/pnas.96.19.10575

Cao, F., Zhang, J., Song, L., Wang, S., Miao, D., & Peng, J. (2017). Framing effect in the trolley problem and footbridge dilemma: Number of saved lives matters. *Psychological Reports, 120*(1), 88–101. https://doi.org/10.1177/0033294116685866

Capra, R., Arguello, J., & Scholer, F. (2013). Augmenting web search surrogates with images. In *Proceedings of the 22nd ACM international conference on information & knowledge management* (pp. 399–408). https://doi.org/10.1145/2505515.2505714

Charness, G., & Dave, C. (2017). Confirmation bias with motivated beliefs. *Games and Economic Behavior, 104*, 1–23. https://doi.org/10.1016/j.geb.2017.02.015

Chuklin, A., Markov, I., & de Rijke, M. (2015). Click models for web search. *Synthesis Lectures on Information Concepts, Retrieval, and Services, 7*(3), 1–115. https://doi.org/10.2200/S00654ED1V01Y201507ICR043

Clarke, C. L., Kolla, M., Cormack, G. V., Vechtomova, O., Ashkan, A., Büttcher, S., & MacKinnon, I. (2008). Novelty and diversity in information retrieval evaluation. In *Proceedings of the 31st annual international ACM SIGIR conference on research and development in information retrieval* (pp. 659–666). https://doi.org/10.1145/1390334.1390446

Clemmensen, M. L., & Borlund, P. (2016). Order effect in interactive information retrieval evaluation: An empirical study. *Journal of Documentation, 72*(2), 194–213. https://doi.org/10.1108/JD-04-2015-0051

Cole, M., Liu, J., Belkin, N. J., Bierig, R., Gwizdka, J., Liu, C., Zhang, J., & Zhang, X. (2009). Usefulness as the criterion for evaluation of interactive information retrieval. In *Proceedings of the third workshop on human-computer interaction and information retrieval* (pp. 1–4). HCIR.

Conlisk, J. (1996). Why bounded rationality? *Journal of Economic Literature, 34*(2), 669–700. http://www.jstor.org/stable/2729218

Dungs, S., & Fuhr, N. (2017). Advanced hidden Markov models for recognizing search phases. In *Proceedings of the ACM SIGIR international conference on theory of information retrieval* (pp. 257–260). https://doi.org/10.1145/3121050.3121090

Eickhoff, C. (2018). Cognitive biases in crowdsourcing. In *Proceedings of the eleventh ACM international conference on web search and data mining* (pp. 162–170). https://doi.org/10.1145/3159652.3159654

Fuhr, N. (2008). A probability ranking principle for interactive information retrieval. *Information Retrieval, 11*(3), 251–265. https://doi.org/10.1007/s10791-008-9045-0

Füllbrunn, S. C., & Luhan, W. J. (2017). Decision making for others: The case of loss aversion. *Economics Letters, 161*, 154–156. https://doi.org/10.1016/j.econlet.2017.09.037

Ge, Y., Zhao, S., Zhou, H., Pei, C., Sun, F., Ou, W., & Zhang, Y. (2020). Understanding echo chambers in e-commerce recommender systems. In *Proceedings of the 43rd international ACM SIGIR conference on research and development in information retrieval* (pp. 2261–2270). https://doi.org/10.1145/3397271.3401431

Harman, D. (2011). Information retrieval evaluation. *Synthesis Lectures on Information Concepts, Retrieval, and Services, 3*(2), 1–119. https://doi.org/10.2200/S00368ED1V01Y201105ICR019

He, T. S. (2020). The framing effect of tax–transfer systems. *Journal of the Economic Science Association, 6*(2), 213–225. https://doi.org/10.1007/s40881-020-00095-0

Ingwersen, P. (1996). Cognitive perspectives of information retrieval interaction: Elements of a cognitive IR theory. *Journal of Documentation, 52*(1), 3–50. https://doi.org/10.1108/eb026960

Kahneman, D. (2003). Maps of bounded rationality: Psychology for behavioral economics. *American Economic Review, 93*(5), 1449–1475. https://doi.org/10.1257/000282803322655392

Kahneman, D., & Tversky, A. (2013). Prospect theory: An analysis of decision under risk. In *Handbook of the fundamentals of financial decision making: Part I* (pp. 99–127). World Scientific.

Kappes, A., Harvey, A. H., Lohrenz, T., Montague, P. R., & Sharot, T. (2020). Confirmation bias in the utilization of others' opinion strength. *Nature Neuroscience, 23*(1), 130–137. https://doi.org/10.1038/s41593-019-0549-2

Kato, M. P., Ohshima, H., Liu, Y. H., & Chen, H. L. (2020). Overview of the NTCIR-15 data search task. In *Proceedings of the NTCIR-15 conference on evaluation of information access technologies*.

Kazai, G., Craswell, N., Yilmaz, E., & Tahaghoghi, S. M. (2012). An analysis of systematic judging errors in information retrieval. In *Proceedings of the 21st ACM international conference on information and knowledge management* (pp. 105–114). ACM. https://doi.org/10.1145/2396761.2396779

Kelly, D., & Azzopardi, L. (2015). How many results per page? A study of SERP size, search behavior and user experience. In *Proceedings of the 38th international ACM SIGIR conference on research and development in information retrieval* (pp. 183–192). https://doi.org/10.1145/2766462.2767732

Khattab, O., & Zaharia, M. (2020). Colbert: Efficient and effective passage search via contextualized late interaction over BERT. In *Proceedings of the 43rd international ACM SIGIR conference on research and development in information retrieval* (pp. 39–48). https://doi.org/10.1145/3397271.3401075

Klayman, J. (1995). Varieties of confirmation bias. *Psychology of Learning and Motivation, 32*, 385–418. https://doi.org/10.1016/S0079-7421(08)60315-1

Li, Y., & Belkin, N. J. (2008). A faceted approach to conceptualizing tasks in information seeking. *Information Processing & Management, 44*(6), 1822–1837. https://doi.org/10.1016/j.ipm.2008.07.005

Lilleholt, L. (2019). Cognitive ability and risk aversion: A systematic review and meta-analysis. *Judgment and Decision making, 14*(3), 234–279. https://psycnet.apa.org/record/2019-32086-002

Liu, J. (2017). Toward a unified model of human information behavior: An equilibrium perspective. *Journal of Documentation, 73*(4), 666–688.

Liu, J. (2021). Deconstructing search tasks in interactive information retrieval: A systematic review of task dimensions and predictors. *Information Processing & Management, 58*(3), 102522. https://doi.org/10.1016/j.ipm.2021.102522

Liu, J., & Han, F. (2020). Investigating reference dependence effects on user search interaction and satisfaction: A behavioral economics perspective. In *Proceedings of the 43rd international ACM SIGIR conference on research and development in information retrieval* (pp. 1141–1150). https://doi.org/10.1145/3397271.3401085

Liu, J., & Shah, C. (2019). Interactive IR user study design, evaluation, and reporting. *Synthesis Lectures on Information Concepts, Retrieval, and Services, 11*(2), i-93. https://doi.org/10.2200/S00923ED1V01Y201905ICR067

Liu, J., Liu, C., & Belkin, N. J. (2016). Predicting information searchers' topic knowledge at different search stages. *Journal of the Association for Information Science and Technology, 67*(11), 2652–2666. https://doi.org/10.1002/asi.23606

Liu, M., Mao, J., Liu, Y., Zhang, M., & Ma, S. (2019a). Investigating cognitive effects in session-level search user satisfaction. In *Proceedings of the 25th ACM SIGKDD international conference on knowledge discovery & data mining* (pp. 923–931). https://doi.org/10.1145/3292500.3330981

Liu, J., Mitsui, M., Belkin, N. J., & Shah, C. (2019b). Task, information seeking intentions, and user behavior: Toward a multi-level understanding of web search. In *Proceedings of the 2019 ACM SIGIR conference on human information interaction and retrieval* (pp. 123–132). ACM. https://doi.org/10.1145/3295750.3298922

Lodder, P., Ong, H. H., Grasman, R. P., & Wicherts, J. M. (2019). A comprehensive meta-analysis of money priming. *Journal of Experimental Psychology: General, 148*(4), 688–712. https://doi.org/10.1037/xge0000570

Luan, M., & Li, H. (2017). Good enough—Compromise between desirability and feasibility: An alternative perspective on satisficing. *Journal of Experimental Social Psychology, 70*, 110–116. https://doi.org/10.1016/j.jesp.2017.01.002

Luo, J., Zhang, S., & Yang, H. (2014, July). Win-win search: Dual-agent stochastic game in session search. In *Proceedings of the 37th international ACM SIGIR Conference on Research & Development in Information Retrieval* (pp. 587–596). ACM.

Malenka, D. J., Baron, J. A., Johansen, S., Wahrenberger, J. W., & Ross, J. M. (1993). The framing effect of relative and absolute risk. *Journal of General Internal Medicine, 8*(10), 543–548. https://doi.org/10.1007/BF02599636

Mansourian, Y., & Ford, N. (2007). Search persistence and failure on the web: A "bounded rationality" and "satisficing" analysis. *Journal of Documentation, 63*(5), 680–701. https://doi.org/10.1108/00220410710827754

Mao, J., Luo, C., Zhang, M., & Ma, S. (2018). Constructing click models for mobile search. In *41st international ACM SIGIR conference on research & development in information retrieval* (pp. 775–784). ACM. https://doi.org/10.1145/3209978.3210060

Markle, A., Wu, G., White, R., & Sackett, A. (2018). Goals as reference points in marathon running: A novel test of reference dependence. *Journal of Risk and Uncertainty, 56*(1), 19–50. https://doi.org/10.1007/s11166-018-9271-9

Martin, V. (2017). When to quit: Narrow bracketing and reference dependence in taxi drivers. *Journal of Economic Behavior & Organization, 144*, 166–187. https://doi.org/10.1016/j.jebo.2017.09.024

Mullen, B., Brown, R., & Smith, C. (1992). Ingroup bias as a function of salience, relevance, and status: An integration. *European Journal of Social Psychology, 22*(2), 103–122. https://doi.org/10.1002/ejsp.2420220202

Murphy, J., Olaru, D., Schegg, R., & Frey, S. (2003). The bandwagon effect: Swiss hotels' web-site and e-mail management. *The Cornell Hotel and Restaurant Administration Quarterly, 44*(1), 71–87. https://doi.org/10.1016/S0010-8804(03)90048-6

Nadeau, R., Cloutier, E., & Guay, J. H. (1993). New evidence about the existence of a bandwagon effect in the opinion formation process. *International Political Science Review, 14*(2), 203–213. https://doi.org/10.1177/019251219301400204

Novin, A., & Meyers, E. (2017). Making sense of conflicting science information: Exploring bias in the search engine result page. In *Proceedings of the 2017 conference on human information interaction and retrieval* (pp. 175–184). https://doi.org/10.1145/3020165.3020185

O'Donoghue, T., & Somerville, J. (2018). Modeling risk aversion in economics. *Journal of Economic Perspectives, 32*(2), 91–114. https://doi.org/10.1257/jep.32.2.91

Rabin, M., & Thaler, R. H. (2001). Anomalies: Risk aversion. *Journal of Economic Perspectives, 15*(1), 219–232.

Sakai, T., & Zeng, Z. (2019). Which diversity evaluation measures are "good"? In *Proceedings of the 42nd international ACM SIGIR conference on research and development in information retrieval* (pp. 595–604). https://doi.org/10.1145/3331184.3331215

Sayed, M. F., & Oard, D. W. (2019). Jointly modeling relevance and sensitivity for search among sensitive content. In *Proceedings of the 42nd international ACM SIGIR conference on research and development in information retrieval* (pp. 615–624). https://doi.org/10.1145/3331184.3331256

Scholer, F., Kelly, D., Wu, W. C., Lee, H. S., & Webber, W. (2013). The effect of threshold priming and need for cognition on relevance calibration and assessment. In *Proceedings of the 36th international ACM SIGIR conference on research and development in information retrieval* (pp. 623–632). https://doi.org/10.1145/2484028.2484090

Sels, L., Ceulemans, E., & Kuppens, P. (2019). All's well that ends well? A test of the peak-end rule in couples' conflict discussions. *European Journal of Social Psychology, 49*(4), 794–806. https://doi.org/10.1002/ejsp.2547

Shokouhi, M., White, R., & Yilmaz, E. (2015). Anchoring and adjustment in relevance estimation. In *Proceedings of the 38th international ACM SIGIR conference on research and development in information retrieval* (pp. 963–966). https://doi.org/10.1145/2766462.2767841

Simon, H. A. (1955). A behavioral model of rational choice. *The Quarterly Journal of Economics, 69*(1), 99–118. https://doi.org/10.2307/1884852

Singh, A., & Joachims, T. (2018). Fairness of exposure in rankings. In *Proceedings of the 24th ACM SIGKDD international conference on knowledge discovery & data mining* (pp. 2219–2228). https://doi.org/10.1145/3219819.3220088

Sokol-Hessner, P., & Rutledge, R. B. (2019). The psychological and neural basis of loss aversion. *Current Directions in Psychological Science, 28*(1), 20–27.

Stoffel, S. T., Yang, J., Vlaev, I., & von Wagner, C. (2019). Testing the decoy effect to increase interest in colorectal cancer screening. *PLoS One, 14*(3), e0213668. https://doi.org/10.1371/journal.pone.0213668

Szabo, A., & Kocsis, Á. (2017). Psychological effects of deep-breathing: The impact of expectancy-priming. *Psychology, Health & Medicine, 22*(5), 564–569.

Thaler, R. H. (2016). Behavioral economics: Past, present, and future. *American Economic Review, 106*(7), 1577–1600. https://doi.org/10.1257/aer.106.7.1577

Tipper, S. P. (1985). The negative priming effect: Inhibitory priming by ignored objects. *The Quarterly Journal of Experimental Psychology, 37*(4), 571–590. https://doi.org/10.1080/14640748508400920

Tversky, A., & Kahneman, D. (1991). Loss aversion in riskless choice: A reference-dependent model. *The Quarterly Journal of Economics, 106*(4), 1039–1061.

Tversky, A., & Kahneman, D. (1992). Advances in prospect theory: Cumulative representation of uncertainty. *Journal of Risk and Uncertainty, 5*(4), 297–323.

Voorhees, E. M. (2001). The philosophy of information retrieval evaluation. In *Workshop of the cross-language evaluation forum for European languages* (pp. 355–370). Springer.

Voorhees, E. M. (2018). On building fair and reusable test collections using bandit techniques. In *Proceedings of the 27th ACM international conference on information and knowledge management* (pp. 407–416). https://doi.org/10.1145/3269206.3271766

Wadhwa, S., & Zamani, H. (2021). Towards system-initiative conversational information seeking. In *Proceedings of the second international conference on design of experimental search and information retrieval systems. DESIRES'21* (pp. 102–116).

Warwick, C., Rimmer, J., Blandford, A., Gow, J., & Buchanan, G. (2009). Cognitive economy and satisficing in information seeking: A longitudinal study of undergraduate information behavior. *Journal of the American Society for Information Science and Technology, 60*(12), 2402–2415. https://doi.org/10.1002/asi.21179

White, R. (2013). Beliefs and biases in web search. In *Proceedings of the 36th international ACM SIGIR conference on research and development in information retrieval* (pp. 3–12). https://doi.org/10.1145/2484028.2484053

Wildemuth, B. M. (2004). The effects of domain knowledge on search tactic formulation. *Journal of the American Society for Information Science and Technology, 55*(3), 246–258. https://doi.org/10.1002/asi.10367

Wu, C., & Cosguner, K. (2020). Profiting from the decoy effect: A case study of an online diamond retailer. *Marketing Science, 39*(5), 974–995. https://doi.org/10.1287/mksc.2020.1231

Yechiam, E. (2019). Acceptable losses: The debatable origins of loss aversion. *Psychological Research, 83*(7), 1327–1339. https://doi.org/10.1007/s00426-018-1013-8

Zhai, C. (2016). Towards a game-theoretic framework for text data retrieval. *IEEE Data Engineering Bulletin, 39*(3), 51–62.

Zhang, T., & Zhang, D. (2007). Agent-based simulation of consumer purchase decision-making and the decoy effect. *Journal of Business Research, 60*(8), 912–922. https://doi.org/10.1016/j.jbusres.2007.02.006

Zhang, Y., Zhao, Q., Zhang, Y., Friedman, D., Zhang, M., Liu, Y., & Ma, S. (2016). Economic recommendation with surplus maximization. In *Proceedings of the 25th international conference on world wide web* (pp. 73–83). ACM.

Chapter 2
Formally Modeling Users in Information Retrieval

Abstract Formally modeling user behavior and predicting interaction events is essential for evaluating and advancing IR systems. This chapter focuses on the ways in which IR researchers formally model users and their behaviors in IR activities and introduces two main groups of formal models: (1) *single-event-focused models*, especially basic click models and enhanced versions of click models with additional user characteristics and result factors being represented and parameterized, and (2) *models of search interactions*, especially the ones underpinning offline evaluation metrics and search phase models. The review on existing models, rational assumptions, and related empirical studies in this chapter will enhance our understanding of the similarities and connections between related models presented in varying ways and serve as a basis for the further investigation and discussion on how to better characterize user traits, especially their biases and cognitive limits, in modeling search sessions and evaluating the performance of IR systems.

2.1 Introduction

Modeling user behavior and predicting interaction events is essential for evaluating and advancing information retrieval (IR) systems. For instance, models developed to predict single interaction events or a sequence of events (e.g., click models) can help researchers and engineers characterize users' patterns of browsing and navigation on search engine result pages (SERPs) and understand the distribution of attention and cognitive resources during search interactions (Chuklin et al., 2015; Guo et al., 2009). Knowledge learned through the modeling process can facilitate the organization of information on the search interface and enhance search effectiveness through effective ranking and search recommendations.

Evaluation is a central topic of IR research. In addition to interaction event predictions, in the context of search evaluation, IR researchers also develop *user models* with varying explicit or implicit assumptions to define user behavioral patterns (e.g., querying, browsing, search continue or stop, skip, or click) and propose evaluation metrics of varying types, including both online process-oriented metrics (e.g., dwell time on result pages, query formulation) and offline

J. Liu, *A Behavioral Economics Approach to Interactive Information Retrieval*, The Information Retrieval Series 48, https://doi.org/10.1007/978-3-031-23229-9_2

outcome-based metrics (e.g., relevance-based precision, recall, discounted cumulative gain), based on simulated user models (Azzopardi et al., 2018; Zhang et al., 2017a). The evaluation metrics, once developed and applied, determine how researchers and adaptive algorithms (e.g., reinforcement-learning-based re-ranking systems) grade system performance and which ranking strategies and result presentation patterns would receive higher scores and be encouraged in following information seeking episodes. Also, the evaluation metrics as a part of the optimization functions also affect the process and results of training ranking algorithms when researchers conduct experiments on large-scale commercial Web search logs and standard test collections.

This chapter focuses on the ways in which IR researchers formally model users and their behaviors in IR activities and introduces two main groups of formal models: (1) *single-event-focused models*, especially basic click models and enhanced versions of click models with additional user characteristics and result factors being incorporated and represented (e.g., Chuklin et al., 2015), and (2) *models of search interactions*, especially the ones underpinning offline evaluation metrics and search phase models (e.g., Azzopardi et al., 2018; Chen et al., 2017; Dungs & Fuhr, 2017; Liu et al., 2017; Tran & Fuhr, 2013; Zhang et al., 2017a). To define and test a model, researchers need to characterize observed and hidden variables, relations between the variables and the associated assumptions, as well as how these relations depend on the model parameters. This chapter will introduce the assumptions and goals of these models, the research problems these models seek to address, basic function structure and key parameters, as well as their limitations in characterizing users' behaviors and search experiences, especially in the context of task-based whole-session interactive IR. Review on existing models, terminologies, and related empirical studies in this chapter will enhance our understanding of the similarities and connections between related models presented in varying ways and serve as a basis for the further investigation and discussion on how to better characterize user traits, especially their biases and cognitive limits, in modeling search sessions and evaluating system performances. In particular, based upon the discussion on the limitations and restrictions of existing formal models of user and associated evaluation measures in IR (e.g., difficulties in characterizing and predicting real-time search actions and user satisfaction; unable to capture the variations across different search intentions, task states, in situ reference points and search expectations), the following chapters will discuss the potential ways in which these models can be adjusted and extended to at least partially address the limitations and take into consideration the role and impacts of user bounded rationality for facilitating user-centered search system design.

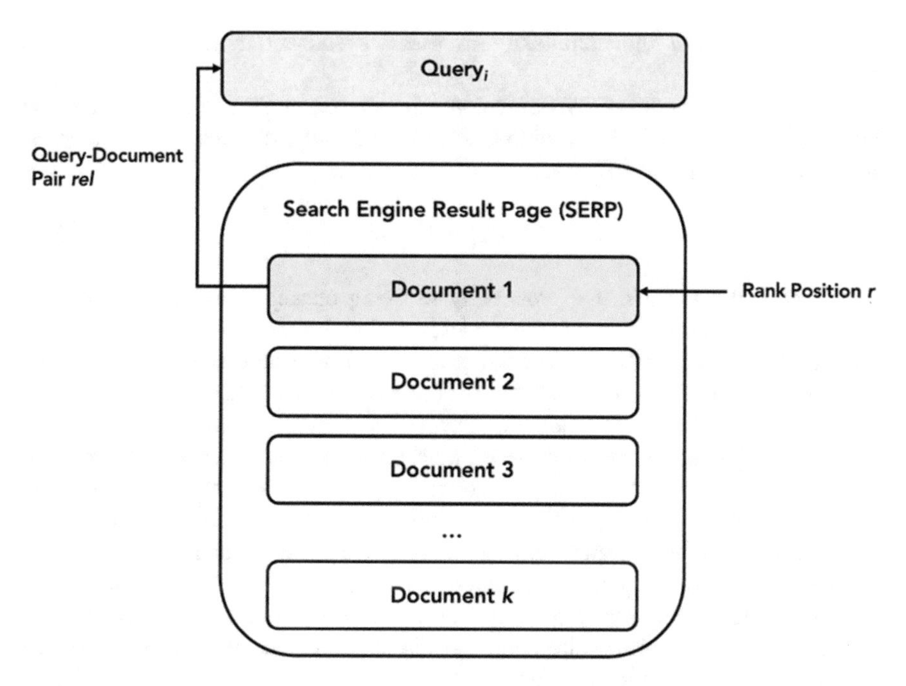

Fig. 2.1 Click models built upon query-document pair and rank position

2.2 Basic Click Models

A user model essentially defines a set of rules that enable researchers to simulate user actions on a SERP. One of the main types of observable user interaction with a search system is clicks. To understand and simulate user click patterns and estimate document features from click behavior, researchers have developed varying types of *click models* to facilitate simulation and evaluation experiments. In addition, some click models also seek to represent and simulate the effects of user biases (e.g., position bias, attention bias, and novelty bias) in search evaluation and aim to debias the process of relevance estimation for obtaining a more effective, fairer re-ranking of retrieved search results. This section focuses on the basic click models built upon which advanced click models with additional signals and user trait parameters are developed.

The first set of click models have the simplest form compared to other models and set simulation rules mainly based on the rank of a document or the query-document pair (see Fig. 2.1). This batch of baseline click models includes random click model (RCM), rank-based click-through rate models (RCTR), and document-based click-through rate models (DCTR). These models only have a small set of parameters and thus have the potential to be widely applied in various types of search datasets (especially the large-scale search logs that do not have rich annotation labels) and face less risk of overfitting in training. Meanwhile, however, these models cannot capture or estimate the complexity in users' systematic biases and cognitive variations.

Random click model (RCM) only contains one parameter and does not include any representations of rank position, document feature, and user characteristics. RCM can be defined as follows:

$$P(C_d = 1) = p \tag{2.1}$$

For each document d, the probability of being clicked remains the same and equals to parameter p. Although the model is straightforward and has faced minimal risk of overfitting in training (Chuklin et al., 2015), it cannot capture the potential variations and errors caused by the facets of document quality (e.g., query-document relevance, task-document usefulness, information credibility, and accessibility) and users' cognitive biases and limits (e.g., rank position bias, loss aversion, limits of current knowledge structure). These factors may lead to significant changes in the value of p across different queries, results, and user populations and thus may need to be estimated with more parameters. In addition, the value of parameter p may also change across different points of a search session as users' search intentions and in situ expectations about search gains and efforts may vary overtime. When developing more advanced, bias-aware click models, RCM could be used as one of the baseline models for evaluation purposes.

Compared to RCM, RCTR and DCTR models take a step forward by including document rank and query-document pair, respectively (see Fig. 2.1). One commonly studied and estimated user bias is *rank position bias*. Specifically, users tend to consider top ranked results as relevant and credible, and the results ranked on the top generally have a higher click-through rate compared to lower ranked documents. In this sense, users' raw click logs as a relevance feedback could be biased, and this bias can in turn negatively affect the performance of click model in predicting future clicks. RCTR touches on this user bias and is built on the assumption that the click probability is not a constant value across all results. Instead, it depends on the rank of the document being retrieved and browsed. Thus, the focus of RCTR is on estimating the click-through rate for each rank position based on available training data. Compared to RCM, RCTR moves click models slightly closer to real users by recognizing the impact of rank position bias on click-through probability. There are also other cognitive biases that are closely associated with positions of rank and evaluation sequences, such as reference dependence (Liu & Han, 2020), threshold priming (Scholer et al., 2013), and anchoring effect (Chen et al., 2022). For better estimating users' click-through behavior and search experience, it is critical to properly represent and estimate the effect of these biases and limits in future click models.

Similarly, DCTR introduced by Craswell et al. (2008) added one parameter compared to RCM for estimating the click-through rates for each query-document pair. DCTR recognizes the perceived connection between query and document on users' click behaviors and offers click models more flexibility in capturing the dynamic relationship between query-document relevance and users' implicit rules

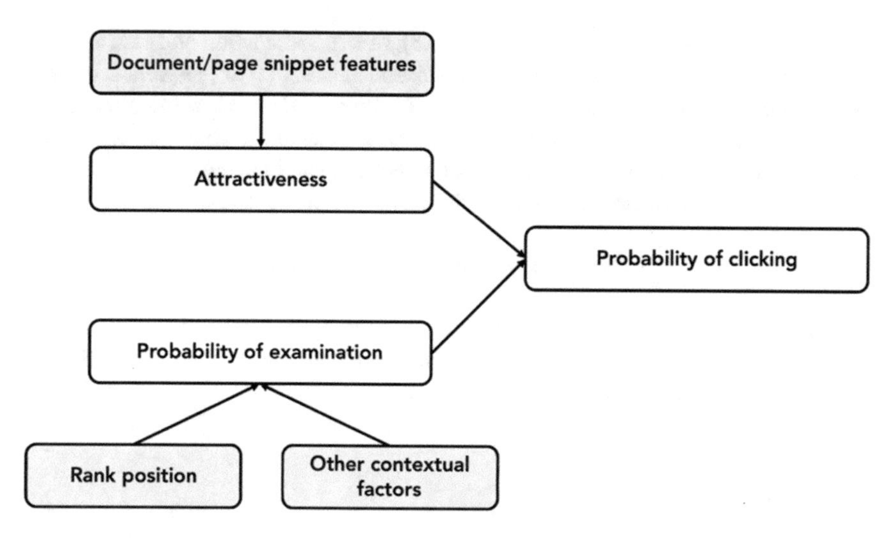

Fig. 2.2 Click models built upon examination hypothesis

and thresholds regarding document clicking. One main limitation is that the performance of DCTR model heavily relies on the documents and queries encountered and included in training click logs, and may not be able to estimate user clicks on new, previously unseen documents or under significantly different queries or topics. Another limitation, from user perspective, is that DCTR does not recognize the systematic biases that may lead to significant deviations in user feedback (e.g., clicks, prolonged dwell time on pages) from the actual connections in query-document pairs.

The three basic click models introduced above serve as useful baselines for further advancing and evaluating click models, especially in terms of combining rank position bias and document biases and capturing more aspects of user bounded rationality and actual information search strategies.

Built upon the three basic models above, IR researchers take a step forward and incorporate the probability of examination and document attractiveness into click models for modeling click behaviors and estimating document relevance. These more advanced models, such as position-based model (PBM), cascade model (CM), user browsing model (UBM), and dependent click model (DCM), were designed based on *examination hypothesis*: A user clicks a document only if they *examined* the document and were *attracted* by the retrieved document. As it is shown in Fig. 2.2, attractiveness is closely related to document or Web page snippet features, not the characteristics of the full text, which cannot be directly presented on SERPs. The probability of a user examining a presented result snippet highly depends on the rank position and is also affected by other contextual factors (e.g., format and textual features of result snippets). The effects of probability of examination E and document snippet attractiveness A may also be moderated by different aspects of users' bounded rationality, such as the impacts of previous relevance judgment experiences and dynamic thresholds (Scholer et al., 2013), in situ satisfaction and loss aversion bias (Liu & Han, 2020), time constraints (Crescenzi et al., 2016), as well as existing beliefs and anchoring biases (Chen et al., 2022; White, 2013). How to represent and measure the potential effects of bounded rationality factors in click models and the associated evaluation experiments still remains an open challenge.

Built upon examination hypothesis, the PBM can be written as follows:

$$P(C_d = 1) = P(E_d = 1) * P(A_d = 1) \tag{2.2}$$

where E_d represents examination behavior and A_d measures attractiveness. C_d refers to click on the document d. Furthermore, given that both the probability of examination and the probability of attractiveness are affected by contextual factors, we can use the following functions adapted from Craswell et al. (2008) to represent these contextual impacts:

$$P(A_d = 1) = \alpha_{dq} \tag{2.3}$$

$$P(E_d = 1) = \beta_{dr} \tag{2.4}$$

where α_{dq} and β_{dr} represent two sets of parameters that affect $P(A_d)$ and $P(E_d)$, respectively. While understanding the features of document snippets and rank positions is critical for estimating the probability of attractiveness and examination behavior, incorporating these traits into click models still cannot fully explain the discrepancy between predicted clicks and actual explicit feedback. Taking a step forward, researchers may be able to reduce the gap by investigating and representing user-side systematic biases, especially the ones caused by cognitive and perceptual factors. These effects can be written as follows:

$$P(A_d = 1) = U_b(\alpha_{dq}) \tag{2.5}$$

$$P(E_d = 1) = U_b(\beta_{dr}) \tag{2.6}$$

$$U_b = U(b_1, b_2, \ldots b_n) \tag{2.7}$$

where U_b represents a bias-aware user model that captures the impacts of document snippets, rank positions, and other system-side factors (e.g., textual features, interface design, and layout) under the influence of different dimensions of users' bounded rationality $b_1, b_2, \ldots b_n$.

As it is shown in Fig. 2.3, document and result snippet features affect the probabilities of attractiveness and examination under the influence of user characteristics, especially dimensions of bounded rationality, such as cognitive biases, perceptual biases, and situational limits (e.g., time constraints, task urgency) (cf. Azzopardi, 2021; Kahneman, 2003). Also, different types of user biases (e.g., reference dependence biases, decoy effects, peak-end evaluation biases) may interact with and even reinforce each other in decision-making scenarios, including the ones in search interactions (e.g., clicking, query reformulation, search stopping). In

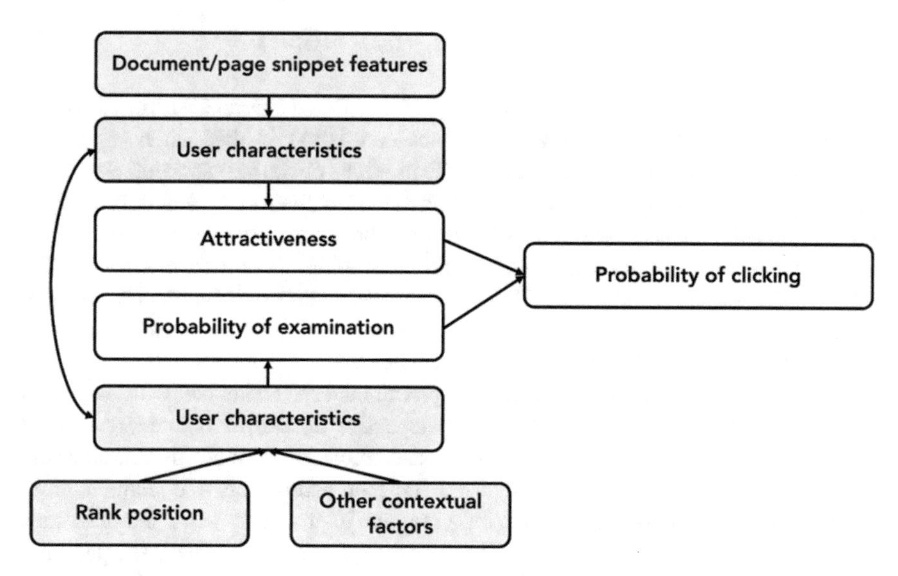

Fig. 2.3 Clicks under the impacts of user characteristics

addition, within the function U_b, the *weights* of different dimensions may differ from each other and change during the transitions of information search intentions, cognitive states, and task types (Liu & Yu, 2021). How to estimate the weights of different dimensions of bounded rationality and measure the interactions between human biases of varying types would be two key open questions for constructing bias-aware click models. While our discussion under this current section will continue with other types of existing click models, how to characterize and represent the impacts of bounded rationality will be discussed in the following chapters.

Similar to PBM, cascade model (CM) also considers attractiveness and examination in modeling clicks. According to Craswell et al. (2008), CM is built upon the assumption that a user scans results on a SERP sequentially from top to bottom until they find a relevant document that fulfills the information need in mind. Moreover, documents at rank 2 or lower are examined *only if* the previous document is examined but not clicked. This core assumption of CM can be written as Formula (2.8). CM enables simple estimation as it assumes that all documents before first click on the SERP are examined by the user. However, this assumption also restricts CM to one-click and linear examination sessions (Chuklin et al., 2015). This model setup could not explain the potential impacts of information gains and search efforts accumulated during search sessions on following search result clicking and evaluation behaviors. Also, with the increasing diversity in search result presentation on SERPs in Web search, it is also critical to investigate and predict the information gain obtained directly from non-clicked search result snippets for better understanding clicks and evaluating the quality of SERPs under queries with varying intentions (Azzopardi et al., 2018).

$$P\left(E_r = 1 \mid E_{r-1} = 1,\ \ C_{r-1} = 0\right) = 1 \tag{2.8}$$

To partially address these limitations, UBM and DCM extend CM from different perspectives. Specifically, the main idea behind UBM is that when estimating examination probability, we should also take previous clicks into account, especially the rank of the previously examined and clicked document. DCM is developed to model interactive search sessions with multiple clicked documents. The assumption is that a user may continue to examine and click other documents after clicking a document. If a document is clicked but does not lead to user satisfaction, the user will continue their examination of following documents and click the ones that may be relevant to the expressed information need. Given the above assumptions on click dependence, UBM and DCM could be presented and estimated with Bayesian network (Chuklin et al., 2015). From the perspective of real-life boundedly rational users, these assumptions and new setups also allow researchers to examine and represent the connections between users' current actions on a document (e.g., examination, click, continuation) with previous interactions (e.g., examinations and clicks on higher ranked documents under the query) and thus have the potential to incorporate and model some of the user biases that rely on accumulated in situ information gains, efforts, associated user expectations, and interaction experiences (e.g., reference dependence biases, loss aversion biases).

Figure 2.4 illustrates the click model framework extended with the assumptions and parameters from DCM and UBM discussed above. The extended framework connects current examination with previous clicks, examination, and user satisfaction and thus has the potential to handle more complex, multi-click search sessions. In addition to the extensions from DCM and UBM, the framework also highlights the potential moderating effects from user characteristics (especially user biases and other dimensions of bounded rationality) on the impacts of previous clicks and examinations. For instance, anchoring effects may motivate users to put higher weights on the examined and clicked documents that are aligned with their

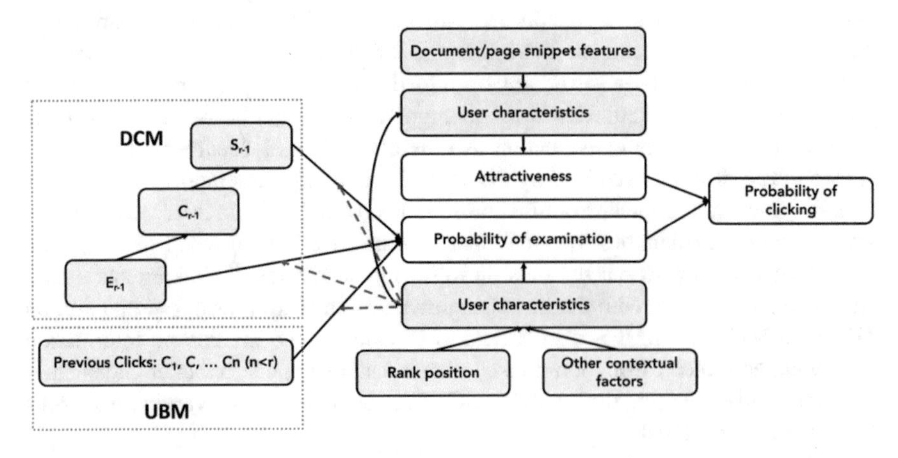

Fig. 2.4 Click modeling extended with DCM and UBM

pre-search beliefs and expectations, which may also lead to biased evaluations (e.g., overestimation on document relevance and usefulness) (Chen et al., 2022). In addition, recency effects may lead to higher weights on most recently clicked and viewed documents and associated interaction experience (e.g., satisfied or dissatisfied; overall document usefulness and information search efforts) (Liu et al., 2019a, b). Also, the limits of a user's knowledge structure, search skills, and topical familiarity may lead to difficulties and errors in judging document relevance and credibility, which leads to unexpected clicks that deviate from the formal predictions made based on document ranks and relevance scores. These aspects of bounded rationality play an essential role in the interplay of user perception and cognition, system and document features (including the traits of search result snippets), and different aspects of search interactions (e.g., click, query formulation, document evaluation). Although the current click models with associated Bayesian framework may be useful to at least partially capture this dependence relationship, it is important to systematically examine the role of users' bounded rationality at different phases and components of click models in order to predict user clicks and estimate true document relevance in a more accurate manner. To achieve this, researchers need a deeper exploration and reflection on user characteristics and leverage the insights from behavioral economics and cognitive psychology in modeling and representing the clicking, SERP examination, and document evaluation strategies of boundedly rational users.

Click models are a major form of formal modeling that characterizes and simulates user behavior in online information seeking and retrieval. Click actions connect search interactions (e.g., query formulation and reformulation, browsing and examination, and associated document features) and information evaluations (document relevance, usefulness, attractiveness) and thus can serve as a critical hub for studying the role and impacts of user biases and contextual factors. In addition, document examination and clicking are also shaped by the features of motivating tasks and affect users' in situ information gain (e.g., new facts and knowledge learned, new ideas and interests generated) and overall task performance and decision-making outcome. The next section will summarize more recent and advanced click models that enhance the basic click models discussed above by incorporating new parameters and utilizing new data and search signals, especially the ones that employ state-of-the-art machine learning techniques. We will also discuss the potentials and limitations of advanced click models, especially in terms of capturing the impacts of users' bounded rationality on search decision-making and judgment as well as other session-level contextual features (e.g., search task facets, system interface, and search recommendations). Discussions on click models and other user models in IR modeling and simulation serve as part of the preparation for representing bounded rationality and developing bias-aware user models and search evaluation metrics.

2.3 Advanced Click Models

Inspired by Chuklin et al. (2015) and Wang et al. (2015a, b), this section discusses a series of advanced click models that extend basic model setups and characterize beyond-one-query sessions and explore richer user characteristics and behavioral signals. Methodologically, while the major goals remain similar to basic models (e.g., estimating/learning document relevance and predicting users' clicks on SERPs), the advanced click models further incorporate feature-based machine learning and fine-grained interaction signals (e.g., eye tracking and mouse movement) into click model training and evaluation and may have better potential in capturing the nuance and temporal variations in users' cognitive states, relevance thresholds, and in situ expectations regarding informational gains and search efforts. Differing from traditional SERPs consisting of organic search results only, SERPs in *aggregated* or *federated search* paradigm often include multiple sources and forms of information, which are usually called as *verticals* (e.g., answer card, images, video clips, apps, and products; see Fig. 2.5). As it is shown in the example, SERPs include not only organic results (e.g., introductions of Washington state and salmon from Wikipedia pages; Web page explaining salmon recipes) but also different verticals, such as frequently asked questions, images, news from media outlets, and videos from different sources.

Adding and presenting multiple verticals become common for contemporary commercial Web search engines and have changed the way in which users click and interact with search results (Kopliku et al., 2014). For instance, some verticals may offer direct answers or salient cues to users, which do not require users to click and further examine for more details. This "good abandonment" behavior is less common on traditional SERPs where the regular search result snippets may only serve as an initial indicator of topical relevance and do not have the direct answers or key facts presented. In addition, the presence of vertical blocks also affects the attention distribution on other nearby results and causes certain attention bias and divergence in eye fixations and mouse movements (Liu et al., 2016). According to Chen et al. (2012), results that are presented near a vertical (e.g., image, answer card, news stories) could receive higher chance of being clicked than their counterparts that are ranked near regular organic results. This diversification of result form as a fundamental change of search result presentation on SERPs also affect search evaluation and user behavior modeling, especially the modeling of browsing activities (Arguello & Capra, 2012; Arguello et al., 2012; Bron et al., 2013; Liu et al., 2015; Xie et al., 2020). To partially address this problem, IR researchers have developed novel evaluation frameworks for properly measuring the utility of SERPs consisting of diverse verticals and components in addition to organic results (e.g., Azzopardi et al., 2018; Zhou et al., 2012). The presence of diverse types of verticals leads to varying interaction patterns and may create extra challenges for capturing the impacts of human biases and cognitive limits (e.g., attention bias, salience bias, effects of click baits). Researchers may need to include additional parameters for representing levels of impacts from individual biases and model user

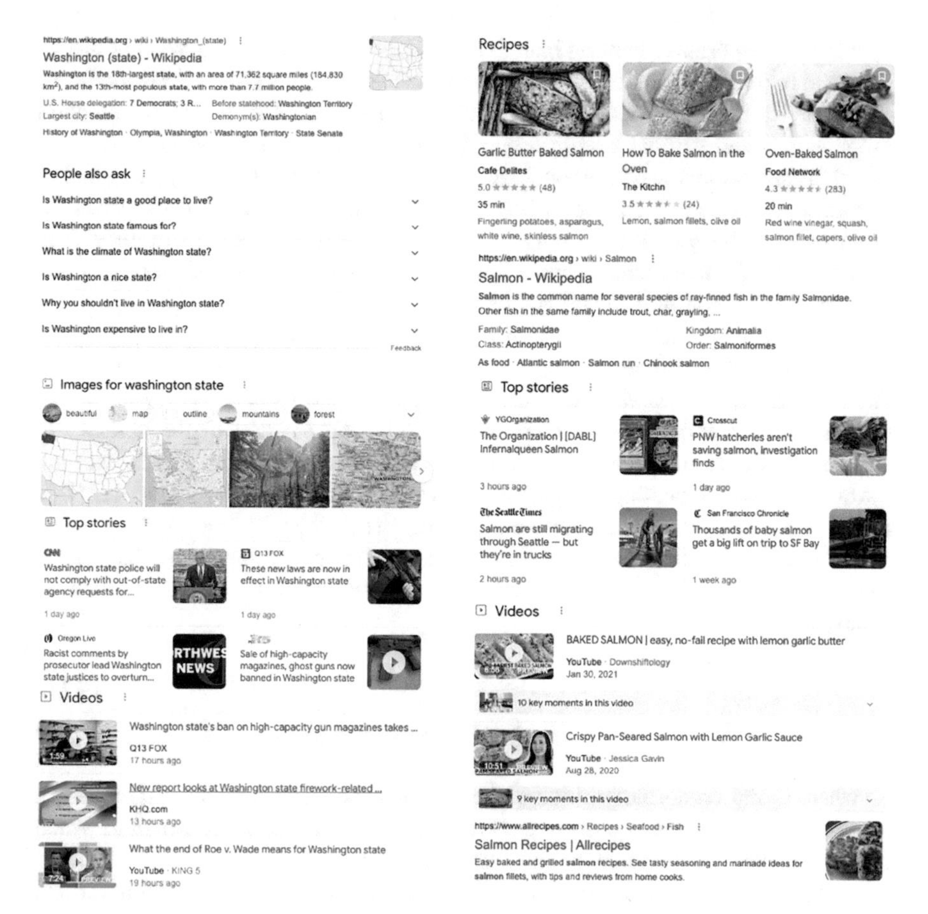

Fig. 2.5 Two examples of search engine result pages (SERPs) retrieved with queries "Washington state" (left) and "salmon" (right), respectively

behavioral patterns on traditional non-vertical documents and verticals of varying types separately on SERPs.

To model and predict users' clicks in aggregated search, IR researchers have developed and evaluated click models of varying complexities to cover potential cognitive and behavioral biases caused by verticals on SERPs. According to Chen et al. (2012), apart from rank position bias, results presented near vertical documents (e.g., images, videos, news) usually attract more attention from users due to higher saliency, which results in higher click-through rate. Based on this finding, Chen et al. (2012) develop federated click model (FCM), which includes a parameter that accounts for the attention bias associated with vertical results. The basic FCM model can be written as follows:

$$P\left(E_r = 1 \mid A = 0,\ \ E_{<r}, S_{<r}, C_{<r}\right) = \varepsilon_r \tag{2.9}$$

$$P\left(E_r = 1 \mid A = 1,\ \ E_{<r}, S_{<r}, C_{<r}\right) = \varepsilon_r + (1 - \varepsilon_r)\beta_d \tag{2.10}$$

where A represents attention bias. If A = 1, then the results near vertical blocks receive a higher examination rate. Similar to that of previous basic click models, E, S, C represents the interaction history before result r. ε_r refers to the examination probability when vertical attention bias is absent. β_d measures the impact of the actual distance from the current document to the nearest vertical document. A higher β_d value represents either a short distance from current result to the nearest vertical block or a relatively high sensitivity to vertical results in attention distribution. The actual parameters that shape examination probability can be estimated based on click through data, mouse movement, and eye movement signals.

To model the probability of attention bias $P(A = 1)$, Chen et al. (2012) propose two different assumptions or approaches, namely, *position attention model* and *document attention model*. Under the position attention model, the attention bias on a SERP is assumed to be determined only by the position of the vertical. In contrast, under document attention model, the attention bias is associated with the intrinsic features (including the relevance level r_d) of the vertical document d. This model is designed to account for the situation where when different vertical documents are placed at the same rank position, the attention bias values are still different. The position attention model and document attention model can be written as follows:

$$P\ (A = 1\ |P_d) = att_d \tag{2.11}$$

$$P\ (A = 1\ |d) = att_d \tag{2.12}$$

where P_d represents the position of the document being examined and d refers to a set of rank-independent document parameters. att_d characterizes the extent to which a user's attention is attracted by and spent on the target document.

Compared to basic click models, FCM examines the complexity from vertical blocks on SERPs and accounts for vertical-related attention biases, in addition to widely examined rank position biases. Knowledge learned about this attention bias may also be valuable for researchers to develop more dynamic and realistic weight discount distributions for offline evaluation metrics, instead of monotonically increasing by rank (e.g., normalized discounted cumulative gain, nDCG). Taking multiple aspects and forms of attention biases into consideration would enhance our understanding of the intrinsic nonlinearity in users' browsing and examination activities, especially on SERPs that contain diverse vertical blocks, and thereby facilitate the associated evaluation experiments. Apart from examination probability, features of vertical blocks (e.g., color, form, font size, image) may generate similar effects as characteristics of regular search result snippets and thereby affect result attractiveness. Results presented as or near vertical blocks on SERP (even not ranked as top search results) may be more likely to attract users' attentions during browsing processes. Furthermore, according to Chuklin et al. (2015) and Chen et al. (2012), FCM model can also be extended to represent individual differences in vertical-related attention biases (e.g., some users may be more sensitive to vertical results in examination under certain tasks) and measure the impacts of multiple vertical blocks.

While FCM model considers attention bias related to vertical features, users' clicks are also affected by other types of cognitive and perceptual biases at both global (i.e., whole SERP) and local (i.e., individual results). To address this challenge, Wang et al. (2013) develop an extended vertical click model (VCM) that takes into account four types of biases, some of which correspond to the cognitive biases and dimensions of bounded rationality examined in behavioral economics and decision-making experiments. Specifically, Wang et al. (2013) analyzed both large-scale click-through log data and laboratory eye-tracking data and examined four types of biases, including attraction bias, global bias, first place bias, and sequence bias.

The assumption behind *attraction bias* is that when there is a vertical block presented on the SERP, there is a chance that users examine the vertical result first. This assumption highlights the additional attraction associated with the saliency of vertical results (compared to regular organic search results) and can be written as follows:

$$P\left(F=1\right)=\varnothing_{t_v,p_v} \tag{2.13}$$

where F as a binary variable represents the probability of the vertical result being examined first on the SERP. t_v and p_v represent the type and position of the vertical result, respectively. $\{\varnothing\}$ refers to a set of customized global parameters that vary across different classes and positions of vertical blocks.

Global bias defines the "spillover effect" of vertical results on browsing activities. Specifically, it assumes that if a vertical is presented in a SERP and user examines it first, this examination event will generate a global impression on the whole SERP, which will affect the user's examination and click probability of all other results on the SERP. The formalization and representation of global bias can help partially address the limitation of models and metrics, assuming that different results on a SERP are examined independently. Also, the assumption regarding global bias could also be extended to cover the effects of motivating tasks, contextual constraints (e.g., time limit, available system support, and query recommendations), and the examination and click events in previous queries or search intervals under the same session.

Regarding *first place bias*, Wang et al. (2013) assume that if a vertical result is placed at the first position in a SERP, there is probability that the user examines and clicks more on vertical results and less on other types of results in search interactions. This assumption to some extent echoes *reference dependence* and *anchoring biases* (cf. Kahneman, 2003) in that it focuses on the possible impacts of first encountered results and experience on following interaction behaviors. According to Wang et al. (2013), both global bias and first place bias can be represented and written as:

$$P\left(E_i=1 \mid F=1\right)=P\left(E_i=1 \mid F=0\right)+\theta_{q,i} \tag{2.14}$$

$$P\left(A_i=1 \mid E_i=1, F=1\right)=P\left(A_i=1 \mid E_i=1, F=0\right)+\beta_{q,i} \tag{2.15}$$

where $P\left(E_i = 1 | F = 0\right)$ measures the probability of examination on document I when the presented vertical is not examined first. The additional global impression generated by the vertical result ($F = 1$) on examination and attractiveness events, compared to the situation where the vertical result is not examined first, is measured by the parameter sets $\{\theta\}$ and $\{\beta\}$. Apart from the document and position features, this hypothesized additional impression may also be shaped and moderated by individual users' characteristics, such as their current information seeking intention (e.g., finding a known item or exploring an unfamiliar topic), levels of search skills, and search environments (e.g., desktop search or mobile search, levels of unexpected interruptions, urgency of the search task at hand) (Arguello et al., 2012).

According to the assumption of sequence bias, if a user's examination on the SERP starts from the vertical block, the user will revisit the results ranked above the vertical in either top down or reversed order. The four types of biases discussed above are supported by the empirical evidences extracted from click-through and eye-tracking data and could serve as initial basis for exploring and modeling more complex and individualized cognitive biases. The impacts of human biases, tasks, and contextual constraints need to be systematically examined and could be represented as part of the global parameters. The detailed description and result discussion associated with the VCM can be found in the original research conducted by Wang et al. (2013).

In addition to the effects of rank positions and features of vertical blocks, users' information needs, intents, or information seeking intentions under each query may also affect the examination and click probabilities as well as evaluation criteria on search results presented in the SERP (Chuklin et al., 2015; Mitsui et al., 2017). For instance, users under different motivating tasks (e.g., browsing news about a trending topic, learning knowledge about a natural scenery) may have different preferences and levels of attention on different types of results and verticals (e.g., news, images, videos) (Chuklin et al., 2013). Also, under different information seeking intentions (e.g., exploring a new domain, finding a known fact or item, comparing collected information and evaluating credibility), users' click and examination patterns across different result types and rank positions may vary largely (Mitsui et al., 2017; Liu et al., 2019a, b) and thus would require separate click models and metrics for supporting parameter estimation and search system evaluation.

According to Chuklin et al. (2013)'s intent-aware click model, assuming the query-level intents are independent from each other, then click probability can be written as follows:

$$P\,(C_1, C_2 \ldots C_n) = \sum\nolimits_i P\,(I = i) * P(C_1, C_2 \ldots C_n | \, I = i) \tag{2.16}$$

where users may have different click and examination probability distributions under different intent i. Also, the biases associated with verticals discussed above may interact with the intent-related biases and generate mixed effects on browsing and search result examination events. This concept of intent and other similar query-level driving factors (e.g., information seeking or search intention) could help connect local search activities with global motivating tasks and help explain and model the effects of search task characteristics and session-level contextual constraints on examination and click probabilities on different SERPs and rank positions. In addition, the intent-aware model can also be integrated with other click models (e.g., FCM, UBM) for examining the impacts of different intents while taking other factors and parameters into consideration, and this integration could lead to significant improvements in terms of perplexity (Chuklin et al., 2015).

One of the key challenges of modeling clicks in an intent-aware fashion is to predict intents and learn intent distributions from search log data and available annotations. The intention distribution across different queries may differ across different sessions, tasks, and user populations, and within each query segment, a user may have multiple intents (e.g., an information need that requires multiple types of information objects) and information seeking intentions (Mitsui et al., 2017). This diversity in intents and relationships between different intentions may add extra difficulties for estimating intent presence probabilities and developing generalizable intent models. Therefore, instead of representing intents and user biases as individual items and binary variables (i.e., presence or absence), researchers may need to develop vector representation of *intent combinations* in order to accommodate possible multi-intent search scenarios (Liu et al., 2020). This can be written as follows:

$$I_i = I\,(intent_1, \;\; intent_2, \;\; \ldots intent_n) \tag{2.17}$$

$$P\,(C_1, C_2 \ldots C_n) = \sum\nolimits_i P\,(I = I_i) * P(C_1, C_2 \ldots C_n | \, I = I_i) \tag{2.18}$$

$$P\,(I = I_i) = f(T, U, S) + \varepsilon \tag{2.19}$$

where I_i represents different intent or user intention combinations. Estimating $P\,(I = I_i)$ would require richer knowledge of task features T, user characteristics U, and local search state S. Differing from the single-intent assumption, this revised model assumes that different queries or states of search are associated with significantly different intent combinations. Therefore, researchers and system designers may need to learn different intent combinations from search interaction data and explore the associations between intent combinations and click probabilities.

Recent studies on search intent and intention modeling (e.g., Liu et al., 2019a, b; Mitsui et al., 2016, 2017; Ruotsalo et al., 2014) and state-aware search evaluation and recommendation (e.g., Liu & Yu, 2021; Liu et al., 2020; Liu & Shah, 2022; Luo et al., 2014) could be useful initial steps toward addressing this open question. In particular, Liu et al. (2020) found that although there might be a large number of possible intention combinations from search sessions, the overall distributions could be clustered into a relatively small number of search task states, which makes it possible to identify main types of intent combinations and develop state-aware adaptive recommendations.

2.4 Clicks and Examinations in Multi-query Search Sessions

Under complex, intellectually challenging tasks, users often need to engage in a sequence of queries, rather than a single query or SERP, in addressing their information needs under the same task (Byström & Hansen, 2005; Liu, 2021). Within a task-oriented *search session*, two consecutive query intervals may have different intents and click probabilities at different rank positions. Also, users' actions and evaluations in previous query intervals may also affect their current examination and click probabilities and contribute to certain cognitive biases (e.g., anchoring biases, reference dependence, and loss aversion biases). These cross-query connections, query reformulation activities, and associated behavioral impacts in search sessions would not be captured if we consider and investigate each query separately.

To model document clicking patterns in multi-query search sessions, Zhang et al. (2011) develop a task-centric click model (TCM). TCM is built upon two assumptions defined according to the empirical results regarding within-session browsing and clicking patterns. While there are different definitions and operationalizations of tasks and search sessions, Zhang et al. (2011) adopted the method of setting up default time and similarity thresholds for identifying and segmenting individual task-based sessions (Piwowarski et al., 2009). The two assumptions include:

- *Query bias*: If there is a mismatch between current query and the user's search intent, the user will reformulate a new query based on the information learned from search results without clicking any of the retrieved results.
- *Duplicate bias*: If a previously examined document appear again under a new query, it will have a lower probability to be clicked.

Based on these two assumptions, Zhang et al. (2011) formulize TCM as follows:

$$P\left(M=1\right)=\theta_1 \tag{2.20}$$

$$P\left(N=1 \mid M=1\right)=\theta_2 \tag{2.21}$$

$$P\left(F_{m,n}=1 \mid H_{m,n}=1\right)=\theta_3 \tag{2.22}$$

$$P\left(E_{m,n}=1\right)=\varnothing_n \tag{2.23}$$

$$P\left(R_{m,n}=1\right)=r_d \tag{2.24}$$

$$P\left(N_m=1 \mid M_m=0\right)=1 \tag{2.25}$$

$$P\left(F_{m,n}=1 \mid H_{m,n}=0\right)=1 \tag{2.26}$$

$$P\left(C_{m,n}=1 \mid M_m=1, \quad E_{m,n}=1, R_{m,n}=1, F_{m,n}=1\right)=1 \tag{2.27}$$

The notations used in TCM are defined as follows:

- *M*: whether a user's current search intent matches with the current query. M = 0 (mismatch between query and intent) is part of the prerequisites that trigger query reformulation behavior.
- *N*: whether a user is going to reformulate a new query.
- *H*: whether the document presented under query m at the n-th rank position occurred in an earlier query interval or session. When H = 1, the probability of examination would be lower than that of the situation where the document is new and has never been presented to the user before.
- *F*: whether the document is considered as "fresh" to the user. When H = 0, the document will be considered as a fresh document (see Formula 2.26).
- *E*: Examination of the document presented under query m at the n-th rank position in a search session.
- *R:* Relevance of the document. Formula (2.24) models the position bias in relevance evaluation.
- *C*: Whether the document presented under query m at the n-th rank position is clicked by the user. According to TCM and the assumptions, click probability is affected by not only the intrinsic feature of the document (e.g., $R_{m,\ n}$, other document factors that affect attractiveness A and examination E) but also by the comparison of the current document with previous documents (e.g., $F_{m,\ n}$, $H_{m,\ n}$) as well as the nature of the query in the session (M_m) (see Formula 2.27).

Compared to basic individual-SERP-based click models, the new parameters included in TCM (e.g., M_m, $F_{m,\ n}$) take into account the role of the document and query within the context of entire interactive search session (instead of treating them as separate disconnected items) and connects current click decisions to the user's previous search and browsing activities. In addition, similar to VCM, TCM can also be modified to be integrated with existing basic click models (Zhang et al., 2011).

To better leverage fine-grained session information in relevance estimation and click prediction, Chen et al. (2020) propose the context-aware click model (CACM), which is built upon an *end-to-end* neural network. CACM as a neural-based model jointly learns the relevance score and click probabilities of each specific document in sessions. CACM includes a relevance estimator and an examination predictor. In the relevance estimator, both the inter-session context information (*query context* and *click context*) and features of the current documents are encoded for supporting context-aware relevance estimation. Intra-session context is utilized to predict the examination probability. Then, with a combination layer, the relevance estimator and examination predictor are integrated together for predicting click activities at different documents, ranks, and moments of search sessions.

Differing from the top-down setup of TCM and other related click models, CACM adopts a *data-driven* approach and learns query-level and session-level contexts through the raw connections in search log data, such as *query-query* edge (i.e., reformulation relationship between two consecutive search queries), *URL-URL* edge (i.e., the similarity of two contiguous results and their rank positions), as well as *query-URL* edge (i.e., a query and each of the retrieved documents under the query). To facilitate relevance estimation and examination prediction, researchers applied *node2vec* technique (Grover & Leskovec, 2016) to learn the embeddings of query and URL vectors based on the *session-flow graph* consisting of diverse edges and nodes. Chen et al. (2020) found that CACM achieves significantly better performance compared to existing best-performing click models in terms of both relevance estimation and click prediction and that incorporating session context information into click model can enhance the process of relevance estimation, which also leads to significant improvements in document ranking performance measured by nDCG scores at different rank positions.

Compared to traditional click models, models that utilize neural network and pre-trained models can better characterize the rich connections and nuances among queries and URLs which occur at different moments of search sessions. In addition to CACM, Lin et al. (2021) also go beyond traditional click models built upon probabilistic graphical models and oversimplified, manually designed dependencies among variables and leverage neural network techniques in developing a *graph-enhanced* click model (GraphCM) for Web search. To better capture and utilize inter-session and intra-session contextual information for click prediction, researchers construct *query homogeneous graph* and *document homogeneous graph*, respectively, based on session log data. The two graphs extract and model dependencies in user search behaviors and cover four types of edges in session-flow graphs:

- *Query multi-hop edge*, which connects queries that include clicks on the same document on the SERP
- *Query-query edge*, which refers to each pair of two consecutive queries from the same search session
- *Doc multi-hop edge*, which characterizes the relationship between documents that are clicked under the same query
- *Doc-doc edge*, which focuses on rank position information and connects two consecutive documents in a ranked result list

Figure 2.6 illustrates the general structure of graph-based session click models. In addition to the explicit connections (e.g., consecutive queries in sessions, adjacent documents in ranked result lists) and click behaviors that connect individual queries and retrieved documents (represented by arrows in Fig. 2.6), there are also implicit connections (e.g., multi-hop edge in Lin et al., 2021) that characterize the relationships between queries under which the same document is clicked and the relationships between documents that are clicked under the same query (represented by red

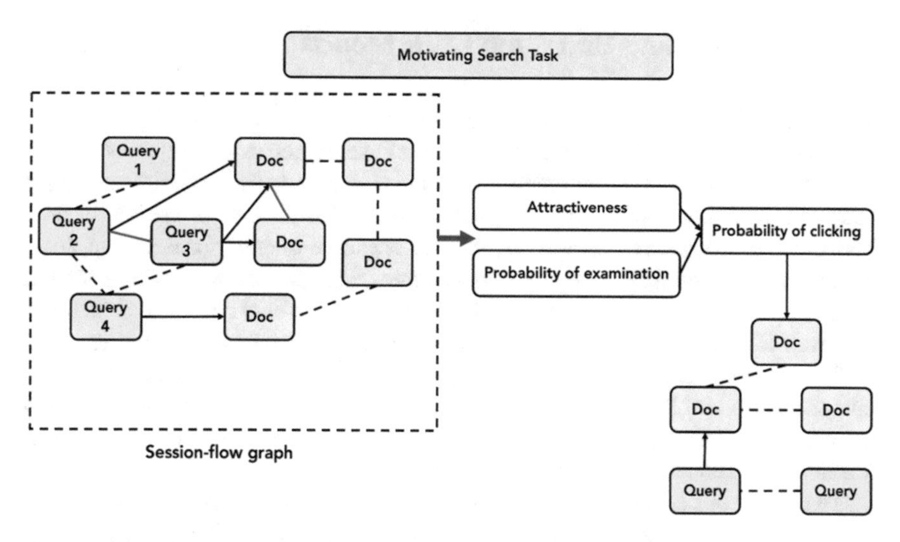

Fig. 2.6 General structure of graph-based session click models

edges). Neural-based models can help extract large amounts of explicit and multi-hop edges from search logs consisting of queries, clicks, and documents and turn them into features that can help estimate attractiveness scores, probability of examination, relevance levels, and ultimately the probability of clicking. Based on the results from extensive experiments on three real-life search session datasets, Lin et al. (2021) found that the constructed graphs and edges can effectively utilize the intra-session and inter-session information in estimating examination probabilities and attractiveness scores and help address data sparsity and cold-start problems in model training.

As discussed above, neural-network-based click models can better capture the diverse connections among queries, URLs, and user activities and thus can extract richer information behind click decisions (e.g., through learning embeddings of query and URL vectors) than manually designed dependencies in basic click models (see Fig. 2.4). However, the application of advanced neural networks in estimating relevance and predicting examination and click events also bring explainability challenges to researchers and system engineers, especially in terms of how exactly the hidden signals (e.g., edges, previous click patterns) in Web search logs are utilized and what user biases (if any) are captured or represented in the trained click models. Also, investigating the dimensions of users' bounded rationality and incorporating the learned knowledge into formal user models would be critical for measuring the actual contributions of neural models to characterizing click behaviors and, more importantly, clarifying the *reusability boundary* of session search datasets and trained click models across different user groups and search task contexts (Liu, 2022).

2.5 Incorporating Users into Click Models

While both the manually designed and learned dependencies and edges in many click models reflect certain aspects and levels of user search strategies, most of them did not explicitly include user characteristics into click models. Instead, they mainly focus on the features of documents and issued queries as well as the connections between them (*explicit connections*, e.g., consecutive queries, consecutive documents on the same SERP; *implicit connections*, e.g., pair of queries that include clicks on the same document; pair of documents that are clicked in the same query interval). It is unclear how the interactions between documents and queries, especially the ones that are learned from large-scale search logs, help characterize user characteristics and behavioral patterns and how the learned knowledge or empirically confirmed theories regarding users' search actions could be reused and generalized in a broader range of search scenarios.

To address this challenge and explore ways to represent user characteristics, Shen et al. (2012) propose a personalized click model (PCM) to define and characterize user-centered click preferences in search sessions. PCM assumes that the attractiveness parameter α_{uq} has a Gaussian prior that is defined by three factors, including document matrix D_d, query matrix Q_q, and user matrix U_u. Figure 2.7 illustrates the structure of PCM, which can also be connected to previous basic click models. PCM adopts the basic structure of *matrix factorization click model* (MFCM) that describes the interactions between queries and documents through their latent feature vectors and extends MFCM by including an additional matrix into the model to denote the latent factors of user domain. According to Shen et al. (2012), PCM can be written as:

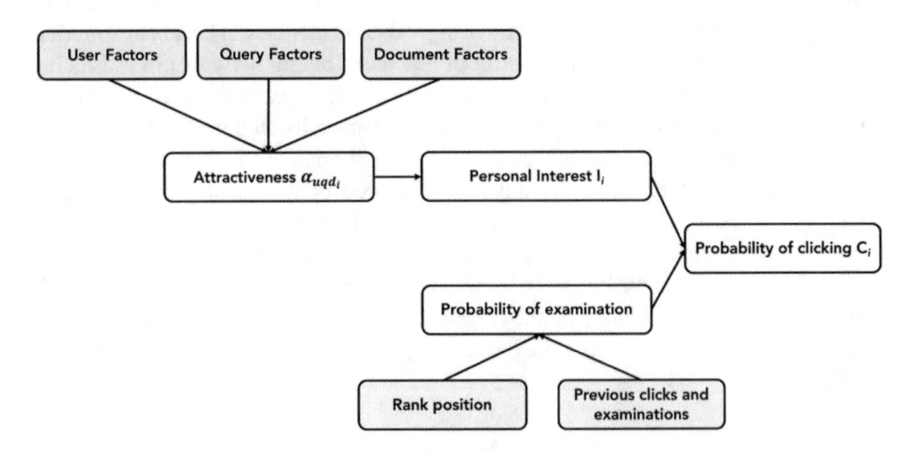

Fig. 2.7 Factors of personalized click models

$$P\ (A=1)=\alpha_{uqd_i} \tag{2.28}$$

$$P\ \left(\alpha_{uqd_i} \mid U_u, Q_q, D_d, \sigma\right) \sim N\left(\left(U_u \circ D_d \circ Q_q\right), \sigma^2\right) \tag{2.29}$$

$$P\ (U_u \mid \sigma_u) \sim N\left(0, \sigma_u^2\right) \tag{2.30}$$

$$P\ \left(Q_q \mid \sigma_q\right) \sim N\left(0, \sigma_q^2\right) \tag{2.31}$$

$$P\ (D_d \mid \sigma_d) \sim N\left(0, \sigma_d^2\right) \tag{2.32}$$

where $U_u \circ D_d \circ Q_q = \sum_{f=1}^{F} U_{fu} Q_{fq} D_{fd}$ is defined as a canonical tensor factorization. In PCM, while the probability of examining a document, $P\ (E_d = 1)$, is determined by the assumptions and variables defined in previous click models, a user's personal interest (affected by attractiveness scores) on document i, I_i, is represented with a probability function based upon the latent factors of queries, documents, and users. Compared to existing click models, PCM takes a step forward by modeling the interactions among users, queries, and documents in search interactions. However, it is also acknowledged in Shen et al. (2012) that PCM could suffer from overfitting problem, especially in some factual and navigational searches where the impact of personal difference is insignificant in click and examination events.

To partially address this overfitting issue and balance the represented impacts of query-document pairs and user characteristics, Shen et al. (2012) develop a hybrid personalized click model (HPCM), which re-focuses on the connections between queries and documents and only factorize residuals using user latent factors. In HPCM, the factorized residuals and user latent factors are used to describe the individual users' deviations from the "global model" defined by query-document interactions. The distribution of α_{uqd_i} in HPCM can be written as:

$$P\ \left(\alpha_{uqd_i} \mid U_u, Q_q, D_d, \sigma\right) \sim N\left(\left(\tilde{D}_d \circ \tilde{Q}_q + U_u \circ D_d \circ Q_q\right), \sigma^2\right) \tag{2.33}$$

where $\tilde{D}_d \circ \tilde{Q}_q$ denotes query-document interactions, which can be considered as a *relevance bias*, and $U_u \circ D_d \circ Q_q$ depicts the biases and deviations from user side. Differing from PCM, HPCM adds the local personalization factor after the global inference of query-document relevance. More details regarding the model setup of PCM and HPCM can be found in the original published paper.

PCM and HPCM explicitly integrate user domain into click models and allow researchers to directly estimate the potential impacts of user factors, especially on attractiveness. Future research on users' bounded rationality could further specify the Gaussian prior associated with user domain and define the distribution functions according to the knowledge of human biases and cognitive limits confirmed through behavioral experiments. For instance, due to the presence of reference dependence biases and peak-end evaluation rule (cf. Liu & Han, 2020), the impacts of user domain may vary across different queries within a session. Documents that presented in the first query segments and last query segments have achieve higher attractiveness scores compared to documents with similar quality and textual features retrieved under other queries because of higher level of user attention allocated. Thus, we may need to include a position parameter p to denote the position of current query within the associated search session. This position information could help estimate the true effects of user features, especially their cognitive and perceptual biases (cf. Azzopardi, 2021), in a more accurate manner. The modified function can be written as follows:

$$P\left(U_{up} \mid \sigma_u\right) \sim N\left(\tau_p, \sigma_u^2\right) \tag{2.34}$$

In addition to the potential biases associated with query positions in session sequences, users may also be affected by other biases related to the features of search result snippets and vertical blocks. As it is suggested in vertical-based click models, researchers may need to define separate priors for different components of SERPs (e.g., organic search results, ads, different forms of vertical results) and estimate the effects of user factors, query factors, and document factors on clicks across different components separately.

Similar to Shen et al. (2012), Xing et al. (2013) also investigate the heterogeneity among different users in terms of search result browsing patterns and incorporates user preferences into click models. Based on eye tracking and click through log analyses, researchers found that users have diverse examination and browsing strategies, which is difficult to capture for any uniform click model. Based on this observation, Xing et al. (2013) propose two *preference factors* to partially characterize the uniqueness of individual users in click and browsing.

- *Examination preference*, which refers to the probability of a document being examined by different users. Specifically, when encountering the same or similar documents ranked at the same position on SERPs, different users may still have largely different preferences or probability of examination. This examination preference could be affected by a series of contextual factors, such as a user's patience, search task urgency, local information seeking intentions, topic familiarity and interest, as well as cognitive biases. Users who have high examination preference may examine more documents on the ranked search result list.
- *Click preference*, which measures the probability of a document being clicked when the document is already examined. Similar to examination preference, click preference also denotes an aspect of users' individual characteristics and is associated with different users' individual thresholds of relevance judgment and clicks. The assumption associated with this preference factor is that users with high click preference is more likely to click a document. Click preference as part of user features is also assumed to be consistent within all search interactions of a user.

Figure 2.8 illustrates the structure of preference-based click model discussed above. Built upon these two preference factors, Xing et al. (2013) develop new

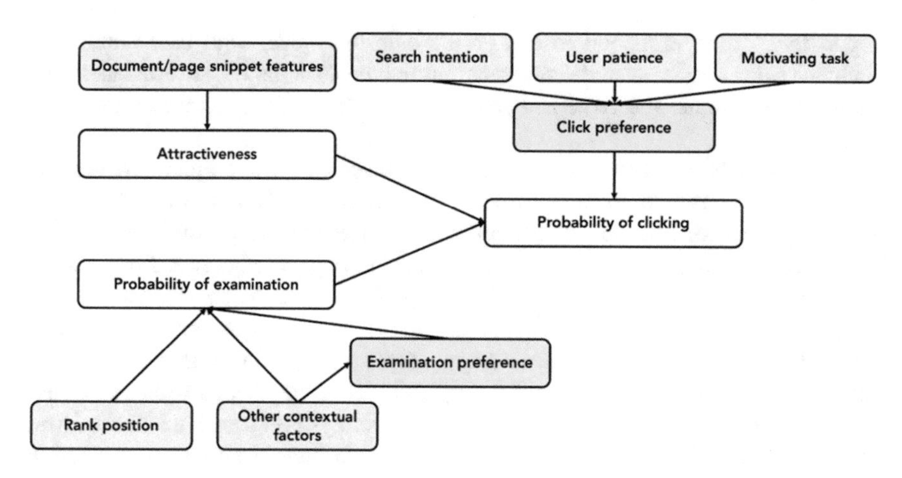

Fig. 2.8 Preference-based click models

preference-aware click models by incorporating examination preference parameter and click preference parameter into existing click models. Specifically, the researchers assume that the examination preference EP and click preference CP both follow Bernoulli distribution in click models. Thus, the probability distribution for user p can be written as follows:

$$P\,(EP|\,p) = \delta_p^{EP}(1-\delta_p)^{1-EP} \tag{2.35}$$

$$P\,(CP|\,p) = \varnothing_p^{HP}(1-\varnothing_p)^{1-HP} \tag{2.36}$$

where EP indicates whether the examination preference is met and CP measures whether the click preference is met. Based upon the two preference distribution functions above, the click probability can be written as:

$$P\,(C\mid d, q, r, l, p) = \partial_{d,q}\,\beta_r\delta_p\varnothing_p \tag{2.37}$$

where d, q, r, and p denote document, query, rank position, and user, respectively. l represents the distance of current document to the last clicked document. Following the basic setup of user browsing model, ∂ measures the probability of the target document being relevant to the query, and β represents the probability of the document being examined by the user.

In addition, according to Xing et al. (2013), user preference factors can also be incorporated into logistic model. The adjusted model can be written as:

$$P\,(C\mid d, q, r, p) = \mu(\beta_r + \delta_p)\mu(\partial_{d,q} + \varnothing_p) \tag{2.38}$$

where $\mu(x)$ represents the logistic function. More details regarding the model design and experimental setup can be found in the original paper. Xing et al. (2013)

report that the experimental results on the adjusted model with user preferences included show consistent and significant improvements in model performances. This finding demonstrates the value and potential of integrating explicit user factors with click modeling.

More broadly, the user-aware click models discussed above open new research space for scientists to explore different formal representations of user factors, including facets of bounded rationality, and evaluate their respective contributions to the tasks of document examination and clickthrough predictions. For instance, both the examination preference and click preference could be affected by both individual cognitive biases and situational factors. When a user aims to explore an unfamiliar domain or seek to learn a group of new skills, the user may be open to a diverse set of results and topics, which may lead to relatively higher examination and click preferences. Also, with the change of local, query-level search intentions (from exploring a new domain to finding a specific known item; from verifying a simple fact to evaluating different pieces of information), the examination preference and click preference, especially on topically diversified search results, might also change even within the same search session for the same user (Liu & Han, 2022). Without the knowledge of this change in user preference on topically diversified information, researchers may not be able to properly debias the behavioral feedback (e.g., browsing and examination, document clicking, annotation or bookmarking). As a result, the associated evaluation and learning to rank may be biased and do not accurately reflect the relevance of retrieved results. This temporal variation in examination and click thresholds during information seeking episodes still cannot be captured or estimated by existing click models.

Besides, task-related factors, such as task urgency and time constraints, may also affect users' examination and click activities. Users under limited search time and urgent information needs (e.g., navigational and medical information need under certain conditions) may be less patient with retrieved search results and tend to click less results on SERPs and stop search sessions at satisficing documents (Crescenzi et al., 2021; Maxwell et al., 2015; Wu & Kelly, 2014). Thus, it might be useful to integrate task facet features (e.g., Jiang et al., 2014; Li & Belkin, 2008; Liu, 2021) with user factors (e.g., user preferences, user interests, user patience) in modeling click and examination probabilities (e.g., Edwards & Kelly, 2017; Lu et al., 2018; Tang & Sanderson, 2010), as task characteristics may have a strong moderating effect on user cognitive impacts during browsing and search evaluation. For this, future researchers could start with exploring the integration of user-aware click models (e.g., different versions of user preferences and personalized click models) with task-aware click models (e.g., TCM) and include appropriate representations for key user factors (especially human biases and mental shortcuts) and search task characteristics for achieving more accurate relevance estimation and click-through rate prediction.

2.6 User Models and IR Evaluation Metrics

Evaluation has been a central research focus in IR community (Sanderson, 2010). Apart from estimating document relevance and predicting click events in search sessions, researchers have also developed a series of formal user models as fundamental assumptions for supporting offline IR evaluation experiments.

Cranfield evaluation methodology has been widely applied in IR experiments and allows researchers to test and compare the performances of search systems based on standard test collections (Voorhees, 2001). To reduce the cost of developing test collections and improve reproducibility of evaluation experiments, researchers often reuse established test collections to evaluate multiple search systems, including the ones that are developed after the experimental test collections are accumulated (Carterette et al., 2010; Hashemi et al., 2015; Liu, 2022). To facilitate large-scale reproducible IR evaluation experiments, researchers have proposed and meta-evaluated a variety of evaluation metrics that are built upon different assumptions or formal user models (e.g., Chen et al., 2017; Liu & Yu, 2021; Liu et al., 2021). Most of these user models adopt relatively simplified forms and mainly rely on *document relevance* and *rank position* for defining simulated browsing behaviors. These simplified formal models allow researchers to incorporate relevance scores and rank positions into evaluation metrics and also reduce the computational complexity in parameter estimation, evaluation of ranked result lists, and training new ranking algorithms. Because of these benefits, many of the implicit formal user models and associated evaluation metrics (e.g., normalized discounted cumulative gain, expected reciprocal rank, mean average precision, U measure) have been adopted in comparing the performances of submitted search systems and algorithms in IR evaluation conferences and competition tracks (Azzopardi et al., 2021; Kekäläinen, 2005; Sakai, 2008), such as Text REtrieval Conference (TREC),[1] NII Testbeds and Community for Information access Research (NTCIR),[2] and Conference and Labs of the Evaluation Forum (CLEF).[3] In addition to standard evaluation tracks and conferences, the widely applied offline evaluation metrics and related user models have also been employed in a variety of user studies and interactive IR experiments to evaluate customized interactive search systems, result ranking algorithms, and graphical user interfaces (Chen et al., 2017; Kelly, 2009; Liu & Shah, 2019). For IR studies that focus on developing new evaluation metrics, the mainstream offline evaluation metrics are often employed (with parameters being fine-tuned, if applicable) as standard baselines for meta-evaluating the effectiveness of the proposed metrics (e.g., Luo et al., 2017; Yilmaz et al., 2010; Zhang et al., 2017a, b).

Existing user models underpin a broad range of evaluation metrics, including both *process-oriented* online evaluation metrics and *outcome-oriented* offline

---

[1] https://trec.nist.gov/

[2] https://research.nii.ac.jp/ntcir/index-en.html

[3] https://www.clef-initiative.eu/

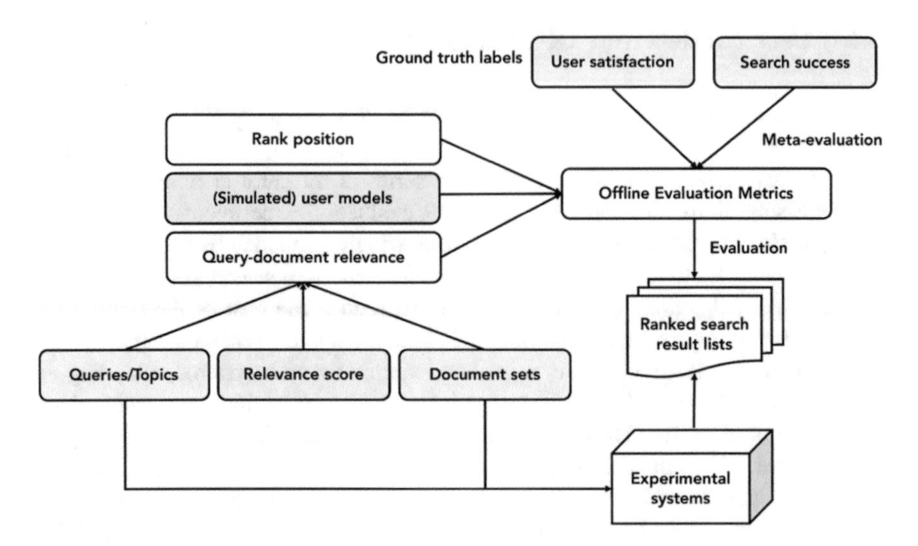

Fig. 2.9 Offline evaluation metrics in IR evaluation and meta-evaluation experiments

evaluation metrics (Chen et al., 2017; Järvelin, 2009; White, 2016). Meanwhile, however, they also limit the performance of these evaluation metrics as many hidden impacts of user characteristics are not examined or represented through the user models (Liu & Han, 2020; Zhang et al., 2017a). Some researchers have conducted *meta-evaluation experiments* on a broad scope of IR evaluation metrics and found that (1) most evaluation metrics, especially offline evaluation metrics, are weakly correlated with user satisfaction during search sessions (Chen et al., 2017; Zhang et al., 2018) and (2) the performances of evaluation metrics in terms of capturing in situ user satisfaction vary across different search states (e.g., exploration search state, known-item search state) and query-level user intentions (Liu & Yu, 2021).

Figure 2.9 illustrates the structure of offline evaluation metrics and shows the ways in which they are applied in search evaluation and examined in user-feedback-based meta-evaluation experiments. As it is shown in the figure above, most offline evaluation metrics are built upon two key components, query-document relevance ("qrel") and rank position. The *simulated user models* underpinning evaluation metrics essentially assume different browsing and interaction patterns, including examination preference, click threshold, *post-click* actions, as well as search stopping rules. The different (assumed) behavioral patterns then determine the *weights* of document relevance and rank position (e.g., role of first relevant document, discounted utility associated with different rank positions), which fundamentally define what a "good system" actually means in evaluation and what kind of search outputs are "encouraged," especially in iterative learning and training progresses. The actual effectiveness of these evaluation metrics, in terms of both capturing in situ user satisfaction and reflecting user search experience in general, is largely affected by two main factors: (1) the extent to which a user's search experience and outcome are shaped by document relevance and rank positions, instead of other factors (e.g., document usefulness, document interestingness), and (2) the extent to which the way in which document relevance factor and rank position factor are connected and represented in user models reflects users' actual search decision-making strategies. In this chapter, we will mainly focus on the second question, which is associated with the quality and effectiveness of existing user models. The first question speaks to a more fundamental issue: what ground truth labels we should use to better capture the actual support of a search systems that are *perceived* and *accepted* by a system user. Similar to click decisions discussed above, the overall perception, adoption, and use of search results and recommendations are also affected by users' bounded rationality in different aspects, search stages, and situations. This topic will be discussed in later chapters.

Going beyond traditional desktop search contexts and study settings, users engaging in other modalities of search interactions, such as mobile search (e.g., Hoeber et al., 2022; Luo et al., 2017), conversational search (e.g., Sekulić et al., 2022; Lipani et al., 2021), and tangible and augmented reality-based search (e.g., Büschel et al., 2018; Jansen et al., 2010) may be affected by other additional cognitive, perceptual, as well as situational factors (e.g., search interruptions and resumptions, multi-tasking activities, recommendations from other mobile applications and collaborators, social information seeking episodes). These factors may cause additional challenges for standard IR system evaluation as well as meta-evaluation of existing evaluation metrics both within and outside simulated search tasks and laboratory settings (Borlund, 2016; Kelly et al., 2015; Wang & Shah, 2022).

To address this challenge, IR researchers need to incorporate richer user features into formal models and offer these models a more behaviorally realistic foundation. This effort would allow researchers to better model boundedly rational users in real-life search scenarios and diverse task environments. In addition, built upon new enhanced user models, researchers will need to update the overall structure and specific parameters of evaluation metrics and develop new evaluation metrics that better reflect user experience and the quality of search system support. To achieve this, we need to start with investigating existing assumptions regarding user behaviors and ways in which researchers formally model users in the context of IR evaluation.

Zhang et al. (2017a) examined a number of existing evaluation metrics as well as the implicit assumptions or user models behind the metrics, aiming to improve current metrics and develop a general formal framework for supporting IR evaluation. Specifically, Zhang et al. (2017a) first defined the basic components of their new session evaluation framework, including simulator, interaction reward and cost, lap, action and interface card, user state, user action model, and interaction sequences. Among these components, *simulator* refers to a simulated user with a search task in mind. Other components, such as reward and cost, action, state, and interaction sequences, depict different aspects of the search interactions (e.g., querying, browsing and examination, clicks) that the (synthetic) user engages in. Based on the new components and integrated evaluation framework, the researchers revisited and characterized the nature and assumption of a series of widely used offline evaluation metrics.

According to Zhang et al. (2017a), given a list of ranked results retrieved by a system, *Precision* can be characterized as the ratio of search interaction reward and cost of a simulated user. Also, the simulator would keep scanning results until the whole result list is browsed and scanned. The precision measure focuses on the reward (measured by document relevance) per unit of cost in search evaluation. Another basic metric, *Recall*, can be characterized as task completion percentage, or the obtained reward relative to the best possible reward measured by total number of relevant documents. The assumed task behind recall is that the user or simulator aims to find *all* relevant documents available in the corpus based on which the search system operates.

$$Precision = \frac{D_r \cap D_R}{D_R} \tag{2.39}$$

$$Recall = \frac{D_r \cap D_R}{D_r} \tag{2.40}$$

In the formulas above, D_r represents the total set of relevant documents in the corpus, and D_R refers to the total set of retrieved documents under the current query or search iteration. Differing from precision, the recall measure focuses on the total collected reward or relevance-based utility only and does not consider cost or predefine search cost budget at all. Given this assumed user model, recall measure may be closer or more applicable to open-ended exploratory searches where users aim to broadly explore a new domain or area of knowledge, rather than known-item factual or navigational searches where users formulate specific queries and know exactly what they are looking for. Also, due to the restrictions associated with human biases, imperfect information, and situational limits, users may have different preferences, levels of urgency and patience, as well as implicit "cost budgets" across different search states and problematic situations (Liu & Han, 2022). As a result, they may only continue browsing and examination up to certain point or rank position, instead of exhausting all retrieved documents through search systems (Chen et al., 2017). Also, their implicit thresholds for relevance may also change over time due to the variations in their search intentions and in situ search expectations.

To incorporate the idea of cost budget into offline evaluation metrics, researchers have developed several *metrics@K* metrics to characterize partial examination behavior on SERPs. For instance, *Precision@K* and *Recall@K* both assume that a user would stop browsing or viewing documents when the accumulated interaction cost reaches the predefined budget *K*. This measure of cost budget can also be considered as a representation of user patience or tolerance of browsing efforts. *Metrics@K* models search cost based on rank position and evaluates the utility from retrieved results within a certain range of search browsing. The cost budget assumption also echoes the empirical finding that users often pay more attention to top ranked results and are less likely to interact with lower ranked search results on SERPs (Jiang et al., 2014; Matthijs & Radlinski, 2011). Thus, focusing on system performance up to certain *cost budget point* may allow search systems to measure users' search satisfaction and overall interaction experience in a more accurate manner. More broadly, the framework of cost-reward analysis provides a useful tool for simulating users' judgments and search decision-making rules and inspired many other IR research and offline evaluation experiments built upon a variety of user simulations (e.g., Azzopardi, 2014; Azzopardi & Zuccon, 2016; Brown & Liu, 2022).

However, it is worth noting that rank position is merely one of the possible aspects of users' perceived costs. Within each individual query-based search iteration, users may also be sensitive to the *dwell time* spent on examining search result snippets, moving cursor when browsing the SERP, and reading clicked documents or Web pages. In addition, within the scope of search sessions, users may also perceive higher cognitive and memory loads when formulating and reformulating search queries, judging query recommendations, and deciding overall search strategies (Gwizdka, 2010; Rieh et al., 2012; Wang et al., 2015a). Many of these hidden aspects of perceived cost are difficult to capture, especially in real-time search settings, as their connections to explicit behavioral signals and implicit cognitive changes still need to be further explored in IR research community. Besides, users' perceptions of different search events (e.g., issuing a query, clicking a document, continuing or exiting a search iteration) and overall task load are also affected by their cognitive and perceptual biases at both query and search session levels. The actual impacts of these biases and the dynamic gaps between *actual* cost (e.g., rank of relevant results, length, and readability of documents) and *perceived* cost are difficult to predict or simulate with offline evaluation metrics only and may require additional, more fine-grained physiological signals in measurements.

Following the cost-reward analytical framework, *Average Precision* (AP) can be interpreted as the average ratio of the search interaction reward and cost across a group of different retrieval tasks or simulated users (Zhang et al., 2017a). By comparing multiple retrieval results under different tasks and users from two or more search systems, AP may be more effective in differentiating good-performing search systems with the other ones compared to single SERP-based metrics, such as precision and recall. Based on this, *AP@K* can be defined as average reward-cost ratio under a predefined cost budget for a group of simulators.

Apart from costs and rewards in search interactions, another key component of simulated user model is *stopping rule*. *Metrics@K* defines a pre-search cost budget as a static stopping point. In contrast, *Mean Reciprocal Rank* (MRR) connects the stopping rule with document relevance and assumes that the precision-oriented simulator aims to find only one relevant document and then stop searching. Consider the rank position, r, of the first relevant document on a SERP. MRR measures the average performance measured by RR across multiple queries or topics, which can be written as follows:

$$MRR = \frac{1}{Q} \sum_{n=1}^{Q} \frac{1}{r_n} \tag{2.41}$$

where Q refers to a set of queries and r_n represents the rank of the first relevant document of query n. This simulated user models echoes many simple, fact-finding, and ad hoc retrieval tasks, where users aim to find one document or page that provides the needed factual or navigational information and then stop. In these short, factual search sessions, documents that are ranked below the first relevant document may not affect users' actions or perceived search utility that much.

$$DCG_k = \sum_{n=1}^{k} \frac{rel_n}{log_2(n+1)} \tag{2.42}$$

$$IDCG_k = \sum_{n=1}^{REL_k} \frac{rel_n}{log_2(n+1)} \tag{2.43}$$

$$nDCG_k = \frac{DCG_k}{IDCG_k} \tag{2.44}$$

Although RR and MRR can characterize and evaluate some of the simple, factual retrieval tasks, they have limited effectiveness for evaluating search systems under complex tasks where users often need to issue multiple queries under varying intentions and click and assess documents obtained at multiple rank positions. Under this circumstance, users are less likely to stop searching at the first relevant document. Instead of assuming a static stopping point or constant stopping rate, *normalized Discounted Cumulative Gain* (nDCG) includes a *discounting factor*, assuming that users' stopping rate increases as the rank order goes down on the SERP. In Formulas (2.42)–(2.44), *rel* measures the relevance of each document up to the search stopping or cost budget point k. *IDCG* as the denominator of nDCG represents the ideal DCG value given the relevance of retrieved documents under a perfect ranking algorithm (all documents are ordered by their relevance). Based on this setup, the nDCG score measures the *expected reward* over all rank positions and stopping points. Using this normalized value of DCG allows researchers to compare and evaluate the performance of retrieval algorithms across different corpora and test collections in a fairer manner.

Similar to other basic metrics, researchers have also applied *nDCG@K* to evaluate system performances against certain baselines within a certain reasonable range of SERP browsing by rank. These simplified user models behind offline evaluation metrics allow researchers to some extent mimic real users' decision-making activities based on search costs, gains, and diverse stopping rules and also achieve certain levels of computational convenience. Figure 2.10 summarizes the key components of the cost-reward evaluation framework and shows how each individual component is connected to document relevance and result rank position via different constructs or parameters designed by researchers.

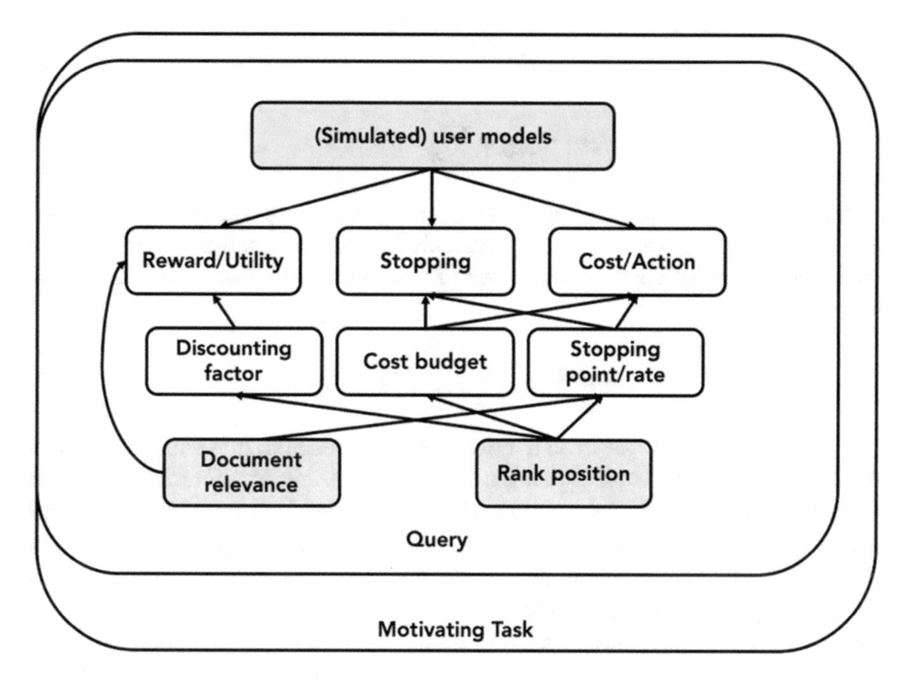

Fig. 2.10 Structure of simulated user models

In addition to the evaluation framework proposed by Zhang et al. (2017a), Moffat et al. (2017) develop a *C/W/L* framework for modeling different components of search interactions and characterizing different types of existing offline evaluation metrics based upon their respective focuses (e.g., search action, search utility). Within the framework, $C(\cdot)$ defines a user browsing model and characterizes the way in which "a user *consumes* the items in the SERP." This component can be deconstructed into separate functions that measure the fraction of users that examine the document at each rank position r. Similarly, $W(\cdot)$ represents the fraction of attention paid to retrieved search results and can also be deconstructed by rank. $L(\cdot)$ is associated with the stopping rule and defines the probability that the retrieved item at a rank position will be the last one viewed by a given user. Then, similar to the general framework discussed above, Moffat et al. (2017) deconstruct and re-examine individual offline evaluation metrics within C/W/L framework and explored the intrinsic connections among these measures. More details regarding the specific C/W/L functions and the comparison of evaluation metrics are offered in the original published paper.

Apart from the general evaluation frameworks, IR researchers have also attempted to employ click models as a basis for building *behavioral-aware* evaluation metrics. According to Chuklin et al. (2013b), based on the nature of different click models, researchers can develop two sets of click model-based evaluation metrics: *utility-based* metrics and *effort-based* metrics. Regarding utility, evaluation metrics can focus on the utility that a user accumulates through examining relevant documents on SERPs. The utility-based evaluation metrics can be defined as follows:

$$Metrics_{utility} = \sum_{r} P\left(C_r = 1\right) u_r \tag{2.45}$$

where u_r represents the utility accumulated from the document ranked at r-th position. Similarly, evaluation metrics can also be designed based on the efforts on search before the user's information need is satisfied. The effort-based metrics can be written as follows:

$$Metrics_{effort} = \sum_{r} P\left(S_r = 1\right) e_r \tag{2.46}$$

where e_r indicates the search efforts at r-th position in search evaluation. According to Chuklin et al. (2013b), a common representation of rank-based effort measure is the inverse of rank $\frac{1}{r}$: as the rank position goes deeper, the user is assumed to spend more efforts on document examination. This form of rank-based presentation and its variants are widely used in existing offline evaluation metrics, such as reciprocal rank, expected reciprocal rank (ERR), and nDCG (cf. Chapelle et al., 2009). In online evaluation studies, dwell-time-based behavioral features and cursor movement trajectories can also be considered as representations of search efforts (Chen et al., 2017). It is also critical to leverage the knowledge about users' cognitive and perceptual traits, especially their biases, in modeling the dynamic gap between actual efforts spent and perceived search efforts. For instance, apart from the content of information objects, the ways in which the target information is presented and framed also have significant impacts of users' perception and evaluation (framing effects). For SERPs with more diverse forms of information items (e.g., organic search results, vertical blocks, advertisements, search engine answer box), researchers may incorporate more sophisticated click models with evaluation tasks and estimate the utility and efforts associated with different result types, respectively (Wang et al., 2013). More details regarding the gap between perception and objective outcomes, as well as other types of biases and cognitive deviations, will be further discussed after we introduce and explain the mainstream theories and major empirical progresses on human biases and decision-making.

As discussed above, existing offline metrics and associated user models are mainly built upon rank position and document relevance factors. Based on these factors, researchers made several implicit and explicit assumptions regarding search costs and actions, interaction rewards, as well search stopping rule or rate. While the simulated user models consisting of these three major components provide a formal basis for building offline evaluation metrics and conducting evaluation experiments, many real-life user characteristics, especially the factors that contribute to their bounded rational decision-making, are not properly represented in these models. Incorporating these understudied factors (e.g., human biases, user patience, situational limits) into simulators would cause extra challenges for predicting user actions and estimating parameter values and also create new opportunities for developing more realistic, bias-aware user models and search evaluation metrics. Meanwhile, it is important to acknowledge that more parameters and greater model complexity cannot guarantee better performances in estimating document relevance or predicting user search behavior (Chuklin et al., 2015). Understanding the implicit multidimensional gap between rational agent and boundedly rational real-life users is a starting point toward building more behaviorally and psychologically realistic user models and offline evaluation metrics.

In addition, as most of the existing evaluation metrics are tested in traditional Cranfield style and employed mainly in ad hoc retrieval tasks, it is still unclear how to evaluate search sessions or a sequence of task-driven query segments from a user-oriented perspective (Liu et al., 2020). To achieve this, researchers need to not only connect single-SERP measures to session context (e.g., session-DCG, Järvelin et al., 2008) but also address unique challenges associated with sessions, such as simulation of query reformulation (e.g., Ganguly et al., 2011; Jiang et al., 2012), modeling changes of local search intentions (e.g., Mitsui et al., 2017), and developing adaptive intention-aware search evaluation (Liu & Shah, 2022; Mehrotra & Yilmaz, 2017; Ruotsalo et al., 2014). Also, it is worth noting that different queries in a session may address different aspects or serve different intentions at varying stages, and thus may not be equally important to a motivating task. Therefore, system performances under different queries and task states may need to be evaluated separately over different evaluation metrics (Liu & Yu, 2021). These subtasks under session-based evaluation require a deeper understanding of users' biases, intentions, and situational limits within specific search tasks, problematic situations, as well as diverse information seeking and search environments (e.g., workplace, everyday life search contexts).

Apart from evaluation metrics and click models, researchers have also applied economic analytical framework in examining the relationships among search cost, search performance, and user actions (e.g., clicking, query formulation and reformulation, browsing, and examination). For example, Azzopardi (2014) proposes an extended model of search costs and predict user actions based on the optimization of search efficiency. The extended cost model covers multiple aspects of search activities, such as query formulation cost, assessment cost, page reading cost, and cost associated with search result snippets, and provides a richer representation of search interactions compared to other existing economic search models (e.g., Azzopardi, 2011; Pirolli & Card, 1999). More broadly, adopting methods of economic analysis in IR research allows researchers to develop quantifiable and statistically testable hypotheses regarding different aspects of interactive search activities and offers a useful and theoretically rich basis for formally modeling optimized search activities, which in some cases (e.g., known-item ad hoc search, navigational search) may serve as a good proxy of real-life search interactions. However, to enhance the predictive power and explainability of IR models, researchers need to reflect on the assumptions made in economic search theories and further extend formal user models by reducing the gap between rational man assumptions and real-life boundedly rational users. Knowledge on boundedly rational decision-making and human biases from behavioral economics and cognitive psychology could help achieve these goals.

Regarding formally modeling users' search sessions, some researchers sought to connect different search actions, decisions, and states together, in order to build a computational model and reproducible evaluation tool of interactive IR. Among varying types of search actions, *query reformulation* has been identified as a key search phase and useful indicator of search state transitions. For instance, Azzopardi (2011) has simulated search costs and benefits based on users' actions, seeking to explain and predict users' decisions in sessions, such as choosing between query reformulation and continuing browsing, from an economic perspective. Dungs and Fuhr (2017) employed both discrete and continuous behavioral features and proposed a *Hidden Markov Model* (HMM) for identifying search phases or states and modeling the phase transition patterns. To build a formal model of search interactions, Fuhr (2008) developed a formal framework (i.e., IIR-PRP) for extending probabilistic IR to the context of interactive IR based on a cost model of interaction. Yue et al. (2014) applied HMM in analyzing collaborative Web search sessions. With the behavioral data collected from a lab study, the researchers empirically demonstrated that HMM can help identify users' search interaction patterns.

The idea of dividing interactive search sessions into different phases (especially with the support of Markov decision process model) and modeling the phase transitions has also been adopted and extended in other IR research (e.g., Cole et al., 2014; Hendahewa & Shah, 2013), especially for facilitating reinforcement-learning (RL)-based IR simulations and offline evaluations of adaptive search recommendations (e.g., Guan et al., 2013; Luo et al., 2014; Liu & Shah, 2022). Luo et al. (2014) combined document features (e.g., relevance) with term changes in query reformulation in identifying state transitions and demonstrated that the knowledge about users' implicit search states behind query reformulation behaviors can be leveraged in enhancing the performance of document re-ranking algorithms. Liu and Shah (2022) focused on the usefulness side of documents and developed state-based search path recommenders that can adjust the best recommendation strategies according to task states and help users collect useful documents and complete search tasks sooner. The search phase and state-based models go beyond traditional single-query-based ad hoc retrieval models and help connect adaptive ranking and recommendation algorithms with decisions in interactive IR sessions (e.g., query reformulation, browsing, and search stopping) at simulation level.

Taking a *game-theoretic* approach to modeling search interaction processes, Zhai (2016) formulates the problem of text data retrieval as a cooperative and interactive game between a user and a search engine. During the game, the shared goal between the two sides is satisfying the user's information need or supporting their motivating task while minimizing the user's actual search efforts and optimizing the operation efficiency of the retrieval system. In contrast to previous economics and session modeling approach, Zhai (2016)'s game-theoretic approach can optimize the overall utility over a whole search session, instead of merely improving a traditional ranking algorithm under individual queries or topics. The game-theoretic framework has also been implemented in improving interface retrieval decisions, where the optimization goal is to maximize the gain-cost ratio in users' interactions with certain search interfaces (Zhang & Zhai, 2015, 2016). This optimization approach also echoes the *expected utility theory* (cf. Harrison, 1994), which underpins a variety of rational decision-making models. Zhang and Zhai (2015)'s interface card model developed under the game-theoretic approach not only extends the traditional *probability ranking principle* (PRP) of IIR but also facilitates the adaptive optimization of navigational interfaces in interactive search interactions. Furthermore, going beyond simulation-driven experiments, Zhang and Zhai (2015)'s findings from a follow-up user study demonstrate that the proposed interface card model can effectively generate adaptive navigational interface for users engaging in search sessions, which can significantly outperform several fixed predesigned baseline interfaces.

Although the formal models and frameworks discussed above provide a valuable starting point for developing scalable computational models of interactive IR and simulating user search sessions for reproducible evaluation experiments, they abstract out user characteristics and situational factors that play important roles in search interactions. Consequently, existing formal models of search may not be able to properly capture the potential behavioral impacts associated with individuals' biases and seemingly irrational search actions and document judgment strategies. Also, the gap between the actual costs (e.g., dwell time and search actions) and users' perceived costs, which is often influenced by human biases and mental shortcuts in judgments (Kahneman, 2003), may lead to systematic errors in the predictions of formal models and in situ evaluations of user experiences and thus need to be taken into consideration with model users' actual decision-making and search evaluation activities.

2.7 Summary

This chapter offers a brief overview of the main approaches that researchers utilize to formally model users in IR as well as the associated simplified assumptions. Our overview mainly includes two types of formal models: click models and user models associated with evaluation metrics. Based on individual formal models, we synthesized the common components shared by different models (e.g., attractiveness, examination, cost budget, discount rate) and also discussed the unique assumptions, components, and parameters for individual models. Although different types of assumptions and model design allow researchers to model and simulate different parts and types of search interactions and judgments, they also lead to a variety of limitations in modeling and approximating real-life user actions, especially in interactive search sessions and click sequences. More details regarding formal model design and findings from evaluation experiments are provided in respective original papers cited above.

Although factors associated with bounded rationality (e.g., biases and heuristics) and mental shortcuts often reduce the efforts and difficulty of information seeking, retrieval, as well as everyday life decision-making tasks in general, they increase the complexity of modeling interaction processes and predicting search actions of boundedly rational users in real-world settings. Methodologically, unlike traditional standardized components of search contexts (e.g., retrieval algorithms, queries, factual tasks), user biases are difficult to measure or simulate even in controlled laboratory settings. In the following chapters, we will further discuss the research progress on understanding factors related to users' bounded rationality and their impacts in information seeking and retrieval activities and explain how the knowledge of users' bounded rationality from behavioral economics contradict with the assumptions made in IR evaluation experiments. This discussion will shed light on the question of how we should incorporate these factors into user modeling, system evaluation, and customized recommendation design.

References

Arguello, J., & Capra, R. (2012). The effect of aggregated search coherence on search behavior. In *Proceedings of the 21st ACM International Conference on Information and Knowledge Management* (pp. 1293–1302). ACM. https://doi.org/10.1145/2396761.2398432

Arguello, J., Wu, W. C., Kelly, D., & Edwards, A. (2012). Task complexity, vertical display and user interaction in aggregated search. In *Proceedings of the 35th International ACM SIGIR Conference on Research and Development in Information Retrieval* (pp. 435–444). ACM. https://doi.org/10.1145/2348283.2348343

Azzopardi, L. (2011). The economics in interactive information retrieval. In *Proceedings of the 34th International ACM SIGIR Conference on Research and Development in Information Retrieval* (pp. 15–24). ACM. https://doi.org/10.1145/2009916.2009923

Azzopardi, L. (2014). Modelling interaction with economic models of search. In *Proceedings of the 37th International ACM SIGIR conference on Research & Development in Information Retrieval* (pp. 3–12). ACM. https://doi.org/10.1145/2600428.2609574

Azzopardi, L. (2021). Cognitive biases in search: A review and reflection of cognitive biases in information retrieval. In *Proceedings of the 2021 ACM SIGIR Conference on Human Information Interaction and Retrieval* (pp. 27–37). ACM. https://doi.org/10.1145/3406522.3446023

Azzopardi, L., Mackenzie, J., & Moffat, A. (2021). ERR is not C/W/L: Exploring the relationship between expected reciprocal rank and other metrics. In *Proceedings of the 2021 ACM SIGIR International Conference on Theory of Information Retrieval* (pp. 231–237). ACM. https://doi.org/10.1145/3471158.3472239

Azzopardi, L., Thomas, P., & Craswell, N. (2018). Measuring the utility of search engine result pages: An information foraging based measure. In *Proceedings of the 41st International ACM SIGIR Conference on Research & Development in Information Retrieval* (pp. 605–614). ACM. https://doi.org/10.1145/3209978.3210027

Azzopardi, L., & Zuccon, G. (2016). An analysis of the cost and benefit of search interactions. In *Proceedings of the 2016 ACM International Conference on the Theory of Information Retrieval* (pp. 59–68). ACM.

Borlund, P. (2016). Framing of different types of information needs within simulated work task situations: An empirical study in the school context. *Journal of Information Science, 42*(3), 313–323. https://doi.org/10.1177/0165551515625028

Bron, M., Van Gorp, J., Nack, F., Baltussen, L. B., & de Rijke, M. (2013). Aggregated search interface preferences in multi-session search tasks. In *Proceedings of the 36th International ACM SIGIR Conference on Research and Development in Information Retrieval* (pp. 123–132). ACM. https://doi.org/10.1145/2484028.2484050

Brown, T., & Liu, J. (2022). A reference dependence approach to enhancing early prediction of session behavior and satisfaction. In *Proceedings of the 22nd ACM/IEEE Joint Conference on Digital Libraries* (pp. 1–5). ACM. https://doi.org/10.1145/3529372.3533294

Büschel, W., Mitschick, A., & Dachselt, R. (2018). Here and now: Reality-based information retrieval: Perspective paper. In *Proceedings of the 2018 Conference on Human Information Interaction & Retrieval* (pp. 171–180). ACM. https://doi.org/10.1145/3176349.3176384

Byström, K., & Hansen, P. (2005). Conceptual framework for tasks in information studies. *Journal of the American Society for Information Science and Technology, 56*(10), 1050–1061. https://doi.org/10.1002/asi.20197

Carterette, B., Gabrilovich, E., Josifovski, V., & Metzler, D. (2010). Measuring the reusability of test collections. In *Proceedings of the Third ACM International Conference on Web Search and Data Mining* (pp. 231–240). ACM. https://doi.org/10.1145/1718487.1718516

Chapelle, O., Metlzer, D., Zhang, Y., & Grinspan, P. (2009). Expected reciprocal rank for graded relevance. In *Proceedings of the 18th ACM Conference on Information and Knowledge Management* (pp. 621–630). ACM. https://doi.org/10.1145/1645953.1646033

Chen, D., Chen, W., Wang, H., Chen, Z., & Yang, Q. (2012). Beyond ten blue links: Enabling user click modeling in federated web search. In *Proceedings of the Fifth ACM International Conference on Web Search and Data Mining* (pp. 463–472). ACM. https://doi.org/10.1145/2124295.2124351

Chen, J., Mao, J., Liu, Y., Zhang, M., & Ma, S. (2020). A context-aware click model for web search. In *Proceedings of the 13th International Conference on Web Search and Data Mining* (pp. 88–96). ACM. https://doi.org/10.1145/3336191.3371819

Chen, N., Zhang, F., & Sakai, T. (2022). Constructing better evaluation metrics by incorporating the anchoring effect into the user model. In *Proceedings of the 45rd International ACM SIGIR Conference on Research and Development in Information Retrieval* (pp. 2709–2714). ACM. https://doi.org/10.1145/3477495.3531953

Chen, Y., Zhou, K., Liu, Y., Zhang, M., & Ma, S. (2017). Meta-evaluation of online and offline web search evaluation metrics. In *Proceedings of the 40th International ACM SIGIR Conference on Research and Development in Information Retrieval* (pp. 15–24). ACM. https://doi.org/10.1145/3077136.3080804

Chuklin, A., Markov, I., & de Rijke, M. (2015). Click models for web search. *Synthesis Lectures on Information Concepts, Retrieval, and Services, 7*(3), 1–115. https://doi.org/10.2200/S00654ED1V01Y201507ICR043

Chuklin, A., Serdyukov, P., & de Rijke, M. (2013a). Using intent information to model user behavior in diversified search. In *Proceedings of European Conference on Information Retrieval* (pp. 1–13). Springer.

Chuklin, A., Serdyukov, P., & de Rijke, M. (2013b). Click model-based information retrieval metrics. In *Proceedings of the 36th International ACM SIGIR Conference on Research and Development in Information Retrieval* (pp. 493–502). ACM. https://doi.org/10.1145/2484028.2484071

Cole, M. J., Hendahewa, C., Belkin, N. J., & Shah, C. (2014). Discrimination between tasks with user activity patterns during information search. In *Proceedings of the 37th International ACM SIGIR Conference on Research & Development in Information Retrieval* (pp. 567–576). ACM. https://doi.org/10.1145/2600428.2609591

Craswell, N., Zoeter, O., Taylor, M., & Ramsey, B. (2008). An experimental comparison of click position-bias models. In *Proceedings of the 2008 International Conference on Web Search and Data Mining* (pp. 87–94). ACM. https://doi.org/10.1145/1341531.1341545

Crescenzi, A., Capra, R., Choi, B., & Li, Y. (2021). Adaptation in information search and decision-making under time constraints. In *Proceedings of the 2021 ACM SIGIR Conference on Human Information Interaction and Retrieval* (pp. 95–105). ACM. https://doi.org/10.1145/3406522.3446030

Crescenzi, A., Kelly, D., & Azzopardi, L. (2016). Impacts of time constraints and system delays on user experience. In *Proceedings of the 2016 ACM SIGIR Conference on Human Information Interaction and Retrieval* (pp. 141–150). ACM. https://doi.org/10.1145/2854946.2854976

Dungs, S., & Fuhr, N. (2017). Advanced hidden Markov models for recognizing search phases. In *Proceedings of the ACM SIGIR International Conference on Theory of Information Retrieval* (pp. 257–260). ACM. https://doi.org/10.1145/3121050.3121090

Edwards, A., & Kelly, D. (2017). Engaged or frustrated? Disambiguating emotional state in search. In *Proceedings of the 40th international ACM SIGIR Conference on Research and Development in Information Retrieval* (pp. 125–134). ACM. https://doi.org/10.1145/3077136.3080818

Fuhr, N. (2008). A probability ranking principle for interactive information retrieval. *Information Retrieval, 11*(3), 251–265. https://doi.org/10.1007/s10791-008-9045-0

Ganguly, D., Leveling, J., & Jones, G. J. (2011). Simulation of within-session query variations using a text segmentation approach. In *International Conference of the Cross-Language Evaluation Forum for European Languages* (pp. 89–94). Springer.

Grover, A., & Leskovec, J. (2016). node2vec: Scalable feature learning for networks. In *Proceedings of the 22nd ACM SIGKDD International Conference on Knowledge Discovery and Data Mining* (pp. 855–864). ACM. https://doi.org/10.1145/2939672.2939754

Guan, D., Zhang, S., & Yang, H. (2013). Utilizing query change for session search. In *Proceedings of the 36th International ACM SIGIR Conference on Research and Development in Information Retrieval* (pp. 453–462). ACM. https://doi.org/10.1145/2484028.2484055

Guo, F., Liu, C., & Wang, Y. M. (2009). Efficient multiple-click models in web search. In *Proceedings of the second ACM International Conference on Web Search and Data Mining* (pp. 124–131). ACM. https://doi.org/10.1145/1498759.1498818

Gwizdka, J. (2010). Distribution of cognitive load in web search. *Journal of the American Society for Information Science and Technology, 61*(11), 2167–2187. https://doi.org/10.1002/asi.21385

Harrison, G. W. (1994). Expected utility theory and the experimentalists. In *Experimental Economics* (pp. 43–73). Physica.

Hashemi, S. H., Clarke, C. L., Dean-Hall, A., Kamps, J., & Kiseleva, J. (2015). On the reusability of open test collections. In *Proceedings of the 38th International ACM SIGIR Conference on Research and Development in Information Retrieval* (pp. 827–830). ACM. https://doi.org/10.1145/2766462.2767788

Hendahewa, C., & Shah, C. (2013). Segmental analysis and evaluation of user focused search process. In *Proceedings of the 2013 12th International Conference on Machine Learning and Applications* (Vol. 1, pp. 291–294). IEEE. https://doi.org/10.1109/ICMLA.2013.59

Hoeber, O., Harvey, M., Dewan Sagar, S. A., & Pointon, M. (2022). The effects of simulated interruptions on mobile search tasks. *Journal of the Association for Information Science and Technology, 73*(6), 777–796. https://doi.org/10.1002/asi.24579

Jansen, M., Bos, W., Van Der Vet, P., Huibers, T., & Hiemstra, D. (2010). TeddIR: Tangible information retrieval for children. In *Proceedings of the 9th International Conference on Interaction Design and Children* (pp. 282–285). ACM. https://doi.org/10.1145/1810543.1810592

Järvelin, K. (2009). Explaining user performance in information retrieval: Challenges to IR evaluation. In *Conference on the Theory of Information Retrieval* (pp. 289–296). Springer.

Järvelin, K., Price, S. L., Delcambre, L. M., & Nielsen, M. L. (2008). Discounted cumulated gain based evaluation of multiple-query IR sessions. In *European Conference on Information Retrieval* (pp. 4–15). Springer.

Jiang, J., He, D., & Allan, J. (2014). Searching, browsing, and clicking in a search session: Changes in user behavior by task and over time. In *Proceedings of the 37th International ACM SIGIR Conference on Research & Development in Information Retrieval* (pp. 607–616). ACM. https://doi.org/10.1145/2600428.2609633

Jiang, J., He, D., Han, S., Yue, Z., & Ni, C. (2012). Contextual evaluation of query reformulations in a search session by user simulation. In *Proceedings of the 21st ACM International Conference on Information and Knowledge Management* (pp. 2635–2638). ACM. https://doi.org/10.1145/2396761.2398710

Kahneman, D. (2003). Maps of bounded rationality: Psychology for behavioral economics. *American Economic Review, 93*(5), 1449–1475. https://doi.org/10.1257/000282803322655392

Kekäläinen, J. (2005). Binary and graded relevance in IR evaluations—comparison of the effects on ranking of IR systems. *Information Processing & Management, 41*(5), 1019–1033. https://doi.org/10.1016/j.ipm.2005.01.004

Kelly, D. (2009). Methods for evaluating interactive information retrieval systems with users. *Foundations and Trends in Information Retrieval, 3*(1–2), 1–224. https://doi.org/10.1561/1500000012

Kelly, D., Arguello, J., Edwards, A., & Wu, W. C. (2015). Development and evaluation of search tasks for IIR experiments using a cognitive complexity framework. In *Proceedings of the 2015 International Conference on the Theory of Information Retrieval* (pp. 101–110). ACM. https://doi.org/10.1145/2808194.2809465

Kopliku, A., Pinel-Sauvagnat, K., & Boughanem, M. (2014). Aggregated search: A new information retrieval paradigm. *ACM Computing Surveys (CSUR), 46*(3), 1–31. https://doi.org/10.1145/2523817

Li, Y., & Belkin, N. J. (2008). A faceted approach to conceptualizing tasks in information seeking. *Information Processing & Management, 44*(6), 1822–1837. https://doi.org/10.1016/j.ipm.2008.07.005

Lin, J., Liu, W., Dai, X., Zhang, W., Li, S., Tang, R., He, X., Hao, J., & Yu, Y. (2021). A graph-enhanced click model for web search. In *Proceedings of the 44th International ACM SIGIR Conference on Research and Development in Information Retrieval* (pp. 1259–1268). ACM. https://doi.org/10.1145/3404835.3462895

Lipani, A., Carterette, B., & Yilmaz, E. (2021). How am I doing? Evaluating conversational search systems offline. *ACM Transactions on Information Systems (TOIS), 39*(4), 1–22. https://doi.org/10.1145/3451160

Liu, J. (2021). Deconstructing search tasks in interactive information retrieval: A systematic review of task dimensions and predictors. *Information Processing & Management, 58*(3), 102522. https://doi.org/10.1016/j.ipm.2021.102522

Liu, J. (2022). Toward Cranfield-inspired reusability assessment in interactive information retrieval evaluation. *Information Processing & Management, 59*(5), 103007. https://doi.org/10.1016/j.ipm.2022.103007

Liu, J., & Han, F. (2020). Investigating reference dependence effects on user search interaction and satisfaction: A behavioral economics perspective. In *Proceedings of the 43rd International ACM SIGIR Conference on Research and Development in Information Retrieval* (pp. 1141–1150). ACM. https://doi.org/10.1145/3397271.3401085

Liu, J., & Han, F. (2022). Matching search result diversity with user diversity acceptance in Web search sessions. In *Proceedings of the 45th International ACM SIGIR Conference on Research and Development in Information Retrieval* (pp. 2473–2477). ACM. https://doi.org/10.1145/3477495.3531880

Liu, Y., Liu, Z., Zhou, K., Wang, M., Luan, H., Wang, C., Zhang, M., & Ma, S. (2016). Predicting search user examination with visual saliency. In *Proceedings of the 39th International ACM SIGIR conference on Research and Development in Information Retrieval* (pp. 619–628). ACM. https://doi.org/10.1145/2911451.2911517

Liu, Z., Liu, Y., Zhou, K., Zhang, M., & Ma, S. (2015). Influence of vertical result in web search examination. In *Proceedings of the 38th International ACM SIGIR Conference on Research and Development in Information Retrieval* (pp. 193–202). ACM. https://doi.org/10.1145/2766462.2767714

Liu, M., Mao, J., Liu, Y., Zhang, M., & Ma, S. (2019b). Investigating cognitive effects in session-level search user satisfaction. In *Proceedings of the 25th ACM SIGKDD International Conference on Knowledge Discovery & Data Mining* (pp. 923–931). ACM. https://doi.org/10.1145/3292500.3330981

Liu, Z., Mao, J., Wang, C., Ai, Q., Liu, Y., & Nie, J. Y. (2017). Enhancing click models with mouse movement information. *Information Retrieval Journal, 20*(1), 53–80. https://doi.org/10.1007/s10791-016-9292-4

Liu, J., Mitsui, M., Belkin, N. J., & Shah, C. (2019a). Task, information seeking intentions, and user behavior: Toward a multi-level understanding of Web search. In *Proceedings of the 2019 ACM SIGIR Conference on Human Information Interaction and Retrieval* (pp. 123–132). ACM. https://doi.org/10.1145/3295750.3298922

Liu, J., Sarkar, S., & Shah, C. (2020). Identifying and predicting the states of complex search tasks. In *Proceedings of the 2020 ACM SIGIR Conference on Human Information Interaction and Retrieval* (pp. 193–202). ACM. https://doi.org/10.1145/3343413.3377976

Liu, J., & Shah, C. (2019). Interactive IR user study design, evaluation, and reporting. *Synthesis Lectures on Information Concepts, Retrieval, and Services, 11*(2), 1–93. https://doi.org/10.2200/S00923ED1V01Y201905ICR067

Liu, J., & Shah, C. (2022). Leveraging user interaction signals and task state information in adaptively optimizing usefulness-oriented search sessions. In *Proceedings of the 22nd ACM/IEEE Joint Conference on Digital Libraries* (pp. 1–11). ACM. https://doi.org/10.1145/3529372.3530926

Liu, J., & Yu, R. (2021). State-aware meta-evaluation of evaluation metrics in interactive information retrieval. In *Proceedings of the 30th ACM International Conference on Information & Knowledge Management* (pp. 3258–3262). ACM. https://doi.org/10.1145/3459637.3482190

Liu, Z., Zhou, K., & Wilson, M. L. (2021). Meta-evaluation of conversational search evaluation metrics. *ACM Transactions on Information Systems (TOIS), 39*(4), 1–42. https://doi.org/10.1145/3445029

Lu, H., Zhang, M., & Ma, S. (2018). Between clicks and satisfaction: Study on multi-phase user preferences and satisfaction for online news reading. In *Proceedings of the 41st International ACM SIGIR Conference on Research & Development in Information Retrieval* (pp. 435–444). ACM. https://doi.org/10.1145/3209978.3210007

Luo, C., Liu, Y., Sakai, T., Zhang, F., Zhang, M., & Ma, S. (2017). Evaluating mobile search with height-biased gain. In *Proceedings of the 40th International ACM SIGIR Conference on Research and Development in Information Retrieval* (pp. 435–444). ACM. https://doi.org/10.1145/3077136.3080795

Luo, J., Zhang, S., & Yang, H. (2014). Win-win search: Dual-agent stochastic game in session search. In *Proceedings of the 37th international ACM SIGIR Conference on Research & Development in Information Retrieval* (pp. 587–596). ACM. https://doi.org/10.1145/2600428.2609629

Matthijs, N., & Radlinski, F. (2011). Personalizing web search using long term browsing history. In *Proceedings of the Fourth ACM International Conference on Web Search and Data Mining* (pp. 25–34). ACM. https://doi.org/10.1145/1935826.1935840

Maxwell, D., Azzopardi, L., Järvelin, K., & Keskustalo, H. (2015). Searching and stopping: An analysis of stopping rules and strategies. In *Proceedings of the 24th ACM International on Conference on Information and Knowledge Management* (pp. 313–322). ACM. https://doi.org/10.1145/2806416.2806476

Mehrotra, R., & Yilmaz, E. (2017). Extracting hierarchies of search tasks & subtasks via a Bayesian nonparametric approach. In *Proceedings of the 40th international ACM SIGIR Conference on Research and Development in Information Retrieval* (pp. 285–294). ACM. https://doi.org/10.1145/3077136.3080823

Mitsui, M., Liu, J., Belkin, N. J., & Shah, C. (2017). Predicting information seeking intentions from search behaviors. In *Proceedings of the 40th International ACM SIGIR Conference on Research and Development in Information Retrieval* (pp. 1121–1124). ACM. https://doi.org/10.1145/3077136.3080737

Mitsui, M., Shah, C., & Belkin, N. J. (2016). Extracting information seeking intentions for web search sessions. In *Proceedings of the 39th International ACM SIGIR conference on Research and Development in Information Retrieval* (pp. 841–844). ACM. https://doi.org/10.1145/2911451.2914746

Moffat, A., Bailey, P., Scholer, F., & Thomas, P. (2017). Incorporating user expectations and behavior into the measurement of search effectiveness. *ACM Transactions on Information Systems (TOIS), 35*(3), 1–38. https://doi.org/10.1145/3052768

Pirolli, P., & Card, S. (1999). Information foraging. *Psychological Review, 106*(4), 643–675. https://doi.org/10.1037/0033-295X.106.4.643

Piwowarski, B., Dupret, G., & Jones, R. (2009). Mining user web search activity with layered Bayesian networks or how to capture a click in its context. In *Proceedings of the Second ACM International Conference on Web Search and Data Mining* (pp. 162–171). ACM. https://doi.org/10.1145/1498759.1498823

Rieh, S. Y., Kim, Y. M., & Markey, K. (2012). Amount of invested mental effort (AIME) in online searching. *Information Processing & Management, 48*(6), 1136–1150. https://doi.org/10.1016/j.ipm.2012.05.001

Ruotsalo, T., Jacucci, G., Myllymäki, P., & Kaski, S. (2014). Interactive intent modeling: Information discovery beyond search. *Communications of the ACM, 58*(1), 86–92. https://doi.org/10.1145/2656334

Sakai, T. (2008). Comparing metrics across TREC and NTCIR: The robustness to pool depth bias. In *Proceedings of the 31st Annual International ACM SIGIR Conference on Research and Development in Information Retrieval* (pp. 691–692). ACM. https://doi.org/10.1145/1458082.1458159

Sanderson, M. (2010). Test collection based evaluation of information retrieval systems. *Foundations and Trends in Information Retrieval, 4*(4), 247–375. https://doi.org/10.1561/1500000009

Scholer, F., Kelly, D., Wu, W. C., Lee, H. S., & Webber, W. (2013). The effect of threshold priming and need for cognition on relevance calibration and assessment. In *Proceedings of the 36th International ACM SIGIR Conference on Research and Development in Information Retrieval* (pp. 623–632). ACM. https://doi.org/10.1145/2484028.2484090

Sekulić, I., Aliannejadi, M., & Crestani, F. (2022). Evaluating mixed-initiative conversational search systems via user simulation. In *Proceedings of the Fifteenth ACM International Conference on Web Search and Data Mining* (pp. 888–896). ACM. https://doi.org/10.1145/3488560.3498440

Shen, S., Hu, B., Chen, W., & Yang, Q. (2012). Personalized click model through collaborative filtering. In *Proceedings of the Fifth ACM International Conference on Web Search and Data Mining* (pp. 323–332). ACM. https://doi.org/10.1145/2124295.2124336

Tang, J., & Sanderson, M. (2010). Evaluation and user preference study on spatial diversity. In *European Conference on Information Retrieval* (pp. 179–190). Springer.

Tran, V. T., & Fuhr, N. (2013). Markov modeling for user interaction in retrieval. In *ACM SIGIR 2013 Workshop on Modeling User Behavior for Information Retrieval Evaluation (MUBE 2013)* (Vol. 5, No. 3).

Voorhees, E. M. (2001). The philosophy of information retrieval evaluation. In *Workshop of the Cross-language Evaluation Forum for European Languages* (pp. 355–370). Springer.

Wang, S., Gwizdka, J., & Chaovalitwongse, W. A. (2015a). Using wireless EEG signals to assess memory workload in the *n*-back task. *IEEE Transactions on Human-Machine Systems, 46*(3), 424–435. https://doi.org/10.1109/THMS.2015.2476818

Wang, C., Liu, Y., Wang, M., Zhou, K., Nie, J. Y., & Ma, S. (2015b). Incorporating non-sequential behavior into click models. In *Proceedings of the 38th International ACM SIGIR Conference on Research and Development in Information Retrieval* (pp. 283–292). ACM. https://doi.org/10.1145/2766462.2767712

Wang, C., Liu, Y., Zhang, M., Ma, S., Zheng, M., Qian, J., & Zhang, K. (2013). Incorporating vertical results into search click models. In *Proceedings of the 36th International ACM SIGIR Conference on Research and Development in Information Retrieval* (pp. 503–512). ACM. https://doi.org/10.1145/2484028.2484036

Wang, Y., & Shah, C. (2022). Authentic versus synthetic: An investigation of the influences of study settings and task configurations on search behaviors. *Journal of the Association for Information Science and Technology, 73*(3), 362–375. https://doi.org/10.1002/asi.24554

White, R. (2013). Beliefs and biases in web search. In *Proceedings of the 36th international ACM SIGIR Conference on Research and Development in Information Retrieval* (pp. 3–12). ACM. https://doi.org/10.1145/2484028.2484053

White, R. W. (2016). *Interactions with search systems*. Cambridge University Press.

Wu, W. C., & Kelly, D. (2014). Online search stopping behaviors: An investigation of query abandonment and task stopping. *In Proceedings of the American Society for Information Science and Technology, 51*(1), 1–10. https://doi.org/10.1002/meet.2014.14505101030

Xie, X., Mao, J., Liu, Y., & de Rijke, M. (2020). Modeling user behavior for vertical search: Images, apps and products. In *Proceedings of the 43rd International ACM SIGIR Conference on Research and Development in Information Retrieval* (pp. 2440–2443). ACM. https://doi.org/10.1145/3397271.3401423

Xing, Q., Liu, Y., Nie, J. Y., Zhang, M., Ma, S., & Zhang, K. (2013). Incorporating user preferences into click models. In *Proceedings of the 22nd ACM international Conference on Information & Knowledge Management* (pp. 1301–1310). ACM. https://doi.org/10.1145/2505515.2505704

Yilmaz, E., Shokouhi, M., Craswell, N., & Robertson, S. (2010). Expected browsing utility for web search evaluation. In *Proceedings of the 19th ACM International Conference on Information and Knowledge Management* (pp. 1561–1564). ACM. https://doi.org/10.1145/1871437.1871672

Yue, Z., Han, S., & He, D. (2014). Modeling search processes using hidden states in collaborative exploratory web search. In *Proceedings of the 17th ACM Conference on Computer Supported Cooperative Work & Social Computing* (pp. 820–830). ACM. https://doi.org/10.1145/2531602.2531658

Zhai, C. (2016). Towards a game-theoretic framework for text data retrieval. *IEEE Database Engineering Bulletin, 39*(3), 51–62.

Zhang, Y., Chen, W., Wang, D., & Yang, Q. (2011). User-click modeling for understanding and predicting search-behavior. In *Proceedings of the 17th ACM SIGKDD International Conference on Knowledge Discovery and Data Mining* (pp. 1388–1396). ACM. https://doi.org/10.1145/2020408.2020613

Zhang, F., Liu, Y., Li, X., Zhang, M., Xu, Y., & Ma, S. (2017b). Evaluating web search with a bejeweled player model. In *Proceedings of the 40th International ACM SIGIR Conference on Research and Development in Information Retrieval* (pp. 425–434). ACM. https://doi.org/10.1145/3077136.3080841

Zhang, Y., Liu, X., & Zhai, C. (2017a). Information retrieval evaluation as search simulation: A general formal framework for IR evaluation. In *Proceedings of the ACM SIGIR International Conference on Theory of Information Retrieval* (pp. 193–200). ACM. https://doi.org/10.1145/3121050.3121070

Zhang, Y., & Zhai, C. (2015). Information retrieval as card playing: A formal model for optimizing interactive retrieval interface. In *Proceedings of the 38th International ACM SIGIR Conference on Research and Development in Information Retrieval* (pp. 685–694). NY: ACM. https://doi.org/10.1145/2766462.2767761

Zhang, Y., & Zhai, C. (2016). A sequential decision formulation of the interface card model for interactive IR. In *Proceedings of the 39th International ACM SIGIR conference on Research and Development in Information Retrieval* (pp. 85–94). ACM. https://doi.org/10.1145/2911451.2911543

Zhang, F., Zhou, K., Shao, Y., Luo, C., Zhang, M., & Ma, S. (2018). How well do offline and online evaluation metrics measure user satisfaction in Web image search? In *Proceedings of the 41st International ACM SIGIR Conference on Research & Development in Information Retrieval* (pp. 615–624). ACM. https://doi.org/10.1145/3209978.3210059

Zhou, K., Cummins, R., Lalmas, M., & Jose, J. M. (2012). Evaluating aggregated search pages. In *Proceedings of the 35th International ACM SIGIR Conference on Research and Development in Information Retrieval* (pp. 115–124). ACM. https://doi.org/10.1145/2348283.2348302

Chapter 3
From Rational Agent to Human with Bounded Rationality

Abstract To clarify and address the errors that occur in model parameter estimations and behavior predictions, researchers may need to start with investigating the hidden gaps between rational agent and human that are ignored or covered by oversimplified model assumptions. These gaps could occur in both factual, ad hoc retrieval and whole-session interactive retrieval and involve multiple aspects of search interactions, including not only user characteristics and their search strategies but also search task features, search interfaces, as well as situational factors. In this chapter, we summarize and briefly discuss the gaps we identified between simplified rational assumptions and empirically confirmed human biases and then propose a preliminary bias-aware evaluation framework to describe the connections between different stages of search sessions and diverse types of biases. The identified gaps will serve as the basis for developing bias-aware user models, search systems, and evaluation metrics.

3.1 Background

Formally modeling users often serves as a fundamental step toward predicting users' search activities and evaluating varying aspects of search system performances. Building formal models also facilitates the simulation of user actions and associated system responses, which supports the generation of synthetic evaluation data and enhances the reproducibility and reusability of offline IR evaluation materials. However, from a user-oriented perspective, as discussed in Chap. 2, previous research from both IR and other related fields (e.g., information seeking, human-computer interaction, behavioral economics, and decision-making) calls into question the fundamentals of existing IR user models of varying types (e.g., Agosto, 2002; Azzopardi, 2021; Barnes, 1984; Charness & Dave, 2017; Eickhoff, 2018; Kahneman, 2003; Liu & Han, 2020) and demands revisiting the implicit assumptions upon which formal models and evaluation measures were built. In general, boundedly rational users may not be able to perform accurate computation tasks and complex comparisons among available options due to limited cognitive resources and insufficient information regarding the problematic situation. As a result, users

J. Liu, *A Behavioral Economics Approach to Interactive Information Retrieval*, The Information Retrieval Series 48, https://doi.org/10.1007/978-3-031-23229-9_3

under the impacts of multilevel biases and situational restrictions usually rely on certain *mental shortcuts* for addressing most of the tasks and do not always pursue theoretically optimal outcomes as it is assumed in most formal models and offline evaluation measures. Moreover, these mental shortcuts or biased decision-making strategies may be affected and even reinforced by diverse components of search systems (e.g., ranked search result lists, query recommendations based on different rules, vertical search results) and algorithmic biases in IR, especially in search result ranking (Diaz et al., 2020; Ekstrand et al., 2019; Gao & Shah, 2019).

To clarify and address the errors that occur in model parameter estimations and behavior predictions, researchers need to start with investigating the gaps between rational agent and human that are ignored or covered by oversimplified model assumptions. These gaps could occur in both factual, ad hoc retrieval and whole-session interactive retrieval and involves multiple aspects of search interactions, including not only user characteristics and their search strategies but also search task features, search interfaces, as well as situational factors. Although investigating these implicit gaps alone do not guarantee improved results in behavior prediction and user-oriented search evaluation, it serves as a critical starting point toward developing more accurate, behaviorally realistic formal user models. Building these bias-aware user models may also increase the transparency of advanced machine-learning (ML)-based user models trained based on large-scale behavioral logs and help explain the hidden behavioral traces behind improved performances in relevance estimation, behavioral prediction, and IR evaluation.

3.2 Gaps Between Biased Users and Formal User Models

Regarding click models, although different models have been developed based on diverse assumptions, user models, and parameters, most of the assumptions are associated with the two widely examined components: attractiveness and examination (Chuklin et al., 2015; Zhang et al., 2022). Many of these assumptions, especially the ones regarding the impacts of rank positions, document features and browsing sequences and share similar characteristics with that of offline evaluation metrics (Zhang et al., 2017). For instance, multiple click models were built upon examination hypothesis (e.g., cascade model, position-based model, user browsing model) and assumes that the probability of examination is largely affected by the rank position of retrieved search results. This assumption echoes the implicit user models behind many offline metrics, such as nDCG and ERR, which assign lower weights (or higher stopping or skipping rate) to lower ranked documents. The prediction target of click models, clickthrough events, is associated with clicking activities as online evaluation metrics. Thus, the biases and cognitive limits that affect the robustness of evaluation metrics may also generate impacts on the performance of click models through creating unexpected variations in levels of attractiveness and examination probabilities in SERP browsing. Given these overlaps and similarities, we combined clicks and offline evaluation metrics into the same section of gap analysis to avoid unnecessary duplications. Specifically, we include the discussion on clickthrough events, levels of attractiveness, and examination probabilities under the broader scope of online behavioral metrics, which also include dwell time features, cursor movement, as well as other browsing-related user search activities.

Table 3.1 summarizes the gaps between user biases reported in Chap. 1 and the mainstream behavioral (including clickthrough activities by users) and offline evaluation metrics. By summarizing these gaps, this chapter reveals the inconsistencies between simplified user models and real-life bounded rationality users revealed (both explicitly and implicitly) by existing user studies and evaluation experiments. The first column lists the widely studied human biases, and we interpreted the bias-aware user models in the context of information searching in the second column. We also provide references to related empirical research or conceptual papers for each identified bias so that readers can refer to the original definitions of user biases and bounded rationality through these citations.

Nevertheless, the exploration on boundedly rational users and bias-aware evaluation by us as a research community is still far from complete. Also, at the operationalization level, how to represent different factors associated with boundedly rational search strategies and estimate their impacts in evaluation remains to be a major challenge. Before addressing these broader challenges at both empirical and methodological levels, we need to first review and synthesize the related research progresses made by information seeking, IR, as well as behavioral science researchers on scattered topics and individual specific problems.

To facilitate the analysis, we present the user models derived from the empirical research on user biases and explain how these derived user behavioral models contradict with the existing metrics. The metrics analyzed in the table include not only the basic metrics, such as *nDCG*, *rank-biased precision* (RBP), as well as *metrics@K* but also more recent metrics and evaluation frameworks, such as C/W/L (Azzopardi et al., 2021; Moffat et al., 2017). To cover a broad range of evaluation measures, our analysis includes both process-oriented evaluation measures, which focus on search process and behaviors (e.g., querying, clicking, dwell time measures) (Hofmann et al., 2016), and outcome-oriented evaluation measures, which characterize search result features (e.g., relevance-based metrics, usefulness) (Clarke et al., 2020; Harman, 2011; Sanderson, 2010; White, 2016). Note that process-oriented measures (third column) also include assumptions of click actions, which also involve and overlap some components of click models (e.g., attractiveness, examination probabilities) discussed in the previous chapter.

In the third and fourth columns, we explain how each user bias and the associated user model contradict with the assumptions and parameter setups of different evaluation measures. These gaps are identified based upon both Zhang et al. (2017)'s general evaluation framework and IR studies on individual metrics (e.g., Azzopardi et al., 2018; Chapelle et al., 2009; Moffat & Zobel, 2008). Under each type of user models and metrics, we explain how they conflict with each individual user biases identified in behavioral experiments and what would be the possible changes and adjustments we could make on existing model components or under current frameworks (e.g., rank-based discount rate) to incorporate user biases into

Table 3.1 Gaps between user biases and IR metrics

Empirically confirmed user biases	Derived bias-aware user model/feature	Process-oriented measure (e.g., click, browsing, and dwell time)	Outcome-oriented measure
Reference dependence (Tversky & Kahneman, 1991)	Users evaluate their relative search gains and losses (e.g., increased search efforts, decreased search efficiency) according to certain reference points or pre-search expectations, not merely final outcomes	All process-oriented/ behavioral measures: users may evaluate different search actions based on losses and gains with respect to a reference point or expectation developed in previous interactions, rather than final outcome values. For instance, initially encountered high-quality results may lead to higher thresholds of *attractiveness*, *examination*, as well as *clicks* for following results both within the same SERP and in other query segments	Rank-biased precision (RBP), expected reciprocal rank (ERR): stopping and skipping rate may vary across different ranks due to the changes in references and expectations Normalized discounted cumulated gain (nDCG), utility accumulation model of C/W/L: different users may have different utility discount rates at different moments or states of search sessions due to the variations in reference points. Thus, it may be of help to design and test different utility discount models based upon users' task states and state transition patterns within sessions (Liu et al., 2020a; Liu & Yu, 2021)
Loss aversion (Tversky & Kahneman, 1991; Kahneman, 2003)	Users' evaluations of different search results and search strategies are more sensitive to the variations in perceived or estimated search losses than to gains, which may lead to changes in subsequent search and evaluation tactics	All process-oriented/ behavioral measures: users tend to be more sensitive to perceived losses and try to avoid search actions or results that are likely to result in search time losses and reduced cognitive resources (e.g., increased search efforts, limited useful information)	RBP, ERR: users may have a higher stopping and skipping rate at a rank where they perceive a relatively loss (e.g., less relevant title, confusing search snippet). nDCG, document utility model of C/W/L: a perceived loss at a rank or a search iteration may lead to an increased gain discount rate
	Users' judgments on different search actions	The specific forms and narratives of search	RBP, nDCG, metrics@K,

(continued)

Table 3.1 (continued)

Empirically confirmed user biases	Derived bias-aware user model/feature	Process-oriented measure (e.g., click, browsing, and dwell time)	Outcome-oriented measure
Framing effects (Nelson et al., 1997)	and results are affected not only by the nature of the options but also the ways in which they are framed and presented	result snippets (e.g., organic search results, images, news verticals) with similar or same contents may result in different levels of attractiveness, examination probability, clickthrough rate, as well as document dwell time (if clicked)	document utility model of C/W/L: a result framed or perceived as a loss (relative drops in result quality and clarity, increased difficulty in comprehension) may incur significantly higher stopping and discount rates in browsing processes
Salience bias (Tiefenbeck et al., 2018)	Users often focus on and are more likely to be attracted by the information objects that are especially remarkable and more salient than other objects	All behavioral measures: users may spend longer dwell time and have higher examination and click probabilities on visually salient items and objects	RBP, nDCG, metrics@K, document utility model of C/W/L: salient items (e.g., vertical results, knowledge cards, organic search results near vertical blocks) may have higher click rates and lower stopping or discount rates; salient items, with similar contents to others, may have a higher estimated relevance. Note that these assumptions associated with salience bias partially echo that of vertical click models
Peak-end rule, position bias, order effects; primacy and recency (Kahneman, 2003)	In listwise and session evaluations, a user's overall experience is significantly affected by peak and end/recent points of local experiences	Session behavioral measures: the local search behavior and experience measures at peak and end search moments can better represent session-level experience than traditional sum and average-value-based measures. Knowledge of this bias conflict with the assumption that all moments or search iterations are	Session-level measures, utility accumulation model of C/W/L: the local search result metrics at peak and end search moments can better represent session experience than sum and average-value-based measures, e.g., mean average precision (MAP); users' in situ perception (e.g., query-level search

(continued)

Table 3.1 (continued)

Empirically confirmed user biases	Derived bias-aware user model/feature	Process-oriented measure (e.g., click, browsing, and dwell time)	Outcome-oriented measure
		equally important for a session	satisfaction) at peak and end search moments can better represent session experience
Decoy effect (Zhang & Zhang, 2007)	Users change their preference between different search results when presented with a third option (the decoy) that is asymmetrically dominated	Clicks, browsing (e.g., scrolls, mouse, and eye movements), and dwell time measures: users' implicit feedback (e.g., dwell time) on two similar results could be affected by an implicit decoy option in decision-making	RBP, nDCG, metrics@K, user stopping model of C/W/L: a decoy search result may affect gain discount and stopping rates at adjacent rank positions. Researchers need to look at the implicit connections among different results on a SERP
Priming effect (Tipper, 1985)	A user's exposure to a search result subconsciously affects their evaluation of a subsequent result or recommendation	Previously encountered search result snippets may affect the probability of attractiveness and examination on subsequent search result snippets presented on SERPs. The changes in attractiveness and examination probabilities may also result in variations in clickthrough rates	All relevance- and usefulness-based measures: the relevance and usefulness levels of an encountered landing page may affect the user's evaluation criteria (e.g., thresholds for relevant and usefulness judgment) in following search interactions
Confirmation bias, anchoring bias (Nickerson, 1998)	Users tend to accept the search results that are consistent with their prior beliefs, expected conclusions, and/or the initially encountered search results or documents	Clicks, browsing, and dwell time measures: users tend to spend more time and attention on results that confirm their existing beliefs and expectations; results that echo existing beliefs and in situ search expectations may enjoy a higher clickthrough rate and dwell time	RBP, nDCG, metrics@K, user stopping model and document utility model of C/W/L: lower ranked results and/or later reviewed results that confirm existing beliefs or initially encountered results may be associated with a lower discount rate and skip rate. Thus, researchers may need to measure

(continued)

Table 3.1 (continued)

Empirically confirmed user biases	Derived bias-aware user model/feature	Process-oriented measure (e.g., click, browsing, and dwell time)	Outcome-oriented measure
			the relevance of current result to both the overall topic or query and the user's anchoring point
Ambiguity effects, risk aversion (Pratt, 1978)	Users prefer search results and recommendations with low uncertainty or ambiguity (e.g., Web pages that present "clear facts" or direct answers to queries)	Clicks: users may have a lower click rate on results that seem to be uncertain or ambiguous (although these results may be useful for completing open-ended, intellectually challenging search tasks) Dwell time measures: users may tend to spend less time, have a higher skip rate, or underestimate relevance on seemingly ambiguous results	RBP, nDCG, ERR, metrics@K, document utility model of C/W/L: users may have a higher skip rate and gain discount rate on search results that seem to be ambiguous or uncertain. Thus, the specific discount rate could be written as a function of document relevance, rank position, and content ambiguity of both document itself and the corresponding search result snippet on the SERP
Theory of satisficing (Simon, 1955)	Users tend to stop at satisficing or "good enough" search results, rather than keeping exploring potentially better search results or seeking for theoretically optimized search outcomes	Clicks, browsing, and dwell time measures: users' criteria for satisficing results are affected by their prior interactions and in situ search expectations. Increased search efforts or frustrations may lower the threshold of satisficing	RBP, nDCG, ERR, metrics@K, user stopping model of C/W/L: Instead of having a preexisting cost budget in mind, a user may stop searching once a satisficing result is encountered during SERP browsing. The specific satisficing threshold, however, may vary across different search sessions, and individuals and may be related to both pre-search expectation and in situ outcomes and estimated difficulty

(continued)

Table 3.1 (continued)

Empirically confirmed user biases	Derived bias-aware user model/feature	Process-oriented measure (e.g., click, browsing, and dwell time)	Outcome-oriented measure
Bandwagon effect (Schmitt-Beck, 2015)	Users tend to seek for and accept certain search strategies and search results simply because other users are using them	Click, browsing, and dwell time measures: in search and evaluation contexts where users can observe other users' reactions (e.g., ratings, retweets, and comments in social information seeking), a user may be more likely to react to (e.g., click) or given a higher rating on results and recommendations that are broadly accepted by other users	In social information seeking and search, offline evaluation metrics may need to take into account the impacts of social factors presented in retrieval process, in addition to the widely studied factors, such as features of search result snippets, rank positions, and document relevance. This effect is less relevant in traditional Cranfield experiments, where researchers treat searches as individual, separate events

formal models. More detailed discussions on the extension of model assumptions based on the knowledge of bounded rationality and the development of user models beyond current structures would be provided in the following chapters. In this chapter, our goal is to provide an overview of the major gaps between identified biases and existing formal models, rather than examining the specific metric revision or model extension plan associated with each user bias.

Research on boundedly rational users should not be treated as an independent research topic that is separated from traditional formal models. Similar to the aim of behavioral economics within broader economics research problem space (cf. Kahneman, 2003), our goal behind emphasizing user biases and identifying gaps between rational agents and human is not to replace existing user models or negate the value of widely applied offline evaluation metrics. Instead, as it is presented in Fig. 3.1, the knowledge of these gaps will allow researchers to extend and further generalize existing formal models and metrics in a user-oriented, bias-aware manner, with existing metrics being a special simplified or ideal application scenario (with no or minimized impacts from human biases and situational factors). In other words, the existing formal models and simplified assumptions could be used as the computational basis for incorporating new parameters and representations of human and situational factors and for developing more sophisticated user models. The extent to which the enhanced bias-aware user models could capture the search and judgment strategies of real users depends on both the empirical knowledge of

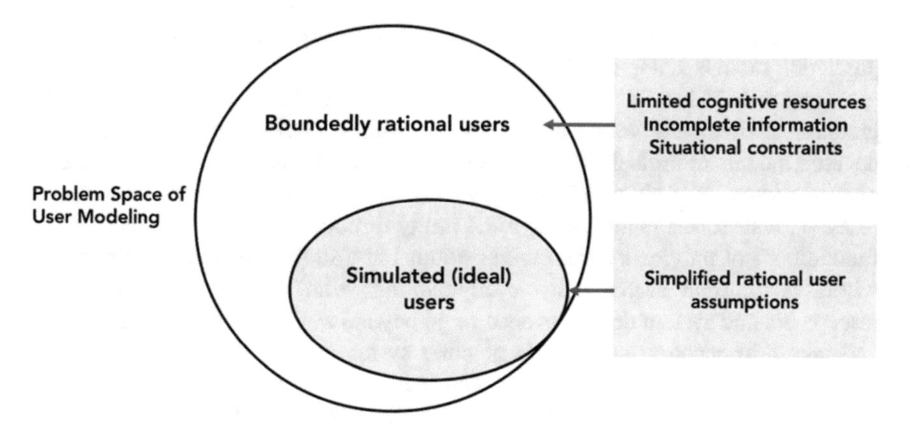

Fig. 3.1 Simulated ideal user and boundedly rational user in IR experiments

human bounded rationality from multiple disciplines and the available resources for model training and validation.

In addition, at practical level, identifying these implicit gaps in research will also inform the design of adaptive, personalized search and recommendation systems that can take into account both algorithmic biases (e.g., Ekstrand et al., 2019; Gao & Shah, 2019) and human biases in search interactions (e.g., Azzopardi, 2021; Liu & Han, 2020). Taking this bias-aware perspective into user modeling, we could further enhance the effectiveness and *multi-dimensional fairness* of existing adaptive and interactive information systems (e.g., Liu & Shah, 2022; Luo et al., 2014; Voorhees, 2008; Zhang et al., 2020a, b).

The summary presented In Table 3.1 focuses on a series of widely used behavioral and offline evaluation metrics proposed and tested in previous research and is by no means exhaustive. Instead, our goal in this chapter is to present and illustrate major *metric-bias gaps* based on the discussions on assumptions and formal user models in Chap. 2 and inform the design of bias-aware user modeling and evaluation framework built upon existing behavioral measures and offline evaluation metrics. The descriptions of derived user models (second column) are developed based on the definitions and empirical evidences on each identified user biases in the first column. More details regarding findings from behavioral experiments, related concepts, and theories, as well as similar cognitive or perceptual biases will be provided and discussed in Chap. 4. In this chapter, our hope is that the readers can have a flavor of existing research on human biases that lead to boundedly rational decisions, as well as their conflicts with the assumptions of formal IR models.

Table 3.1 presents a series of basic boundedly rational user models derived from the knowledge of user biases and bounded rationality in decision-making (e.g., Kahneman, 2003) and points out the ways in which they may conflict with existing components of click models, online behavioral metrics, as well as offline outcome-oriented metrics. The identified gaps between user models associated with existing click models and evaluation metrics and knowledge of human bounded rationality pave new paths toward developing more behaviorally accurate and practically useful prediction models and evaluation measures.

In general, Table 3.1 can serve as a checklist or initial research agenda for graduate students and young researchers to explore available research topics and develop models of critical user biases in the context of interactive IR. For instance, given the knowledge about *reference dependence biases* from behavioral economics research, researchers could redesign the utility discount rates and formulate it as a function of not only query and rank positions but also the dynamic reference level within the current search session. In addition, with respect to *salience bias*, researchers and system designers need to go beyond traditional rank position factor and take into account the impacts of other system output factors and items and examine their levels of saliency compared to adjacent search results and model the possible perceptual biases associated with the visually more salient items. Similar to these biases, exploring the impacts of other cognitive and perceptual biases can also enhance our understanding of search decision-making and potentially pave ways toward more useful user models.

Beyond individual human biases and cognitive limits, it is also critical to explore the in situ interactions among different types of human biases and investigate the ways in which they are affected by algorithmic biases reflected in ranked result lists and jointly decide local search decisions (e.g., query reformulation, clicking, search stopping) and global perceptions and judgments (e.g., whole-session user satisfaction, perceived level of search and task success).

3.3 Hidden Problems Behind Metric-Bias Gaps

Exploring and clarifying the gaps between formal user models (especially the associated implicitly made assumptions) and human biases can help researchers understand and explain different aspects and types of bounded rationality in search-related decision-making. Also, our investigation on the basic assumptions and hidden gaps offers an opportunity to revisit and reflect on the fundamentals of the established IR models, metrics, and the ranking algorithms designed and trained based upon them. Although different user biases, user models, and metrics take different forms and are applied in varying ways, they share many similarities in behavioral and perceptual origins and can be grouped into a small set of gap categories. Specifically, most of the metric-bias gaps (especially the ones related to evaluation and judgment) discussed above are associated with *three main problems*:

- *Problem 1*: dynamic and subjective nature of users' *perceived* rewards and costs, which usually deviate from actual behavior-based events and simulated rewards and costs in click models and evaluation metrics
- *Problem 2*: changing evaluation criteria and thresholds on document relevance, usefulness, and other related dimensions of evaluation across different moments and states of interactive search sessions

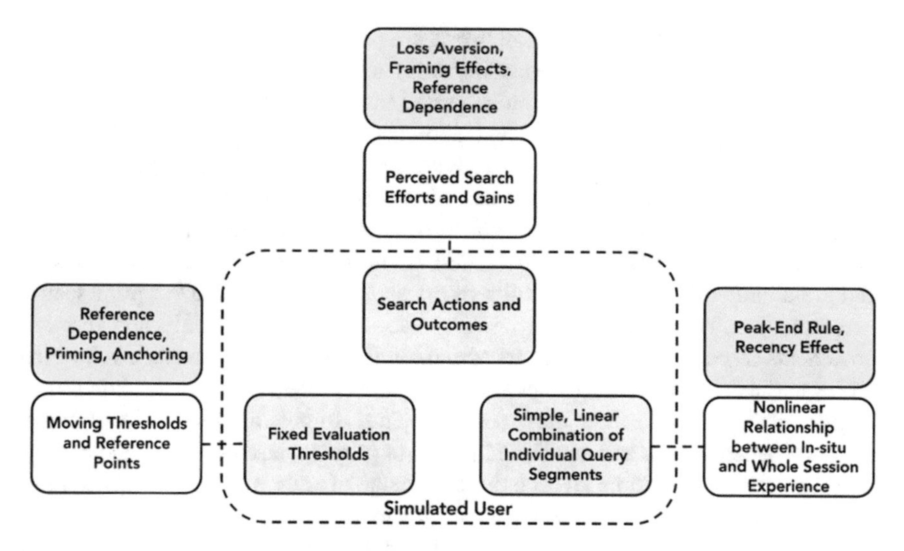

Fig. 3.2 Some gaps between simulated user and boundedly rational user

- *Problem 3*: nonlinear relationship between in situ local evaluation (e.g., query-level search gains, perceived cognitive loads and efforts) and whole-session search evaluation (e.g., session-level user engagement, perceived level of success, and search satisfaction)

The three problems that illustrate the some of the major gaps and conflicts between simulated, formal users and real-life boundedly rational users are summarized in Fig. 3.2. Regarding *Problem 1*, according to findings from behavioral research on reference dependence and loss aversion, users' perceived rewards and costs, which usually serve as the basis for subsequent decision-making, are formed based on dynamic reference points. This thesis conflicts with the final-value-based measures (e.g., total number of clicks and dwell time on SERPs, browsing and cursor movement distances, average nDCG) and assumptions on static costs and gains in search interactions (Azzopardi, 2011, 2014; Azzopardi & Zuccon, 2016). Also, the idea and findings regarding the impacts of reference dependence, anchoring, and framing also challenge the commonly used assumption on cost budget (e.g., metrics@K) as users' in situ perceptions of search cost and implicit acceptable gain-cost ratio may vary over time due to the changes in references and expectations. Built upon the common reference points identified in behavioral economics research (e.g., Kahneman, 2003; Markle et al., 2018; Martin, 2017; Tversky & Kahneman, 1991), Liu and Han (2020) developed a variety of estimated reference-dependent measures and demonstrated their contributions to predicting user behavior and satisfaction. However, how users actually evaluate costs and rewards (e.g., how much time cost equals to or is comparable to the benefits from relevant results) still remains ambiguous and would require further user study efforts to address. To extend existing formal models and evaluation measures, researchers may need to examine more possible reference points or learn personalized reference levels and in situ expectations regarding information gains and efforts from individual users' search interactions and relevance judgments (Liu & Han, 2020).

Taking a step back from diverse evaluation measures, *Problem 2* calls for a revisit on the fundamental ground-truth measures (e.g., relevance, usefulness, user satisfaction) based upon which a large body of outcome-oriented evaluation measures were constructed, especially in the context of whole-session search evaluation. For instance, according to Scholer et al. (2013), users' relevance criteria vary over time and are largely affected by the quality of documents they evaluated in prior search iterations (i.e., threshold priming). Users who are exposed to only non-relevant documents in early sessions tend to assign significantly higher average relevance scores to the documents in later sessions, compared to the users who are exposed to highly relevant documents in early sessions. Thus, to obtain more balanced, unbiased assessment results and avoid the impacts of priming, researchers should expose expert assessors to multiple levels or broader range of relevance score levels early in the evaluation process. This early exposure to diversified documents will help assessors better calibrate the relevance thresholds for judgments. Although the original experiments on this relevance threshold priming effects were conducted in controlled evaluation-only settings, it is possible that threshold priming, as a form of reference dependence in evaluation, also exists in real-life search interactions and may affect not only explicit judgments and evaluations but also implicit feedbacks (e.g., dwell time, cursor movement, browsing, and examination on search results). Also, as an evidence of the complexity of user evaluation, Scholer et al. (2013) also found that users struggled to base their judgments merely on topical relevance and clearly block out the effects of cognitive, situational, and affective relevance. This result indicates that the implicit changes of evaluation thresholds is multidimensional in nature and different dimensions of judgment may interact with each other.

In addition to controlled evaluation-oriented settings, some researchers also examined in situ relevance judgment (e.g., Jiang et al., 2017) and explored the interactions between relevance judgment and usefulness annotations during Web search sessions (Mao et al., 2016). These studies demonstrate the variations in user perceptions and dynamic evaluation thresholds and thereby partially explain why traditional relevance-based evaluation metrics built upon simplified models are not always well aligned with in situ user satisfaction, especially in complex, intellectually challenging search tasks. Compared to document relevance, usefulness as a ground-truth label has the potential to achieve better performance in estimating users' actual search experience and properly evaluating system performances in a user-oriented manner (Cole et al., 2009). External assessors are capable of annotating document usefulness when offered more information about the search context (Mao et al., 2016). However, understanding the nature of usefulness (especially its connections to individual differences and preferences), developing standard and unbiased usefulness-based measures, and applying them in large-scale reproducible experiments are still open challenges to the IR research community (Liu, 2022).

These fundamental challenges in IR evaluation are often bypassed in controlled relevance-based evaluation experiments and user simulations.

Due to the mixed effects generated from multiple sources (e.g., individual human biases, task characteristics, search states, and in situ search session experience), the annotation-based ground-truth measures in IR may act as *moving* targets, rather than *fixed* optimal points that often assumed to be consistent across different search sessions and experimental settings. This dynamic nature introduces fundamental challenges to user-aware IR evaluation and may cause systematic errors in search system evaluation across different contexts. As a result, research on standardizing the documentation and reuse of interactive IR evaluation resources (e.g., tasks, search interaction logs, user judgments, as well as trained models) still face various challenges (Gäde et al., 2021; Liu, 2022). To address this issue and enhance the robustness of IR evaluation, researchers need to further explore the role and impacts of individual differences, especially the systematic user biases and situational limits (e.g., time limit, available system support, quality of information) and capture the systematic effects hidden in seemingly random errors for achieving more accurate user modeling and realistic search system evaluation.

According to findings on anchoring bias (e.g., Chen et al., 2022), users' existing beliefs, biases, and initially encountered information have significant impacts on their subsequent judgments of document usefulness and credibility and information use behavior in search interactions (White, 2013). The variations in in situ evaluation thresholds and users' search expectations also affect users' search stopping and skipping strategies, which calls for revisits and adjustments on related metrics and parameters (e.g., nDCG, ERR, user stopping model of C/W/L), especially in user-oriented session evaluation. Given these findings, researchers can assign adjusted *weights* to documents judged at different points of search sessions to mitigate the impact of user biases on relevance and usefulness labeling and reliability of IR evaluations. To facilitate user-aware reproducible IR evaluation experiments, the possible changes of judgment thresholds, users' references, as well as other impacts associated with bounded rationality should be considered and properly represented as part of the interactive IR test collections (Liu, 2022).

Problem 3 goes beyond individual result evaluation and focuses on the connection between a sequence of local, in situ experience and whole-session evaluation. According to recent research on user biases in search evaluation (Liu & Han, 2020; Liu et al., 2019b), users' experiences at peak and end points usually have higher impacts on session-level evaluations than other search moments. In addition, users' overall experience has no significant correlation with other intuitive search effort measures, such as total dwell time and total number of clicks. This result echoes the findings on peak-end rule from behavioral experiments (e.g., Kahneman, 2003; Sels et al., 2019). Thus, similar to within-SERP evaluation, in interactive session evaluation, the weights of search outcomes and experiences at different moments or under different search states may have largely different impacts on whole-session search experience due to multiple cognitive effects and biases, such as reference dependence biases, peak-end evaluation rule, anchoring biases, and recency effects (Brown & Liu, 2022; Chen et al., 2022; Liu & Han, 2020; Liu et al., 2019b;

Zhang et al., 2020a, b). The specific weight distributions applied in different sessions and evaluation contexts may need to be tailored to different user populations, search task types, as well as distributions of task states and query-level search intentions (Liu et al., 2020a; Mitsui et al., 2017).

In addition to individual click models and evaluation metrics, researchers have also developed a series of formal models to characterize information search interaction. For instance, information foraging theory (IFT) depicts and predicts online information seeking activities based on the assumption that users always try to maximize the rate at which they collect useful information (Pirolli & Card, 1999). This assumption of IFT could be traced back to the economic man assumption behind classical microeconomics theories: individuals have complete, unbiased knowledge about their search costs and gains, and they always seek to optimize the allocation and consumption of limited resources available in order to obtain optimal outcomes. This assumption allows researchers to model the changes of cost-gain ratio in search sessions and calculate expected utility as the basis for evaluating and prediction next-step search decisions, such as continuing browsing, clicking, and search stopping.

Similarly, other researchers have also followed these assumptions in IFT and applied economic models in developing formal models of search gain, cost, and user actions in IR (e.g., Azzopardi, 2011, 2014). Azzopardi (2014) extends search economic theory built in previous works by developing a more comprehensive interaction cost model and derived eight interaction-based hypotheses regarding search behavior. These hypotheses jointly cover different aspects of the interactions among query cost, page cost, assessment cost, snippet cost, assessment probability, and search performance or efficiency. The experimental results obtained on TREC Aquaint Collection show that the economic models of interaction can to some extent predict the observed search behaviors and that the economic approach could provide credible explanations for users' search actions. While the adoption of economic models and assumptions reduce the computational complexity of formal user models in these studies, the assumptions of always maximizing utility contradict with the knowledge of multiple empirically confirmed human biases, such as theory of satisficing, loss aversion, and reference dependence biases (Agosto, 2002; Liu & Han, 2020). Beyond offline system evaluation experiments, researchers also need to examine the components of existing interaction cost models (e.g., costs of formulating queries, reading content pages, browsing search result snippets, and transiting different subtopics) and their deviations from users' perceptions and estimations. Also, when modeling and evaluating search interactions in sessions, researchers need to pay attention to the dynamic gaps between user perception (e.g., perceived time length) and search activities (e.g., actual dwell time on Web pages) (Luo et al., 2017). The outcome-perception gap is associated with both individual differences (e.g., users' tolerance of information uncertainty and tendencies of risk aversion) and in situ changes of search gains, efforts (e.g., relevance of previously examined documents, total elapsed time), as well as search intentions.

Beyond examining specific measures and user models, it is also critical to rethink and revisit the *ground-truth measures* based upon which we evaluate systems and meta-evaluate evaluation metrics in light of individual users' differences and biases (Liu, 2022). *User satisfaction* as a self-reported measure has been widely applied in interactive IR evaluation experiments (e.g., Chen et al., 2017; Liu & Shah, 2019a; Mao et al., 2016) and information systems evaluation in general (Gatian, 1994; Wixom & Todd, 2005; Zviran & Erlich, 2003). According to the empirical findings on peak-end rule and recency effects, researchers need to re-examine the relationship between in situ *experienced satisfaction* and session-level retrospective *remembered satisfaction* (which may significantly deviate from average or total value of in situ satisfaction scores). Besides, user satisfaction as a multifaceted concept may subject to the influence of multiple interrelated factors, such as document relevance, information understandability, emotional state, and task state in information seeking and retrieval (Liu, 2021). Deconstructing user satisfaction measure into separate dimensions may allow researchers to better capture the dynamic nature of user satisfaction and evaluate the multifaceted contributions of IR systems to users and their search tasks in a more accurate manner.

Apart from user biases, there are also other practical challenges associated with above evaluation measures. For instance, it might be reasonable to assume that users have an implicit or subconscious "cost budget" (e.g., the maximum number of clicks and/or time spent) for a search interaction. As discussed in previous chapters, the idea of cost budget serves as an implicit basis for multiple offline metrics (Zhang et al., 2017). However, it is difficult to accurately estimate users' cost budgets, mainly for three reasons:

1. Different users have different levels of topic familiarity, task urgency, and search literacy.
2. Same user may have different cost budgets under varying search intents. For instance, users may have more flexible budgets under exploration stage but become stricter when they have a well-defined target item for search.
3. A user's perceived cost is not always consistent with objectively measured costs and is subject to the influence of contextual factors, such as time pressure, task difficulty, and users' emotional states.

Luo et al. (2017) found that there are gaps between users' perception of time and actual dwell time and that document relevance can significantly affect users' perception of time and their satisfaction feedbacks.

Also, in relevance and usefulness estimation, researchers usually assume a landing page to be useful if a user spent more than 30 s on reading the page (Chen et al., 2017; White & Huang, 2010) or if the page is clicked by two different users under similar search tasks (Hendahewa & Shah, 2017; Shah & González-Ibáñez, 2011). However, depending on the nature of the motivating task, users' topic familiarity and domain knowledge, and the availability of "direct answers" on SERPs, this assumption, which could be established in laboratory settings, may not always be tenable in real-life search scenarios (Liu & Shah, 2022).

Beyond individuals' information seeking and search contexts, a user's search and evaluation activities are also affected by the information generated and decisions made by other users and social interactions (i.e., Bandwagon effect; Barnfield,

2020). For instance, in the context of social information seeking, users tend to accept information that are widely accepted or used by other users (e.g., tweets that receive a large number of retweets, answers that receive a large number of votes and follow-up comments in social Q&A sites) (Asghar, 2015; Kim et al., 2013). Information from social networks, Q&A sites, and discussion forums is playing an increasingly important role in everyday life tasks and decision-making events (Kairam et al., 2013; Oeldorf-Hirsch et al., 2014). Investigating the role of Bandwagon effect would allow researchers to better understand individuals' information use and decision-making activities.

Although the popularity of information objects may reflect certain aspects of information quality, they may be caused by certain information source exposure biases on the algorithmic side (cf. Diaz et al., 2020), which may end up increasing or reinforcing users' existing biases toward certain pre-search beliefs, perspectives, or political views. To address this issue, next-generation search systems should not only address the task of algorithmic debiasing in ranking and information exposure but also provide *cognitive debiasing* for addressing users' current anchoring and reference dependence biases, which may lead to undesired decision-making outcomes (Croskerry, 2003).

3.4 Preliminary Bias-Aware Interactive User Modeling and Evaluation Framework

This section proposes a general, preliminary bias-aware framework to facilitate the integration of insights regarding user biases with IR research, especially user-oriented search evaluation. Our discussion on the framework includes user behavioral models and assumptions as the foundation, bias-aware extension of online and offline metrics, ground-truth labels and assessors, levels of evaluation (i.e., single-query-level and session/task level), as well as evaluation settings and environments. In Fig. 3.3, we seek to comprehensively cover the overall broad picture and depict the vision of bias-aware user modeling and evaluation. We leave further discussion on the role of each bias and model specifications (e.g., operationalization of costs and rewards, hyperparameters for model learning, structure of loss functions, optimization rules) for the following chapters as well as future research works and experiments. Based on the above discussion on the gaps between formally simulated users and boundedly rational users, the framework presented in Fig. 3.3 can serve as a preliminary work or initial structure within which more detailed user models focusing on different levels and components could be better defined and tested in individual experiments. Chapter 4 will further explain the factors of bounded rationality and human biases presented in Fig. 3.3 and discuss the associated theories and empirical experiments (at both behavioral and neural levels) that support them.

It is worth noting that developing and testing user-oriented bias-aware user models and associated products (e.g., click model, session simulation model, offline

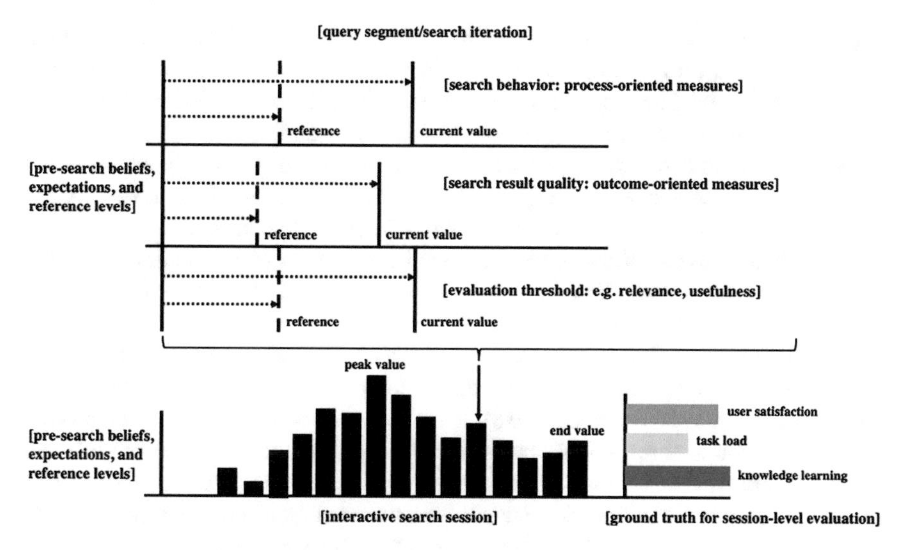

Fig. 3.3 Bias-aware IIR evaluation framework

evaluation metrics) would require extra efforts and more complicated representations than that of traditional Cranfield experiments and offline models (Liu, 2022). To further clarify the knowledge needed for at least partially addressing the gap and specifying bias-aware framework, researchers will need to develop deeper understanding on human biases and bounded rationality in decision-making (Chap. 4) and then leverage the knowledge in revising and improving existing assumptions and formal user models (Chap. 5).

Aligned with the evidence and arguments on metric-bias gaps offered in Sect. 3.2, in our framework, we argue that users' search behaviors and strategies, perceptions of information gains from search results, and evaluation thresholds are affected by both in situ changing references (e.g., reference dependence bias, loss aversion, decoy effect) and pre-search beliefs and expectations (e.g., confirmation bias, anchoring bias). In Fig. 3.3, users' judgments, perceptions, and search decisions are affected by the *delta values* both between current value and moving reference point and between current value and pre-search anchoring point. The perceptual changes or delta values over different dimensions (e.g., perceived search efforts, perceived informational gains) are not only associated with the mathematically calculatable differences in search actions (e.g., changes in number of clicks and dwell time on pages) and search outcomes (e.g., changes in precision and nDCG scores) but also related to the way in which information objects are framed and presented. With similar content and amount of useful information, different types of presentation (e.g., as organic search result or vertical blocks) may attract different levels of user attention and lead to different sizes of changes in perceived efforts.

According to the findings from relevant experiments (e.g., Liu & Han, 2020; Scholer et al., 2013; White, 2013), the weights of different reference points and dimensions in search evaluation vary over time and are associated with search task type and individual characteristics. The hidden pre-search beliefs and moving reference points may contribute to the difficulty in characterizing and predicting user behavior and judgment in session search. This three-dimension part of the framework covers the core metric-bias gap *Problem 1* and *Problem 2*.

Responding to *Problem 3*, we zoom out from individual query segment level and represent users' biased search action and evaluation at whole-session level. Specifically, in addition to the impacts of pre-search beliefs, general references, and loss aversion biases, users' peak- and end-moment experiences (e.g., maximum number of clicks and SERP dwell time in individual queries, SERP dwell time in last query segment) significantly affect their overall session evaluation (Liu & Han, 2020; Liu et al., 2019a). Also, the starting query may play a significant role in deciding the overall search strategies and facilitate early prediction of the characteristics of the overall search task (Mitsui et al., 2018). Knowledge learned from early prediction of task and session features would offer search systems the opportunity to provide and collect in situ feedback on not only *reactive* support but also *proactive* recommendations (e.g., query modification and document recommendation before predicted search failure, proactive search result re-ranking) and search interventions (Koskela et al., 2018; Liu & Shah, 2019b; Shah, 2018; Vuong et al., 2017).

In contrast to the implicit assumptions behind a variety of sum value and average value-based metrics, Liu and Han (2020) found that the total session dwell time do not have a significant impact on whole-session user experience. This result indicates that there are gaps between real-life users' perception of costs, gains, and efforts and the actual search interactions, which often lead to errors in search cost estimation and user satisfaction prediction. Thus, a session-level evaluation model should reflect the *nonlinear* relationship between in situ search experience and session experience and assign different weights to different reference points, rather than simply applying a monotonically decreasing weight function to all SERPs, search sessions, and search task types.

In addition to the three main problems presented in Fig. 3.2, the behavior-based and final-outcome-based measures also deviate from multiple aspects of search experience, which are often labelled and employed as ground-truth measures in meta-evaluation. Regarding this, it is worth noting that researchers can evaluate systems and meta-evaluate evaluation metrics over various dimensions or against different ground-truth measures, such as user satisfaction (Chen et al., 2017; Liu & Yu, 2021; Mao et al., 2016), task/cognitive load (Gwizdka, 2010; Hu & Kando, 2017), knowledge learning (Syed & Collins-Thompson, 2018; Yu et al., 2018), as well as other experience-related measures (e.g., user engagement; O'Brien & Toms, 2008). Some of these ground-truth measures (e.g., user satisfaction) could be deconstructed into separate facets to facilitate more accurate, reproducible user-oriented evaluations (Liu, 2021; J. Liu et al., 2020b). To achieve this, more detailed scales need to be designed and tested based on the knowledge about users' perceptions, their actual behaviors, as well as the human biases that separate them in search interactions. Many of the action-based and perception-based measures, constructs, and scales from management information systems research (e.g., Venkatesh & Davis, 2000; Venkatesh & Bala, 2008) could be adopted and applied to interactive

IR user modeling and system evaluation experiments across a variety of information access and human-computer interaction scenarios (e.g., desktop search, mobile search, chatbot, and spoken search).

3.5 Summary

To better evaluate IR systems and model users' search interactions, we revisit and reflect on the fundamentals of existing user models discussed in the previous chapter and focus on the implicit gaps between boundedly rational users (especially with respect to their cognitive and perceptual biases) and rational assumptions underpinning a variety of formal models and system evaluation metrics. Furthermore, based on the discussions on the limitations of current formal models, this work develops a general bias-aware evaluation framework to roughly characterize the connections between different components and human biases in search sessions. In contrast to the growing research attention on algorithmic biases (e.g., Ekstrand et al., 2019; Zehlike et al., 2017), users' systematic biases and their impacts have been scarcely studied in information seeking and retrieval (Azzopardi, 2021; Liu & Han, 2020). This is a timely opportunity to develop novel concepts, user models, and evaluation measures based on the insights from behavioral economics for this new branch of IR research and complement current IIR evaluations and user modeling. Also, leveraging the knowledge about human-bounded rationality in information seeking (e.g., Agosto, 2002; Chen, 2021) can strengthen the connection between the descriptive user models developed in information seeking community and computational evaluation metrics and techniques proposed in information retrieval community.

Apart from investigating specific models, concepts, and evaluation measures, we are also interested in exploring and enhancing the potential broader impacts of boundedly rational user models. The ultimate goals for this line of research include (1) combining the knowledge learned from user biases and algorithmic biases studies in user modeling and system evaluation, (2) achieving a more comprehensive understanding on how users' biases interact with algorithmic biases and how these two types of biases jointly shape search interactions, and (3) developing unbiased system supports for critical decision-making, such as vaccination, housing, and financial investments. To achieve these goals and explore specific research problems that could be better solved with a bias-aware perspective, the following chapters will review and introduce the research progresses on bounded rationality in decision-making under uncertainty. Reviewing and synthesizing the theories and findings in this area will also provide a richer empirical basis for building formal models of boundedly rational users and developing bias-aware evaluation metrics. As intelligent interactive systems at large become more ubiquitous and complex, research into user biases and bounded rationality is going to be increasingly valuable and may prove to be computationally useful even beyond the field of interactive IR.

References

Agosto, D. E. (2002). Bounded rationality and satisficing in young people's Web-based decision making. *Journal of the American society for Information Science and Technology, 53*(1), 16–27. https://doi.org/10.1002/asi.10024

Asghar, H. M. (2015). Measuring information seeking through Facebook: Scale development and initial evidence of Information Seeking in Facebook Scale (ISFS). *Computers in Human Behavior, 52*, 259–270. https://doi.org/10.1016/j.chb.2015.06.005

Azzopardi, L. (2011). The economics in interactive information retrieval. In *Proceedings of the 34th International ACM SIGIR Conference on Research and Development in Information Retrieval* (pp. 15–24). ACM. https://doi.org/10.1145/2009916.2009923

Azzopardi, L. (2014). Modelling interaction with economic models of search. In *Proceedings of the 37th ACM SIGIR Conference on Research & Development in Information Retrieval* (pp. 3–12). ACM. https://doi.org/10.1145/2600428.2609574

Azzopardi, L. (2021). Cognitive biases in search: A review and reflection of cognitive biases in information retrieval. In *Proceedings of the 2021 ACM SIGIR Conference on Human Information Interaction and Retrieval* (pp. 27–37). ACM. https://doi.org/10.1145/3406522.3446023

Azzopardi, L., Mackenzie, J., & Moffat, A. (2021). ERR is not C/W/L: Exploring the relationship between expected reciprocal rank and other metrics. In *Proceedings of the 2021 ACM SIGIR International Conference on Theory of Information Retrieval* (pp. 231–237). ACM. https://doi.org/10.1145/3471158.3472239

Azzopardi, L., Thomas, P., & Craswell, N. (2018). Measuring the utility of search engine result pages: An information foraging based measure. In *Proceedings of the 41st ACM SIGIR Conference on Research & Development in Information Retrieval* (pp. 605–614). ACM. https://doi.org/10.1145/3209978.3210027

Azzopardi, L., & Zuccon, G. (2016). An analysis of the cost and benefit of search interactions. In *Proceedings of the 2016 ACM SIGIR International Conference on the Theory of Information Retrieval* (pp. 59–68). ACM. https://doi.org/10.1145/2970398.2970412

Barnes, J. H., Jr. (1984). Cognitive biases and their impact on strategic planning. *Strategic Management Journal, 5*(2), 129–137. https://doi.org/10.1002/smj.4250050204

Barnfield, M. (2020). Think twice before jumping on the bandwagon: Clarifying concepts in research on the bandwagon effect. *Political Studies Review, 18*(4), 553–574. https://doi.org/10.1177/1478929919870691

Brown, T., & Liu, J. (2022). A reference dependence approach to enhancing early prediction of session behavior and satisfaction. In *Proceedings of the 22nd ACM/IEEE Joint Conference on Digital Libraries* (pp. 1–5). ACM. https://doi.org/10.1145/3529372.3533294

Chapelle, O., Metlzer, D., Zhang, Y., & Grinspan, P. (2009). Expected reciprocal rank for graded relevance. In *Proceedings of the 18th ACM Conference on Information and Knowledge Management* (pp. 621–630). ACM. https://doi.org/10.1145/1645953.1646033

Charness, G., & Dave, C. (2017). Confirmation bias with motivated beliefs. *Games and Economic Behavior, 104*, 1–23. https://doi.org/10.1016/j.geb.2017.02.015

Chen, T. (2021). A systematic integrative review of cognitive biases in consumer health information seeking: Emerging perspective of behavioral information research. *Journal of Documentation, 77*(3), 798–823. https://doi.org/10.1108/JD-01-2020-0004

Chen, N., Zhang, F., & Sakai, T. (2022). Constructing better evaluation metrics by incorporating the anchoring effect into the user model. In *Proceedings of the 45rd International ACM SIGIR Conference on Research and Development in Information Retrieval*. ACM. https://doi.org/10.1145/3477495.3531953

Chen, Y., Zhou, K., Liu, Y., Zhang, M., & Ma, S. (2017). Meta-evaluation of online and offline web search evaluation metrics. In *Proceedings of the 40th International ACM SIGIR Conference on Research and Development in Information Retrieval* (pp. 15–24). ACM. https://doi.org/10.1145/3077136.3080804

Chuklin, A., Markov, I., & Rijke, M. D. (2015). Click models for web search. *Synthesis Lectures on Information concepts, Retrieval, and Services, 7*(3), 1–115. https://doi.org/10.2200/S00654ED1V01Y201507ICR043

Clarke, C. L., Vtyurina, A., & Smucker, M. D. (2020). Offline evaluation without gain. In *Proceedings of the 2020 ACM SIGIR on International Conference on Theory of Information Retrieval* (pp. 185–192). ACM. https://doi.org/10.1145/3409256.3409816

Cole, M., Liu, J., Belkin, N. J., Bierig, R., Gwizdka, J., Liu, C., Zhang, J., & Zhang, X. (2009). Usefulness as the criterion for evaluation of interactive information retrieval. In *Proceedings of the Third Workshop on Human-Computer Interaction and Information Retrieval* (pp. 1–4). HCIR.

Croskerry, P. (2003). The importance of cognitive errors in diagnosis and strategies to minimize them. *Academic Medicine, 78*(8), 775–780.

Diaz, F., Mitra, B., Ekstrand, M. D., Biega, A. J., & Carterette, B. (2020). Evaluating stochastic rankings with expected exposure. In *Proceedings of the 29th ACM International Conference on Information & Knowledge Management* (pp. 275–284). ACM. https://doi.org/10.1145/3340531.3411962

Eickhoff, C. (2018). Cognitive biases in crowdsourcing. In *Proceedings of the Eleventh ACM International Conference on Web Search and Data Mining* (pp. 162–170). ACM. https://doi.org/10.1145/3159652.3159654

Ekstrand, M. D., Burke, R., & Diaz, F. (2019). Fairness and discrimination in retrieval and recommendation. In *Proceedings of the 42nd International ACM SIGIR Conference on Research and Development in Information Retrieval* (pp. 1403–1404). ACM. https://doi.org/10.1145/3331184.3331380

Gäde, M., Koolen, M., Hall, M., Bogers, T., & Petras, V. (2021). A manifesto on resource re-use in interactive information retrieval. In *Proceedings of the 2021 ACM SIGIR Conference on Human Information Interaction and Retrieval* (pp. 141–149). ACM. https://doi.org/10.1145/3406522.3446056

Gao, R., & Shah, C. (2019). How fair can we go: Detecting the boundaries of fairness optimization in information retrieval. In *Proceedings of the 2019 ACM SIGIR International Conference on Theory of Information Retrieval* (pp. 229–236). ACM. https://doi.org/10.1145/3341981.3344215

Gatian, A. W. (1994). Is user satisfaction a valid measure of system effectiveness? *Information & Management, 26*(3), 119–131. https://doi.org/10.1016/0378-7206(94)90036-1

Gwizdka, J. (2010). Distribution of cognitive load in web search. *Journal of the American Society for Information Science and Technology, 61*(11), 2167–2187. https://doi.org/10.1002/asi.21385

Harman, D. (2011). Information retrieval evaluation. *Synthesis Lectures on Information Concepts, Retrieval, and Services, 3*(2), 1–119. https://doi.org/10.2200/S00368ED1V01Y201105ICR019

Hendahewa, C., & Shah, C. (2017). Evaluating user search trails in exploratory search tasks. *Information Processing & Management, 53*(4), 905–922. https://doi.org/10.1016/j.ipm.2017.04.001

Hofmann, K., Li, L., & Radlinski, F. (2016). Online evaluation for information retrieval. *Foundations and Trends in Information Retrieval, 10*(1), 1–117. https://doi.org/10.1561/1500000051

Hu, X., & Kando, N. (2017). Task complexity and difficulty in music information retrieval. *Journal of the Association for Information Science and Technology, 68*(7), 1711–1723. https://doi.org/10.1002/asi.23803

Jiang, J., He, D., Kelly, D., & Allan, J. (2017). Understanding ephemeral state of relevance. In *Proceedings of the 2017 Conference on Conference Human Information Interaction and Retrieval* (pp. 137–146). ACM. https://doi.org/10.1145/3020165.3020176

Kahneman, D. (2003). Maps of bounded rationality: Psychology for behavioral economics. *American Economic Review, 93*(5), 1449–1475. https://doi.org/10.1257/000282803322655392

Kairam, S., Morris, M., Teevan, J., Liebling, D., & Dumais, S. (2013). Towards supporting search over trending events with social media. In *Proceedings of the International AAAI Conference on Web and Social Media* (Vol. 7, No. 1, pp. 283–292).

Kim, K. S., Sin, S. C. J., & He, Y. (2013). Information seeking through social media: Impact of user characteristics on social media use. *Proceedings of the American Society for Information Science and Technology, 50*(1), 1–4. https://doi.org/10.1002/meet.14505001155

Koskela, M., Luukkonen, P., Ruotsalo, T., Sjöberg, M., & Floréen, P. (2018). Proactive information retrieval by capturing search intent from primary task context. *ACM Transactions on Interactive Intelligent Systems (TIIS), 8*(3), 1–25. https://doi.org/10.1145/3150975

Liu, J. (2021). Deconstructing search tasks in interactive information retrieval: A systematic review of task dimensions and predictors. *Information Processing & Management, 58*(3), 102522. https://doi.org/10.1016/j.ipm.2021.102522

Liu, J. (2022). Toward Cranfield-inspired reusability assessment in interactive information retrieval evaluation. *Information Processing & Management, 59*(5), 103007. https://doi.org/10.1016/j.ipm.2022.103007

Liu, J., & Han, F. (2020). Investigating reference dependence effects on user search interaction and satisfaction: A behavioral economics perspective. In *Proceedings of the 43rd International ACM SIGIR Conference on Research and Development in Information Retrieval* (pp. 1141–1150). ACM. https://doi.org/10.1145/3397271.3401085

Liu, J., Liu, C., & Belkin, N. J. (2020b). Personalization in text information retrieval: A survey. *Journal of the Association for Information Science and Technology, 71*(3), 349–369. https://doi.org/10.1002/asi.24234

Liu, M., Mao, J., Liu, Y., Zhang, M., & Ma, S. (2019b). Investigating cognitive effects in session-level search user satisfaction. In *Proceedings of the 25th ACM SIGKDD International Conference on Knowledge Discovery & Data Mining* (pp. 923–931). ACM. https://doi.org/10.1145/3292500.3330981

Liu, J., Mitsui, M., Belkin, N. J., & Shah, C. (2019a). Task, information seeking intentions, and user behavior: Toward a multi-level understanding of Web search. In *Proceedings of the 2019 ACM SIGIR Conference on Human Information Interaction and Retrieval* (pp. 123–132). ACM. https://doi.org/10.1145/3295750.3298922

Liu, J., Sarkar, S., & Shah, C. (2020a). Identifying and predicting the states of complex search tasks. In *Proceedings of the 2020 ACM SIGIR Conference on Human Information Interaction and Retrieval* (pp. 193–202). ACM. https://doi.org/10.1145/3343413.3377976

Liu, J., & Shah, C. (2019a). Interactive IR user study design, evaluation, and reporting. *Synthesis Lectures on Information Concepts, Retrieval, and Services, 11*(2), i–93. https://doi.org/10.2200/S00923ED1V01Y201905ICR067

Liu, J., & Shah, C. (2019b). Proactive identification of query failure. *Proceedings of the Association for Information Science and Technology, 56*(1), 176–185. https://doi.org/10.1002/pra2.15

Liu, J., & Shah, C. (2022). Leveraging user interaction signals and task state information in adaptively optimizing usefulness-oriented search sessions. In *Proceedings of the 22nd ACM/IEEE Joint Conference on Digital Libraries* (pp. 1–11). ACM. https://doi.org/10.1145/3529372.3530926

Liu, J., & Yu, R. (2021). State-aware meta-evaluation of evaluation metrics in interactive information retrieval. In *Proceedings of the 30th ACM International Conference on Information & Knowledge Management* (pp. 3258–3262). ACM. https://doi.org/10.1145/3459637.3482190

Luo, C., Liu, Y., Sakai, T., Zhou, K., Zhang, F., Li, X., & Ma, S. (2017). Does document relevance affect the searcher's perception of time? In *Proceedings of the Tenth ACM International Conference on Web Search and Data Mining* (pp. 141–150). ACM. https://doi.org/10.1145/3018661.3018694

Luo, J., Zhang, S., & Yang, H. (2014). Win-win search: Dual-agent stochastic game in session search. In *Proceedings of the 37th International ACM SIGIR conference on Research & Development in Information Retrieval* (pp. 587–596). ACM. https://doi.org/10.1145/2600428.2609629

Mao, J., Liu, Y., Zhou, K., Nie, J. Y., Song, J., Zhang, M., Ma, S., Sun, J., & Luo, H. (2016). When does relevance mean usefulness and user satisfaction in web search? In *Proceedings of the 39th*

International ACM SIGIR conference on Research and Development in Information Retrieval (pp. 463–472). ACM. https://doi.org/10.1145/2911451.2911507

Markle, A., Wu, G., White, R., & Sackett, A. (2018). Goals as reference points in marathon running: A novel test of reference dependence. *Journal of Risk and Uncertainty, 56*(1), 19–50. https://doi.org/10.1007/s11166-018-9271-9

Martin, V. (2017). When to quit: Narrow bracketing and reference dependence in taxi drivers. *Journal of Economic Behavior & Organization, 144*, 166–187. https://doi.org/10.1016/j.jebo.2017.09.024

Mitsui, M., Liu, J., Belkin, N. J., & Shah, C. (2017). Predicting information seeking intentions from search behaviors. In *Proceedings of the 40th International ACM SIGIR Conference on Research and Development in Information Retrieval* (pp. 1121–1124). ACM. https://doi.org/10.1145/3077136.3080737

Mitsui, M., Liu, J., & Shah, C. (2018). How much is too much? Whole session vs. first query behaviors in task type prediction. In *Proceedings of the 41st International ACM SIGIR Conference on Research & Development in Information Retrieval* (pp. 1141–1144). ACM. https://doi.org/10.1145/3209978.3210105

Moffat, A., Bailey, P., Scholer, F., & Thomas, P. (2017). Incorporating user expectations and behavior into the measurement of search effectiveness. *ACM Transactions on Information Systems (TOIS), 35*(3), 1–38. https://doi.org/10.1145/3052768

Moffat, A., & Zobel, J. (2008). Rank-biased precision for measurement of retrieval effectiveness. *ACM Transactions on Information Systems (TOIS), 27*(1), 1–27. https://doi.org/10.1145/1416950.1416952

Nelson, T. E., Oxley, Z. M., & Clawson, R. A. (1997). Toward a psychology of framing effects. *Political Behavior, 19*(3), 221–246. https://doi.org/10.1023/A:1024834831093

Nickerson, R. S. (1998). Confirmation bias: A ubiquitous phenomenon in many guises. *Review of General Psychology, 2*(2), 175–220. https://doi.org/10.1037/1089-2680.2.2.175

O'Brien, H. L., & Toms, E. G. (2008). What is user engagement? A conceptual framework for defining user engagement with technology. *Journal of the American society for Information Science and Technology, 59*(6), 938–955. https://doi.org/10.1002/asi.20801

Oeldorf-Hirsch, A., Hecht, B., Morris, M. R., Teevan, J., & Gergle, D. (2014). To search or to ask: The routing of information needs between traditional search engines and social networks. In *Proceedings of the 17th ACM Conference on Computer Supported Cooperative Work & Social Computing* (pp. 16–27). ACM. https://doi.org/10.1145/2531602.2531706

Pirolli, P., & Card, S. (1999). Information foraging. *Psychological Review, 106*(4), 643–675. https://doi.org/10.1037/0033-295X.106.4.643

Pratt, J. W. (1978). Risk aversion in the small and in the large. In *Uncertainty in economics* (pp. 59–79). Academic Press. https://doi.org/10.1016/B978-0-12-214850-7.50010-3

Sanderson, M. (2010). Test collection based evaluation of information retrieval systems. *Foundations and Trends in Information Retrieval, 4*(4), 247–375. https://doi.org/10.1561/1500000009

Schmitt-Beck, R. (2015). Bandwagon effect. *The International Encyclopedia of Political Communication, 1–5*. https://doi.org/10.1002/9781118541555.wbiepc015

Scholer, F., Kelly, D., Wu, W. C., Lee, H. S., & Webber, W. (2013). The effect of threshold priming and need for cognition on relevance calibration and assessment. In *Proceedings of the 36th International ACM SIGIR Conference on Research and Development in Information Retrieval* (pp. 623–632). ACM. https://doi.org/10.1145/2484028.2484090

Sels, L., Ceulemans, E., & Kuppens, P. (2019). All's well that ends well? A test of the peak-end rule in couples' conflict discussions. *European Journal of Social Psychology, 49*(4), 794–806. https://doi.org/10.1002/ejsp.2547

Shah, C. (2018). Information fostering-being proactive with information seeking and retrieval: Perspective paper. In *Proceedings of the 2018 International ACM SIGIR Conference on Human Information Interaction & Retrieval* (pp. 62–71). ACM. https://doi.org/10.1145/3176349.3176389

Shah, C., & González-Ibáñez, R. (2011). Evaluating the synergic effect of collaboration in information seeking. In *Proceedings of the 34th International ACM SIGIR Conference on Research and Development in Information Retrieval* (pp. 913–922). ACM. https://doi.org/10.1145/2009916.2010038

Simon, H. A. (1955). A behavioral model of rational choice. *The Quarterly Journal of Economics, 69*(1), 99–118. https://doi.org/10.2307/1884852

Syed, R., & Collins-Thompson, K. (2018). Exploring document retrieval features associated with improved short- and long-term vocabulary learning outcomes. In *Proceedings of the 2018 ACM SIGIR Conference on Human Information Interaction & Retrieval* (pp. 191–200). ACM. https://doi.org/10.1145/3176349.3176397

Tiefenbeck, V., Goette, L., Degen, K., Tasic, V., Fleisch, E., Lalive, R., & Staake, T. (2018). Overcoming salience bias: How real-time feedback fosters resource conservation. *Management Science, 64*(3), 1458–1476. https://doi.org/10.1287/mnsc.2016.2646

Tipper, S. P. (1985). The negative priming effect: Inhibitory priming by ignored objects. *The Quarterly Journal of Experimental Psychology, 37*(4), 571–590. https://doi.org/10.1080/14640748508400920

Tversky, A., & Kahneman, D. (1991). Loss aversion in riskless choice: A reference-dependent model. *The Quarterly Journal of Economics, 106*(4), 1039–1061. https://doi.org/10.2307/2937956

Venkatesh, V., & Bala, H. (2008). Technology acceptance model 3 and a research agenda on interventions. *Decision Sciences, 39*(2), 273–315. https://doi.org/10.1111/j.1540-5915.2008.00192.x

Venkatesh, V., & Davis, F. D. (2000). A theoretical extension of the technology acceptance model: Four longitudinal field studies. *Management Science, 46*(2), 186–204. https://doi.org/10.1287/mnsc.46.2.186.11926

Voorhees, E. M. (2008). On test collections for adaptive information retrieval. *Information Processing & Management, 44*(6), 1879–1885. https://doi.org/10.1016/j.ipm.2007.12.011

Vuong, T., Jacucci, G., & Ruotsalo, T. (2017). Proactive information retrieval via screen surveillance. In *Proceedings of the 40th International ACM SIGIR Conference on Research and Development in Information Retrieval* (pp. 1313–1316). ACM. https://doi.org/10.1145/3077136.3084151

White, R. (2013). Beliefs and biases in web search. In *Proceedings of the 36th International ACM SIGIR Conference on Research and Development in Information Retrieval* (pp. 3–12). ACM. https://doi.org/10.1145/2484028.2484053

White, R. W. (2016). *Interactions with search systems*. Cambridge University Press.

White, R. W., & Huang, J. (2010). Assessing the scenic route: Measuring the value of search trails in web logs. In *Proceedings of the 33rd International ACM SIGIR Conference on Research and Development in Information Retrieval* (pp. 587–594). ACM. https://doi.org/10.1145/1835449.1835548

Wixom, B. H., & Todd, P. A. (2005). A theoretical integration of user satisfaction and technology acceptance. *Information Systems Research, 16*(1), 85–102. https://doi.org/10.1287/isre.1050.0042

Yu, R., Gadiraju, U., Holtz, P., Rokicki, M., Kemkes, P., & Dietze, S. (2018). Predicting user knowledge gain in informational search sessions. In *Proceedings of the 41st ACM SIGIR Conference on Research & Development in Information Retrieval* (pp. 75–84). ACM. https://doi.org/10.1145/3209978.3210064

Zehlike, M., Bonchi, F., Castillo, C., Hajian, S., Megahed, M., & Baeza-Yates, R. (2017). FA* IR: A fair Top-k ranking algorithm. In *Proceedings of the 2017 ACM on Conference on Information and Knowledge Management* (pp. 1569–1578). ACM. https://doi.org/10.1145/3132847.3132938

Zhang, J., Liu, Y., Mao, J., Xie, X., Zhang, M., Ma, S., & Tian, Q. (2022). Global or local: Constructing personalized click models for Web search. In *Proceedings of the ACM Web Conference* (pp. 213–223). ACM. https://doi.org/10.1145/3485447.3511950

Zhang, Y., Liu, X., & Zhai, C. (2017). Information retrieval evaluation as search simulation: A general formal framework for IR evaluation. In *Proceedings of the ACM SIGIR International Conference on Theory of Information Retrieval* (pp. 193–200). ACM. https://doi.org/10.1145/3121050.3121070

Zhang, F., Mao, J., Liu, Y., Ma, W., Zhang, M., & Ma, S. (2020b). Cascade or recency: Constructing better evaluation metrics for session search. In *Proceedings of the 43rd International ACM SIGIR Conference on Research and Development in Information Retrieval* (pp. 389–398). ACM. https://doi.org/10.1145/3397271.3401163

Zhang, T., & Zhang, D. (2007). Agent-based simulation of consumer purchase decision-making and the decoy effect. *Journal of Business Research, 60*(8), 912–922. https://doi.org/10.1016/j.jbusres.2007.02.006

Zhang, W., Zhao, X., Zhao, L., Yin, D., Yang, G. H., & Beutel, A. (2020a). Deep reinforcement learning for information retrieval: Fundamentals and advances. In *Proceedings of the 43rd International ACM SIGIR Conference on Research and Development in Information Retrieval* (pp. 2468–2471). ACM. https://doi.org/10.1145/3397271.3401467

Zviran, M., & Erlich, Z. (2003). Measuring IS user satisfaction: Review and implications. *Communications of the Association for Information Systems, 12*(1), 5. 10.17705/1CAIS.01205.

Part II
Beyond Rational Agents

Chapter 4
Bounded Rationality in Decision-Making Under Uncertainty

Abstract To better introduce the behavioral economics approach and reinforce the theoretical basis for supporting bias-aware user modeling and evaluation, we need to have a deeper understanding of the concepts, theories, recent progress, and empirical findings on users and their biased decisions in varying scenarios. To achieve this, this chapter takes a step back from specific computational IR models and focuses on explaining the fundamental frameworks (e.g., theories of two systems), research progress, and practical implications of behavioral economics research on boundedly rational decision-making activities. Our review focuses on the major human biases and heuristics that are both widely examined in behavioral economics studies and also clearly contradict one or more assumptions that are explicitly or implicitly made in formal IR models. Although the theories on bounded rationality may not be able to match the precision and quantifiability of formal computational models, as argued by Kahneman, this statement of limitation from the classic economics side is "just another way of saying that rational models are psychologically unrealistic" [Kahneman (American Economic Review 93(5):1449, 2003)]. This argument also serves as part of the motivations for this book and the author's broad research agenda on IR research.

4.1 Background

One of the fundamental research themes of economic studies is how people allocate accessible but limited resources when trying to accomplish some goals and optimize the obtained *utility* (Mankiw, 2014). Classical rational models proposed in economics are practically flexible and have been applied in not only economics studies but also a variety of areas that are not considered as traditional economics research problems. Based on the idea of analyzing costs and optimizing utility, information seeking and retrieval researchers have also applied rational economic models in developing testable hypotheses regarding search interactions, explaining users' actions under different cost and gain scenarios (e.g., Azzopardi, 2014; Pirolli & Card, 1999), and developing basic components of evaluation metrics, such as rank-based discounted utility and cost budget (cf. Zhang et al., 2017). However, under a

J. Liu, *A Behavioral Economics Approach to Interactive Information Retrieval*, The Information Retrieval Series 48, https://doi.org/10.1007/978-3-031-23229-9_4

variety of formal rational models, it is unclear how people make *boundedly rational* decisions with limited resources and incomplete information, especially in complex problematic situations. The ideal assumptions and simulated conditions for analysis, such as complete information about available options, unlimited computational resources, and goal of optimizing measurable utility, are difficult to achieve in real-life decision-making scenarios, which often lead to significant individual differences and systematic deviations from expected optimal options and outcomes.

In contrast to classical economic theories and associated formal models, behavioral economics researchers seek to (1) build the analysis of the rules employed in decision-making under uncertainty on a more realistic behavioral and psychological basis and (2) to differentiate rational man's simulated optimal behavior from people's real-life behavior under various human biases, cognitive limits, and situational constraints (Kahneman, 2003; Thaler, 2016). Furthermore, based on the learned knowledge about bounded rationality in decision-making, researchers also seek to design and develop *cognitive debiasing* tools to mitigate the negative impacts of human biases and heuristics in varying application areas, such as clinical diagnosis, hiring, financial services, and crowdsourcing tasks (Croskerry, 2003; Draws et al., 2021; Ludolph & Schulz, 2018; O'Sullivan & Schofield, 2018). Leveraging the knowledge about human biases and limits accumulated in behavioral economics research could help us better understand and explain the search decision-making and judgments of boundedly rational users.

Previous chapters introduce different types of user models underpinning search models and evaluation metrics and describe the gaps between a series of empirically confirmed human biases and simulated rational user models in varying experimental settings. In particular, Chap. 3 aims to offer readers a preliminary understanding of the deviations of boundedly rational users from simulated formal users. The identified gaps highlight the importance of reflecting on the assumptions and limitations of formal IR models and also encourage us to further explore the cognitive roots, behavioral patterns, and nuances hidden in boundedly rational decisions. To better introduce the behavioral economics approach and reinforce the theoretical basis for supporting bias-aware user modeling and evaluation, we need to have a deeper understanding of the concepts, theories, recent progress, and empirical findings on users and their biased and non-optimal decisions in varying scenarios.

To achieve this, this chapter takes a step back from specific computational IR models and focuses on explaining the fundamental frameworks (e.g., theories of two systems), research progress, and practical implications of behavioral economics research on boundedly rational decision-making activities. A comprehensive overview of all human biases identified in behavioral experiments is beyond the scope of this book. Also, a large portion of identified biases are not mutually exclusive and hard to differentiate from each other in naturalistic settings. Therefore, we focus on the major human biases and heuristics that are both widely examined in behavioral economics studies and also clearly contradict one or more assumptions that are explicitly or implicitly made in formal IR models (see Chap. 3 for a preliminary discussion on the gaps between formal model assumptions and empirical findings on human biases). A more comprehensive list of over 175 individual cognitive biases and mental shortcuts can be found at Benson (2016).[1]

Research on human biases tend to be individualized and sometimes difficult to quantify or formalize based on a set of axioms. Although the theories on bounded rationality may not be able to match the precision and quantifiability of formal economic models, as argued by Kahneman, this statement of limitation from the classic economics side is "just another way of saying that rational models are psychologically unrealistic" (Kahneman, 2003, p.1449). This argument also serves as part of the motivations for this book on IR research.

4.2 Two Systems of Human Cognition: Which One Are We Using?

Depending on the nature of task, individuals often engage in different modes of thinking, judging, and deciding (Sloman, 1996). To characterize the basic structure of human cognition, Kahneman proposed the framework of *Two Systems*, which offers a theoretical umbrella under which various specific decision-making strategies, habits, and heuristics can be categorized, analyzed, and grouped together (Kahneman, 2003; Thaler, 2016). *System 1* often operates in automatic, fast, and effortless manner. The operations of System 1 are often defined by habits, biases, and heuristics as they allow individuals to act fast without consuming much cognitive resources or relying on rich new information. Also, when System 1 operates in decision-making activities, the process is usually difficult to explicitly control or modify. The decision makers' preferences over different options are often established quickly and unconsciously and are also heavily affected by their in situ emotional responses. In contrast, the operations of *System 2* are often associated with careful reasoning and are usually slower, effortful, and under individuals' control. Compared to fast decision-making processes governed by habits and mental shortcuts, System 2 tends to be more flexible and can be integrated with externally obtained rules and predefined plans that could be independent from the individuals' prior beliefs and knowledge. As a result, System 2 consumes more cognitive efforts and slows down decision-making and evaluation processes and sometimes is perceived as unaffordable when quick decision-making is needed on seemingly simple tasks.

Based on the relevant theories and empirical observations (e.g., Evans, 2003; Kahneman, 2003, 2011; Neys, 2006; Tversky & Kahneman, 1992), Table 4.1

[1] After preparing the raw list of all individual biases, Benson (2016) further processed the list by removing duplicates, grouping biases that are similar in nature, and putting together complementary biases (e.g., optimism bias and pessimism bias). After this preprocessing, Benson (2016) obtains a more condensed list with around 20 unique human biases associated with specific mental strategies that decision makers used under different scenarios.

Table 4.1 Two Systems

System	System 1	System 2
Attributes	Fast, automatic, effortless, emotional, unintentional	Slow, controlled, effortful, neutral or rational, intentional, analytical
Cognitive activities	Generate intuitive impressions Produce quick decisions under heuristics and mental shortcuts Simple parallel tasks	Reasoning and calculation Explicit judgments Single, complex tasks and mentally demanding activities

summarizes the features of the dual systems and their respective roles in different cognitive activities. Among different indicators of cognitive activities, the difference in effort is most useful in differentiating the tasks assigned to System 1 and the tasks that are processed under System 2 (Kahneman, 2003; Tversky & Kahneman, 1992). Effortful processes that operate under System 2 tend to disrupt each other. For instance, it is difficult to read a book while monitoring the trending events and news updates on TV. In contrast, effortless processes that do not involve much reasoning or intentionally controlled actions cause little or no interference to other ongoing tasks. For example, a driver can sometimes have a conversation with the passenger while driving on a highway, as the driving task may not consume much attention when the traffic is not too busy.

Note that many real-life work tasks involve the operations of both System 1 and System 2 at multiple stages. According to Kahneman (2011), the perceptual system and intuitive operations under System 1 can generate initial impressions of the features of encountered items or objects. The impressions of objects do not need to be verbally explicit and are not controlled by decision makers. For instance, when searching for information relevant to climate change, people may automatically notice and engage with salient vertical results first (e.g., short videos, trending news and images about natural disasters and economic losses related to climate issues, answer boxes about frequently asked climate questions, social media messages about new scientific experiments on climate effects), rather than regular organic results and Web pages (e.g., Wikipedia page about ongoing climate issues). At this stage, users' impressions and perceptions are heavily influenced by visually salient factors, such as color, vertical boundaries, and font sizes, and this process is not voluntary or effortful. This superficial processing of incoming information may also intensify clickbait issues and biased decisions under unbalanced information exposure (e.g., Jung et al., 2022; Molyneux & Coddington, 2020; Wang et al., 2021).

However, System 2 may operate as the dominant force when users need to evaluate the relevance and usefulness of the contents and synthesize them into usable answers or supporting materials for facilitating subsequent decision-making activities. Under this circumstance, the impressions generated by System 1 has less impacts on users' decision-making activities, and the operation of System 2 supports explicit judgments and slow reasoning needed for the information evaluation task. In addition to operating on complex, cognitively demanding, or intellectually challenging tasks, System 2 in some occasions (when doubts regarding the current decision come to one's mind) can monitor the impressions and intuitive judgments generated by System 1 and proactively correct potential errors (Kahneman, 2003). For instance, a user who has a well-defined evaluation task in mind may voluntarily compare the content of different information items presented on SERPs and check their respective credibility and thus may have a better chance of overcoming the potential biases caused by visual factors and clickbait.

According to Tversky and Kahneman (1974) and Kahneman (2011), another key feature shared by the two systems is that both of them can deal with stored concepts and prior beliefs, and they both can be evoked by language. In contrast of perception, the operation of System 1 is not limited to the processing of current simulations. This broad scope of System 1, compared to human perception, enables its operations on a wider range of tasks and processes where people can leverage accessible heuristics and rules to save cognitive resources and make immediate decisions. However, it also leaves more room for human cognitive biases (cf. Azzopardi, 2021) to operate in decision-making processes, which may interact with biased information presentation and lead to inaccurate understanding and undesired outcomes. While System 2 can monitor the intuitive judgments in some scenarios, the superficial processing of incomplete information under System 1 often plays the dominant role; System 2 monitors immediate judgments and quick decision-making tasks quite lightly (Kahneman, 2003). Thus, it is critical for researchers to study the operations of both systems and leverage the knowledge about dual systems in developing adaptive and useful debiasing interventions and nudging to help people mitigate the negative impacts of various biases (Battaglio et al., 2019; Draws et al., 2021).

Boundedly rational decisions under System 1 are often made quickly through simple rules and mental shortcuts and allow individuals to save cognitive resources in a wide range of tasks. However, due to the intrinsic limitations of System 1, surprising errors could happen when even a simple form of deliberate reasoning is required for completing the task correctly. Kahneman (2003) presents a simple puzzle used for studying cognitive self-monitoring and errors from System 1 in immediate judgments. The original question is:

> A bat and a ball cost $1.10 in total. The bat costs $1 more than the ball. How much does the ball cost?

According to the result reported in the original study, in both of the two groups of college student participants, over 50% of participants yielded to the immediate impulse of answering "10 cents."[2] Errors in simple calculation are not unique to this task. Researchers have also obtained unexpectedly high error rates in other similar tasks and behavioral experiments (e.g., Frederick & Fischhoff, 1998; Kahneman, 2011; Thaler, 2016). This surprisingly high error rate in bat-and-ball question (and other similar puzzles) demonstrates that (1) errors could happen under the immediate impressions or impulses generated by operations of System 1 and (2) the intuitive quick judgments are lightly monitored by System 2. People are not used to think hard, and they are often satisfied with seemingly plausible and straightforward

[2] The correct answer is 5 cents.

judgments that are immediately accessible in their mind. Under simplified assumptions and simulated rational models, it would be challenging to predict or prevent these errors and deviations (that are seemingly easy to avoid) from optimal or correct answers at individual level.

The dual-system architecture and associated empirical experiments demonstrate the complexity of human cognition behind seemingly simple and straightforward decision-making strategies. As discussed above, different systems are associated with different decision-making processes and are subject to the impacts of different external factors and internal biases. The operations of System 1 and System 2 may be triggered by different task types (e.g., simple factual retrieval or open-ended complex retrieval tasks), situational factors (e.g., task urgency), and individual characteristics (e.g., emotional state, prior knowledge on certain domains). Also, at different stages of a motivating task, the two systems may interact with each other (e.g., System 2 may monitor the quick decisions made based on the impressions from System 1).

Although we can differentiate the features and operational processes of the two systems at theoretical level and in highly controlled experimental settings (Evans, 2003; Frederick & Fischhoff, 1998; Kahneman, 2011), it is difficult to clearly separate them and model their operations, respectively, in relatively complex, uncontrolled task settings, such as real-life information seeking and retrieval scenarios. For instance, a user may plan to learn more about the seriousness and actual impacts of heat waves in different regions of the world. Although the user may rely on the operations of System 2 on carefully examining the statistics regarding the impacts of economy, public health, and transportation, their judgments on the seriousness of the situation in different countries may be biased due to the biased presentation of information on SERPs under related queries: Depending on the past search history, geographical location of the user, and the specific personalization algorithms behind the search engine in use, the retrieved search results may be heavily biased toward certain regions and populations. As a result, the user may overestimate the seriousness of the situation in local areas as there are more relevant reports, images, and news stories available on retrieved SERPs and underestimate the gravity of the related problems in other countries and regions.

Another example is about financial decision-making and information processing. Although people who invest in stock markets can sometimes analyze the current situation rationally based on the available information (past stock prices, overall trend of the economy, ongoing and pending policies), this does not mean that System 2 can always be in charge when critical financial decisions need to be made. In some cases where decision makers are not clear about the overall trend of the stock market and have difficulties in predicting the price changes of stocks purchased, they may decide to hold on to the stocks in their accounts and stick to the current status, despite of the uncertain but alarming signals (e.g., ongoing price drops of stocks, fluctuation of interest rates). This *status quo bias* (cf. Fleming et al., 2010; Samuelson & Zeckhauser, 1988) and aversion of risk and ambiguity (cf. Holt & Laury, 2002) allow people to make quick decisions under uncertainty and incomplete information (usually under the operation of System 1); they may lead to inaccurate and irrational decisions regarding "sunk cost" in stock investments and cause even bigger financial losses. Note that people are more likely to rely on intuitive judgments enabled by System 1 and biased decisions when they are required to make choices under high levels of uncertainty and pressure.

Methodologically, although some progress have been made on studying human reasoning and biases in simple crowdsourcing tasks (e.g., Draws et al., 2021; Eickhoff, 2018; Saab et al., 2019), the existing tools (e.g., interfaces, standard tasks, questions, and scales) may not be enough for capturing different aspects of task-based information search interactions. In particular, it is difficult to simulate the contexts, motivations, and situational limits that often trigger the operations of System 1 and create conditions for human biases to play their roles. Although System 1 often offers more room for human biases and rule-of-thumb heuristics to operate, people's decisions made under the operations of System 2 could still be biased and boundedly rational due to the limited capacity of mental efforts and restrictions caused by specific problematic situations (e.g., time limits, constraints, and biases of available information, prior beliefs, and public opinions). Thus, to develop useful, reproducible, bias-aware user models in IR and related fields, researchers need to not only integrate the theories on bounded rationality and human biases with formal models and evaluation metrics but also overcome the methodological challenges of investigating and simulating human biases in user studies and controlled experiments, especially under complex information retrieval tasks.

As discussed above, individuals' decision-making activities are affected by the operations of both System 1 and System 2 in varying ways. The tension and interaction between the two systems often trigger human biases of varying types (Kahneman, 2011), which brings both positive and negative impacts on the process and quality of decisions. Figure 4.1 summarizes the operations of both systems in decision-making activities and illustrates the role of individual human biases within the whole process. As shown in Fig. 4.1, although human biases could generate behavioral impacts under both systems, they usually have higher chance to cause frequent and significant deviations from optimal results under quick, automatic operations of System 1, or in situations where there are conflicts between the impressions generated by System 1 and judgments made under System 2.

The dual-system framework provides an overall conceptual structure for characterizing and explaining different forms of human decision-making activities under varying environments, including the local and global decisions in information seeking and retrieval. Within the operations of two systems, different cognitive and perceptual biases arise and affect different aspects and stages of decision-making and task performances. Knowledge regarding human biases and the operations of System 1 may allow researchers to better understand, explain, and predict the deviations of real-life boundedly rational decisions from optimal decisions, which may require slow deliberate reasoning. To further investigate the details regarding boundedly rational decisions under the impacts of different biases, the following sections will explore a series of widely examined human biases in behavioral economics and explain their implications for information seeking, IR,

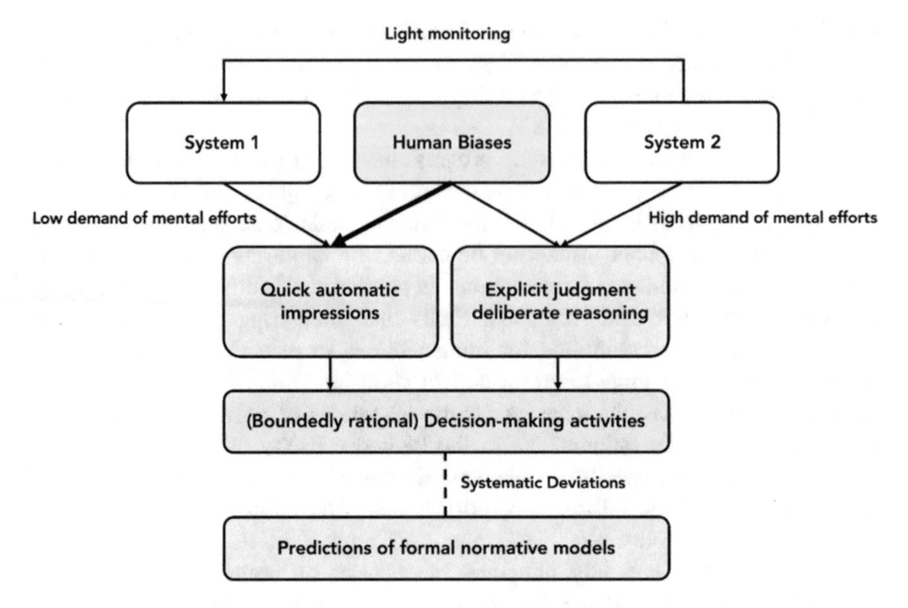

Fig. 4.1 Operations of System 1 and System 2 in decision-making activities

and other closely related research areas, especially in terms of enhancing user models and developing and meta-evaluating bias-aware search evaluations from both user-centered and algorithmic perspectives.

4.3 Reference Dependence

Reference dependence effect is one of the widely studied human biases in option evaluation and decision-making and also connects to or causes several related biases, such as framing effects, loss aversion, and anchoring biases. According to Tversky and Kahneman (1992)'s research on reference dependence, when people make decisions and evaluate available options, they make their judgments based on the gains or losses relative to varying *reference points* in mind, rather than *final absolute outcomes*. Thus, with the same final outcomes associated with choices, different people under different conditions may have largely different judgments and reactions, which may lead to divergent subsequent behaviors. In economics analysis, researchers found that in contrast to the assumptions of standard decision-making models, initial entitlements, which often act as default reference points, do play an important role in determining people's preferences and perception-based evaluations; also, the rate of exchange between products can largely differ depending on which is obtained and which is given up in transactions (Kőszegi & Rabin, 2006; Tversky & Kahneman, 1991).

Fig. 4.2 Reference dependence: an example of moving

The impacts of reference dependence are ubiquitous in real-life decision-making tasks and do not need to involve complex mechanisms or strict conditions. Figure 4.2 presents a simple example that illustrates reference dependence effect. Suppose there are two persons moving from old apartment to new apartment, respectively. The person in situation A is moving from Apartment A to Apartment B. As a result, their work-home distance *decreases* from 30 miles to 15 miles. Meanwhile, in situation B, the person moves from Apartment C to Apartment D. Consequently, the person's work-home distance increases from 2 miles to 10 miles. It would not be surprising to see that the person in situation A is happier (assuming that work-home distance is the only factor that matters here, and levels of happiness and work-home distance are negatively correlated). However, if we merely compare the final outcomes from the two situations, a standard decision-making model would ignore the perceived gains and losses involved in the process and predict that the person in situation B is happier, given the shorter final work-home distance. As argued in reference dependence model, it is the perceived gains and losses relative to the corresponding reference points that matter in decision-making activities and individuals' judgments.

Theories and research on reference dependence cast doubts on the long-standing normative theory of *expected utility*, where individuals' decisions are assumed to be determined by a utility function that includes the expected final outcome and probability associated with each possible situation under the same action. As shown in Formula (4.1), S represents the full set of all possible *situations* or *outcomes* under the *action* A. P and U refer to the measurable *possibilities* and *utility scores* associated with each possible situation. E(A) measures the expected utility of action A, which considers all theoretically possible situations and the related utility that an individual could obtain.

$$E(A) = \sum_{s \in S} P_A(s) U(s) \tag{4.1}$$

In contrast to the findings on reference dependence, the expected utility theory does not involve individual-level factors that are subjective in nature, such as pre-search expectations, changing preferences, and in situ reference levels (Harrison, 1994; Kahneman, 2003). Expected utility or other forms of optimization goals built upon mathematical expectations are widely used in estimating utility and efforts in decision-making processes as this approach offers researchers a tangible way to simplify the analysis of individual choice and quantitatively compute, compare, and evaluate choices, decisions, and possible outcomes (Tversky & Kahneman, 1991). When we apply reference-dependence framework in analyzing and predicting human decisions, one obvious challenge is to estimate and accurately predict people's reference points in mind. In controlled lab settings, researchers can design reference-dependence scenarios by manipulating initial entitlements (e.g., pre-experiment gifts, a certain amount of cash) (Apesteguia & Ballester, 2009; Bateman et al., 1997; Tversky & Kahneman, 1991; Sprenger, 2015) in simulated simple decision-making tasks, with available options, external conditions, and situational restrictions being fully explained and transparent. However, in real-life environments, the estimation of reference points could be difficult and may require deeper knowledge about individuals' knowledge structure, in situ expectation, as well as the perceived gains and efforts from recent and previous similar decisions.

Furthermore, from the reference dependence perspective, researchers also found that the marginal value and impact of both gains and losses decrease with their size (Tversky & Kahneman, 1991). When the changes of gains and losses are far away from the reference points, the impacts of these changes on people's perceived utility and behavior would be smaller compared to the effects of the variations that are close to reference points. For instance, under the impact of inflation, oil prices often increase over time. If the previous long-term stable price range is around \$1.99 to \$2.19, then people tend to be more sensitive to the changes that are close to their initial reference points (e.g., 50 cent price increase from \$2.19 to \$2.69), compared to the same-size marginal changes in a higher price level (e.g., price increase from \$4.49 to \$4.99). On the gain side, this phenomenon of *diminishing sensitivity* can be written as follows:

$$G = d(o, ref) \geq 0 \tag{4.2}$$

$$V(G) \geq 0 \tag{4.3}$$

$$\frac{\partial V}{\partial G} > 0 \tag{4.4}$$

$$\frac{\partial^2 V}{\partial G^2} < 0 \tag{4.5}$$

As shown in the formulas above, G represents the gain that an individual collects or perceives relative to a reference point in mind. Thus, G is determined by the final outcome o and the reference point *ref*. According to the findings on diminishing sensitivity, the first-order derivative is greater than zero as the perceived value or utility keeps increasing as the gain increases. The second-order derivative is negative as the marginal value that each unit of marginal gain brings to the person keeps decreasing as the overall total amount of gain increases. Thus, the relationship between the variations of perceived gains or losses and the corresponding changes in perceived value or utility is nonlinear.

Theories and empirical evidences on reference dependence encourage us to reflect on the simplified assumptions and associated formal models built in a variety of application areas, including information seeking and retrieval. The change from outcome-based perspective to reference-based perspective would motivate researchers to re-examine and revise a large set of existing user models and evaluation metrics. Also, it would be important to investigate the impacts of relative gains and losses (e.g., increases or decreases of dwell time on SERPs and content pages, quality of SERPs measured by nDCG, and difficulty of formulating meaningful queries) on users' in situ search decisions (e.g., changes of search tactics) and levels of satisfaction. However, as discussed above, before we could revise user models and metrics from reference dependent perspective, as the starting basis, researchers need to accumulate solid direct evidences on the roles, changes, and impacts of in situ reference points in search interactions through properly designed user studies. Searchers' reference points could come from their pre-search beliefs and existing knowledge, in situ search expectations, prior search gains and efforts during the same session, as well as past search experience under similar motivating tasks and search scenarios (e.g., a recurring daily task in workplace).

As presented in the examples above, a final outcome could be perceived as either gain or loss, depending on their relative changes to the reference point. Based on the observations on people's responses to perceived gains and losses, researchers have identified another effect related to reference dependence, namely, *loss aversion*, which causes asymmetric sensitivity to gains and losses of the same size (if quantitatively measurable) and other related impacts on decision-making activities, such as endowment effect and status quo bias. The following sections will discuss loss aversion bias as well as other related effects in detail.

4.4 Loss Aversion, Endowment Effect, and Status Quo Bias

According to the empirical evidence (at both behavioral and neural levels) on loss aversion from behavioral science experiments (e.g., Alesina & Passarelli, 2019; Erev et al., 2008; Gächter et al., 2022; Tom et al., 2007; Tversky & Kahneman, 1991), when changes relative to certain reference points occur, people tend to be more sensitive to the losses than to gains. In other words, it is always better to not lose $5 than gain $5. A major increase in product quality may not cause much improvement on customer satisfaction and adoption. However, a slight decrease in product quality from the current status may lead to a quick, major drop in customers' product ratings.

In addition, people are generally more sensitive to the impacts of a difference on a dimension when the difference is perceived as a loss, compared to other dimensions where the same or similar size of changes is perceived as gains. Consider the example presented in Fig. 4.2. Assuming there is only one dimension, work-home distance, considered in decision-making evaluation, then the person in situation A is happy to see the decrease of the distance after moving to apartment B. However, if this apartment moving also involves a perceived loss on another dimension, such as higher rents, increased distances from home to supermarkets, or worse school district, then the option may be viewed differently. If the losses and gains are both quantifiable and can be compared with the same unit (e.g., assuming that both losses and gains could be calculated using dollar amounts), then for the same amount of losses and gains on different dimensions, people are more sensitive to the dimensions where losses compared to the status quo are perceived.

The effect of loss aversion can be written as follows:

$$f'(-\Delta) > f'(\Delta) > 0 \tag{4.6}$$

$$\Delta = o_{gain} - ref \tag{4.7}$$

$$-\Delta = o_{loss} - ref \tag{4.8}$$

$$\omega(-\Delta_a) > \omega(\Delta_b) \tag{4.9}$$

where Δ ($\Delta > 0$) represents the perceived difference between the current outcome being evaluated and the corresponding reference point. We use a and b to denote two different dimensions over which perceived differences are evaluated by decision makers. Note that the changes of perceptions can be caused by both the variations in the outcome (e.g., waiting time in dentist office increases from 15 min to 30 min) and the changes in reference points alone (e.g., expected waiting time increases from 10 min to 35 min). The transitions between gains and losses (not necessarily the changes in outcomes) often lead to significant changes in people's decisions and sensitivity to the variations relative to the reference point. In addition, as it is presented in Formula (4.9), the same difference between two options or statuses is often assigned a greater weight by individuals if the difference is perceived as a difference between two losses or disadvantages relative to a reference point. In naturalistic settings, however, it could be challenging to quantitatively measure and compare the differences which occur on different dimensions of the possible outcome from an option.

To explore the neural basis of loss aversion, Tom et al. (2007) conducted a study on participants' brain activities under simulated gambling tasks. Their results indicate that when potential gain increases in gambles, there was a broad range of areas, including midbrain dopaminergic regions and their targets, showing increased brain activities. Meanwhile, potential losses perceived by the participants were associated with decreasing activity in several of the gain-sensitive regions. Based on this finding, the researchers proposed that individual differences in behavioral-level loss aversion can be estimated and predicted based on neural-level loss aversion signals, such as activities in prefrontal cortex and ventral striatum. Similarly, Canessa et al. (2013) further investigated individual differences in loss aversion tendencies with functional magnetic resonance imaging (fMRI)-based measures and found that behavioral loss aversion is associated with several neural systems and regions, suggesting both structural and functional individual differences that can be related to financial outcomes of decisions under uncertainty.

Apart from loss aversion effect per se, empirical findings from a series of classic and recent behavioral experiments demonstrate that loss aversion has several immediate consequences and impacts in decision-making activities and is associated with several other types of human biases as well. For instance, Kahneman et al. (1986) have conducted a series of experiments on loss aversion in a classroom setting. In one of the experiments, the researchers presented a decorated mug (market value of around $5) to one third of the students who participated in the research study. The participants who received the mug were asked to give an acceptable price for selling the mug to others, ranging from $0.50 to $9.50. For the rest of the participants, researchers offered another questionnaire and asked them to indicate their preferences between a mug and a certain amount of money within the same price range. Under this setting, selling the mug would be considered as a *loss* to the students who already received the mugs. However, for the students who did not receive them (i.e., the "choosers"), they would consider a mug (if they decide by choose or buy it) as a *gain*.

The experimental results echo the findings on loss aversion from other studies and confirmed the effect of *instant endowment*. The median value of the mug evaluated by the sellers (students who received mugs at the beginning) was $7.12. However, for the choosers, the median value was $3.12. The experiment was repeated and yield similar results ($7.00 vs. $3.50). This consequence of loss aversion is defined as endowment effect: the loss of value or utility associated with giving up a valued item is greater than the perceived utility associated with obtaining the item (Kahneman et al., 1986; Tversky & Kahneman, 1991). The significant gap between selling and buying prices demonstrates the effects of endowment and contradicts with many formal economic models where the perceived cost of a product or activity is considered consistent and fixed among different individuals. This endowment effect is also empirically confirmed in several recent studies conducted in various domains and settings (e.g., Hubbeling, 2020; Knetsch & Wong, 2009; Knutson et al., 2008; Morewedge & Giblin, 2015), which partially justifies the importance of examining this effect as well as human biases in general in broader decision-making contexts and more diverse disciplines, including information seeking, retrieval, and recommendation.

Another widely examined consequence associated with loss aversion is *status quo bias* (Tversky & Kahneman, 1991). In many decision-making scenarios, the retention of the status quo is often one of the key options. For instance, traders in stock market can choose to keep current stocks in their accounts. Employees who have been working in a company for years often tend to stay in their positions despite of the possible opportunities of getting promotions and pay raises in different places. When a medical plan or subscription plan is designated as the default plan, employees are more likely to stick to the plan, year after year, despite the opportunities of annual plan review and modifications. This may be because (1) when a status quo as a long-term reference point is fully established in mind, people tend to be highly sensitive to even slight changes near the reference points, especially the ones that are perceived as losses (e.g., increased transportation time after job change; high salary but also higher health insurance premium in a new company), and (2) staying with the status quo option could help people resolve possible *cognitive dissonance* (Akerlof & Dickens, 1982; Bem, 1967; Cooper, 2019; McGrath, 2017) and keep their current behaviors consistent with established habits, beliefs, and perspectives.

In behavioral experiments, researchers found that when an option in a simulated decision-making scenario is designated as the default status quo, participants' choices are systematically biased toward the status quo, especially under the situations where they are not familiar with the decision-making task (Fleming et al., 2010; Kim & Kankanhalli, 2009; Samuelson & Zeckhauser, 1988). Researchers also found that when changes to status quo or default option become inevitable, people would prefer the option that brings slight changes to current status quo than the ones that cause larger changes (Tversky & Kahneman, 1991). For instance, when choosing between different medical plans and retirement plans, employees may be more likely to choose among the ones that are closest to the current default plan offered to them (with minor revisions on a few items), rather than the ones that come with major changes on a broad range of items and restructure the entire plan.

Fleming et al. (2010) explored status quo bias at neural level by investigating the ways in which neural pathways connecting cognitive activities with actions modulate status quo acceptance (or rejection), especially in situations where the status quo is suboptimal and more errors could occur when the default option is selected. The researchers found a selective increase in subthalamic nucleus (STN) when the status quo option is rejected under heightened decision difficulty. Also, researchers found that inferior frontal cortex generates an increased modulatory effect on the STN when individuals switch away from the status quo and choose non-default options. Findings from Fleming et al. (2010) provide a neural-physiological basis for examining the role of status quo, especially in difficult decision-making tasks.

Similarly, Yu et al. (2010) also adopted a neuroscience approach to investigating status quo bias and demonstrated that the increased tendency of moving away from the default option is closely related to the reduced activity in the anterior insula. However, the tendencies and decisions to select the default activated the ventral striatum, which is the same reward area as seen in winning. Yu et al. (2010)'s work emphasizes the aversive processes in insula as the underlying neural mechanism behind the status quo bias and echoes relevant findings from classic behavioral experiments (e.g., Samuelson & Zeckhauser, 1988). More details regarding the experimental design and specific changes in neural metrics under different conditions are reported in the original research papers.

Beyond the impacts of loss aversion, Samuelson and Zeckhauser (1988) noted that status quo bias could also be triggered by other contextual factors, such as switching and transaction costs, mental demands of thinking and evaluation, as well as psychological commitment to prior decisions, even in the cases where loss aversion effect is absent. This finding suggests that there are a variety of motivations

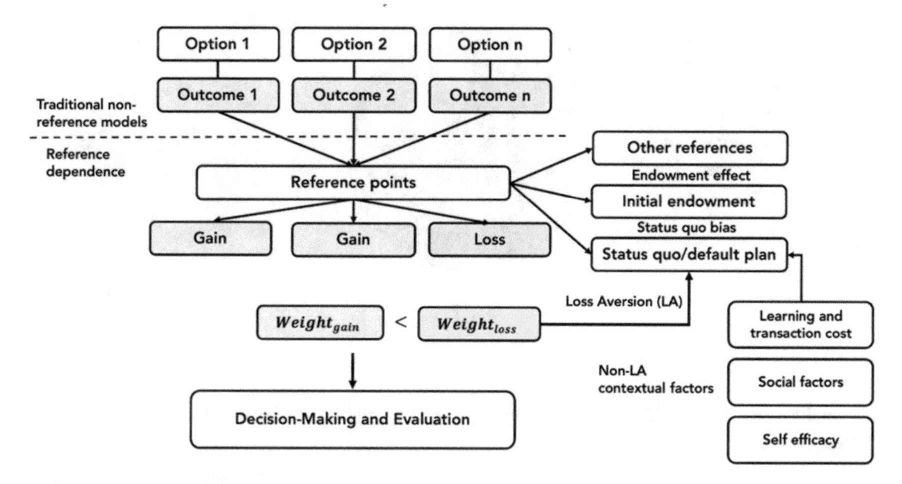

Fig. 4.3 Reference dependence and related human biases

that could push people to existing strategies, options, and default plans and that researchers and designers need to consider a broad range of factors, instead of merely focusing on calculatable losses and gains, when seeking to design effective intervention techniques, nudging tools, and system recommendation to change people's decisions (e.g., Bonnichsen & Ladenburg, 2015; He & Cunha, 2020). For instance, Kim and Kankanhalli (2009) indicate that status quo bias often triggers *user resistance* to the implementation of new information systems and leads to the failure of new systems. To manage and resolve the issue, researchers investigated the formation of status quo bias and also explored the internal and external factors that mediate and reinforce the impacts of status quo bias and user resistance. Based on the survey data collected from the employees of an IT service company where a new enterprise office system is deployed, Kim and Kankanhalli (2009) developed a structural model to characterize user resistance and demonstrated that learning and switching cost mediates the impacts of other factors (e.g., opinions and choices of other employees, self-efficacy) on user resistance. Also, perceived value of the new system and organizational support can also help mitigate status quo bias and reduce user resistance to new systems.

To illustrate the connections among different concepts (e.g., gain, loss, reference point) and biases, Fig. 4.3 presents the structure of reference dependence as well as the associated effects, including loss aversion bias, endowment effect, and status quo bias. Note that the initial endowment and status quo can also be considered as reference points based upon which people compare and evaluate actual or estimated outcomes associated with available options. There are also other types of reference points, such as initial beliefs and knowledge, in situ expectations, and past experiences under the same or similar tasks. Our understanding is that reference dependence can serve as the role of a fundamental framework, which can help us better understand the nature of multiple associated human biases, such as framing effects, anchoring biases, and confirmation biases. We will discuss more diverse types of

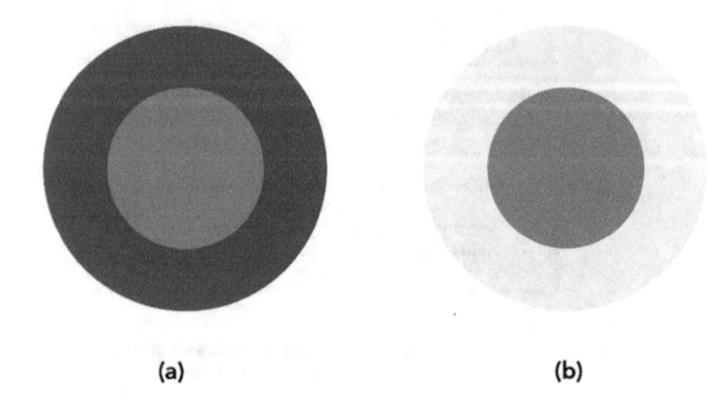

Fig. 4.4 Reference dependence effect in vision [This example is adapted from the reference-dependence vision example offered in Kahneman (2003) (p.1455, Fig. 5)]

possible reference points and corresponding consequences in decision-making in the following sections.

Note that in addition to cognitive impacts, reference-dependence effect also happens at perceptual level. To illustrate the perceptual effects of reference dependence, Fig. 4.4 presents filled circles with different levels of luminance. Although the two enclosed circles have the same level of luminance, they do not seem to be equally bright: the inner circle in Fig. 4.4a seems to be brighter than its counterpart in Fig. 4.4b. This phenomenon demonstrates that the perceived brightness is not only controlled by the absolute luminance of an area but also affected by the background used as an implicit reference. Similar to this example, vision researchers have also explored the role of reference in distance estimation and found that the orientation of the body and the visual environment, both of which can alter the current reference points, have significant impacts on people's perceived distances (Harris & Mander, 2014). Similar reference-dependence effect was also found in the variations in people's perceived sizes of the same object under different reference distances (Barac-Cikoja & Turvey, 1995). This perceptual dimension of reference dependence may also affect other aspects of decision-making and is certainly relevant to graphical user interface (GUI)-based human-information interactions. For example, different color combinations and backgrounds may change the perceived saliency of certain items and thereby affect the distribution of attention and user actions across different rank positions.

In information seeking and retrieval, users' interactions with information and information systems may also be affected by loss aversion bias, endowment effect, and status quo bias. For instance, due to the impacts of loss aversion, a decrease in the quality of current SERP relative to the most recent one may cause local changes in a user's current search strategies (e.g., reformulating a completely new query, abandon current SERP without clicking or careful examining the ranked search results), despite the possibility that the current search path is correct and may eventually lead to a series of useful documents for completing the search task at hand. Also, because of status quo bias, users may choose to stick to the default information sources that they are most familiar with (e.g., a specific online forum, an expert's blog site) and pay less attention to less familiar sites. However, the default status quo options may not cover all necessary information under all tasks. In addition, when users already learned sufficient knowledge and accumulated rich experience regarding the current system they are using, they are less likely to accept or try to learn the operations of a new search system, despite the fact that the new system could be more efficient in processing regular information-intensive work tasks and supporting information sharing and communications among workers and may significantly improve their productivity of information seeking and task performances. Our hope is that through the synthesis and analysis of empirically confirmed behavioral economics theories on biases and bounded rationality, readers can better understand the nature of decision-making under uncertainty and further explore the implicit connections between different factors associated with human biases and components of formal user models.

4.5 Expectation (Dis)confirmation Theory

In addition to the effects discussed above, another bias related to reference dependence is expectation confirmation or disconfirmation, which is widely examined in different application scenarios in the area of management information system (MIS) (e.g., Lankton & McKnight, 2012; McKinney et al., 2002; Oliver, 1980; Venkatesh & Goyal, 2010). Among different applications and subdomains, one of the frequently studied is *information systems adoption*. According to the core arguments in expectation disconfirmation theory (EDT) (Oliver, 1980; Venkatesh & Goyal, 2010), users' acceptance and adoption of a new information system are not only affected by the *perceived performance* of the system but also shaped by their pre-adoption *expectations*. Users' post-adoption satisfaction is determined by the disconfirmation of beliefs, which is closely associated with the difference between pre-adoption expectation (as users' reference points for post-adoption judgments) and users' perceived performance.

Users' continuance intention on information systems is a central topic of study to both information systems research and service providers in online platforms. Many empirical experiments found that users' satisfaction and continuing use of a new information system depend on the status of expectation confirmation (Lankton & McKnight, 2012; Oliver, 1980). Bhattacherjee (2001) proposed an expectation-confirmation model to investigate users' information systems continuance behavior. The study found that users' continuance intention is influenced by their satisfaction with information systems use and perceived usefulness of continued use of the system. User satisfaction with the system is affected by their confirmation of pre-adoption expectation from prior experience of information system use and expected usefulness. Similarly, Venkatesh and Goyal (2010) developed a polynomial modeling of expectation disconfirmation and incorporates multiple related factors into the model, such as cognitive dissonance, job preview, as well as factors of technology acceptance model (cf. Venkatesh & Davis, 2000) and prospect theory, which directly involves the role of reference dependence (cf. Kahneman & Tversky, 2013; Tversky & Kahneman, 1992). Venkatesh and Goyal (2010) showed that

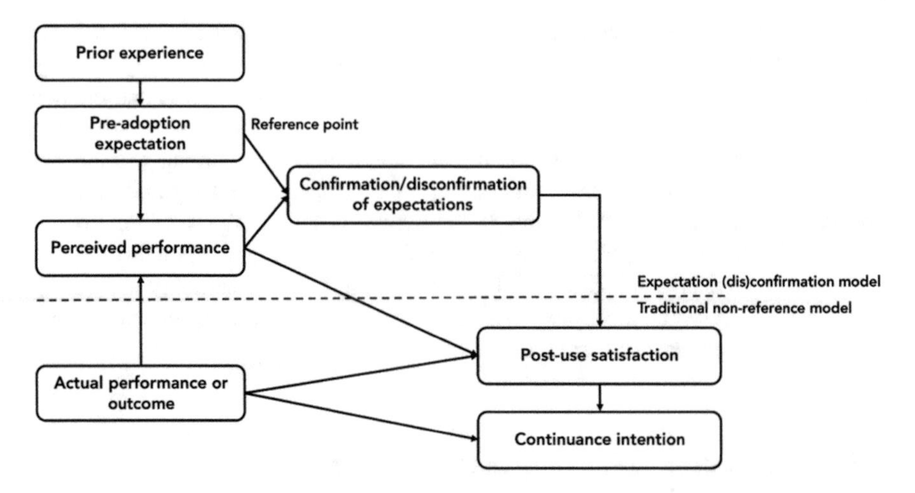

Fig. 4.5 The structure of expectation confirmation theory

expectation disconfirmation is in general bad for information systems adoption and reduces users' behavioral intention to continue their usage of new systems in *both* positive and negative disconfirmation scenarios. Beyond behavioral level, Fadel et al. (2022) conducted an fMRI study on expectation disconfirmation in the context of information filtering in electronic networks of practices. The results of their neuroimaging experiment show that there are neural activation differences between expectation confirmation and disconfirmation states and also between unexpected gains and unexpected losses. Thus, to successfully implement new information systems, researchers and system designers need to systematically examine target users' expectations regarding system layout, performance, as well as other related aspects and their previous experiences and beliefs based on which pre-adoption expectations are built.

Based on previous empirical research and theoretical developments in this area (e.g., Bhattacherjee, 2001; Fadel et al., 2022; Oliver, 1980; Venkatesh & Goyal, 2010), Fig. 4.5 illustrates the structure of EDT under the theoretical umbrella of reference dependence and includes the factors that may affect different aspects of expectation confirmation. Similar to Fig. 4.3, we emphasize the difference between reference dependence model and traditional non-reference model and hope that these highlighted differences could help students and young researchers better identify the gaps between widely used final-outcome-based models in IR and EDT/reference dependence model.

Note that other types of human biases and situational limits may also come into play at different parts of the model. For example, depending on users' knowledge structure, immediate information needs, and existing beliefs and biases, their perceived system performance could systematically deviate from the actual performance (if objective unbiased measurement of performance is possible) to varying degrees. Also, users' perceptions regarding expectation disconfirmation may also be affected by other factors, such as learning costs, emotional states, and the adoption behavior of peer users.

User expectation is an important form of reference point and could affect people's interactions with information systems at both *single-iteration* (e.g., single query-SERP response) and *whole-session* levels. In multi-round user-system interactions, such as interactive information searching, it would be useful to investigate the effects of both *pre-interaction* expectations (e.g., expectation regarding the overall dwell time and efforts based on previous experience under similar tasks) and in situ expectations (the local, temporary expectations established and constantly revised based on the experienced gains and efforts in ongoing sessions). Although we have accumulated rich empirical evidences regarding pre-interaction expectations, such as expected *task difficulty* and *task complexity* measured through pre-search questionnaires (e.g., Arguello, 2014; Capra et al., 2018; Choi et al., 2019; C. Liu et al., 2014; O'Brien et al., 2020), the latter type of expectations, which may play an even more important role in affecting interaction effectiveness, in situ judgments, and whole-session experiences, still remains largely understudied in information seeking, retrieval, and recommender systems research, with few exceptions (e.g., Liu & Shah, 2019).

4.6 Framing Effect, Confirmation Bias, and Anchoring Bias

The sections above discuss several types of perceived quantitative changes under the influence of biases and explain how they might lead to suboptimal and boundedly rational decisions, both within and outside information seeking and retrieval. In addition to the measurable quantitative changes (e.g., price drops and increases, changes of daily work commute time), people's decisions could also be affected by biases and limits in a more qualitative manner, which may not be quantitatively measurable in some decision-making scenarios. For instance, people's perceptions may be affected by the description narrative of the options, which could be framed as either losses or gains. In addition, people are more likely to accept the options or overestimate the usefulness of certain documents if these options or documents are consistent with people's existing beliefs and knowledge. We discuss these types of human biases and their impacts in this section.

In classic economic model, the invariance of individuals' preferences is a fundamental assumption that facilitates the analysis of economic behaviors and enables researchers to represent individuals' preferences with preference indifference curves (Mankiw, 2014; Schumm, 1987). Specifically, microeconomic models often assume that individuals' preferences are not influenced by inconsequential variations in the description of outcomes (when the nature of the outcomes remain the same). This assumption, which has been called *extensionality* and *invariance*, helps researchers bypass the problem of in situ variations of individuals' intents and preferences and reduces the computational complexity of predicting people's preferences for varying combinations of goods (Tversky & Kahneman, 1986). The assumption of preference invariance is also considered as a key aspect of rational decision-making.

While the assumption of extensionality and invariance underpins various formal models of individual choices and decision-making, it contradicts with empirical evidences on real-life individuals' perceptions of options and outcomes. Specifically, some behavioral economics researchers found that individuals' preferences are affected by *framing effects*, where the extensionally equal descriptions of outcomes (only altering the narrative regarding certain salient aspects of the problem, without changing the substances of the problem and outcomes) can lead to systematically difference choices (Kahneman, 2003). Therefore, it would be difficult to map expected utility (cf. Harrison, 1994) to users' preferences as the perceived value of options and potential outcomes could be changed without touching the actual utility or manipulating the nature of decision-making problem. Beyond traditional economic decisions, people's preferences could also be easily altered by changing the layout and framing of accessible options (e.g., the presentation of ranked search results and social media information, different design of advertisements, and clickbait information on SERPs and Web pages).

To better explain framing effects, Tversky and Kahneman (1985) offered a discussion on a hypothetical problem that was presented to their study respondents.

Problem: The Asian Disease

> Imagine that the United States is preparing for the outbreak of an unusual Asian disease, which is expected to kill 600 people. Two alternative programs to combat the disease have been proposed. Assume that the exact scientific estimates of the consequences of the programs are as follows.

To measure the possible impacts of framing, Tversky and Kahneman (1985) designed two different versions of the program descriptions by altering the highlighted salient aspects of the programs but keeping the actual content of the programs unchanged.

Program Description: Version 1

> If Program A is adopted, 200 people will be saved; if Program B is adopted, there is a one-third probability that 600 people will be saved and a two-thirds probability that no one will be saved.

Program Description: Version 2

> If Program A' is adopted, 400 people will die; if Program B' is adopted, there is a one-third probability that nobody will die and a two-thirds probability that all 600 people will die.

Under the same problem statement, the two versions of program descriptions were presented to respondents. Note that under classic economic models, peoples' preferences should not differ between Program A and Program B as they come with the same expected utility score on the dimension over which they were compared. Interestingly, however, the results of this rational mathematical analysis, which seems to be certain and straightforward in formal modeling, clearly contradict with real-life people's preferences and decisions under both versions of program descriptions.

According to the results presented in Tversky and Kahneman (1985), in Version 1, Program A is favored by a significant majority of respondents. This result indicates a general tendency of risk aversion. Then, another group of respondents received the Version 2 of program description, which has no substantial difference from the Version 1. In contrast to the results collected under Version 1, however, researchers found that a substantial majority of respondents favor Program B', which suggested a risk-seeking behavior. According to Kahneman and Tversky (2013), part of the reasons leading to this result is that outcomes that are certain are usually overweighted in people's decision-making compared to the possible outcomes that are associated with high probability. In Version 2, accepting the certain death of people in Program A' seems to be significantly less attractive and even unacceptable compared to the Program B' where there is a chance that all people can be saved. Thus, influenced by the immediate emotional response under overweighted outcomes, people favored B' over A'.

Tversky and Kahneman (1985)'s study demonstrates the pure impacts of framing on people's preferences under the controlled conditions: (1) in both versions, the two programs are associated with the same expected utility, which allows researchers to reveal the gap between real-life individual preferences (and the associated changes) and fixed expected utility; (2) between the two versions, respondents' preferences changed drastically only because the framing of available options were modified (with different salient aspects being emphasized).

Related to status quo bias, researchers also found that when options are framed as default choices, people are more likely to directly accept them in decision-making tasks without deliberate thinking and judgments. For instance, Johnson and Goldstein (2003) examined the enrollment rates in organ donation programs in seven countries and found a significant difference in enrollments depending on the ways in which the organ donation option was framed: in countries where organ donation was framed as the default option, the (automatic) enrollment rate was 97.4%; however, in places where non-enrolment was set as the default choice, the enrollment rate dropped drastically to only 18%. Similarly, Goswami and Urminsky (2016) studied the effect of certain amounts framed as default on charitable donations and found that (1) when setting a low amount as the default donation, it reduces average donation amounts among all donors, and (2) default option as a "distraction" can reduce the impacts of other informational cues, including positive charity information. Both of these studies confirm the impacts of framing certain options as default plans on people's perceptions and decisions.

Figure 4.6 offers a general form of framing effect in the context of decision-making under uncertainty, which is inspired by a series of behavioral experiments conducted by Tversky and Kahneman. Regarding the default or status quo bias (e.g., Johnson & Goldstein, 2003), the option that is set as default can also be considered as a highlighted salient aspect or option, and the change of default option could cause significant changes in people's perceptions and emotional responses to the same option and thereby affects the final decision-making activities.

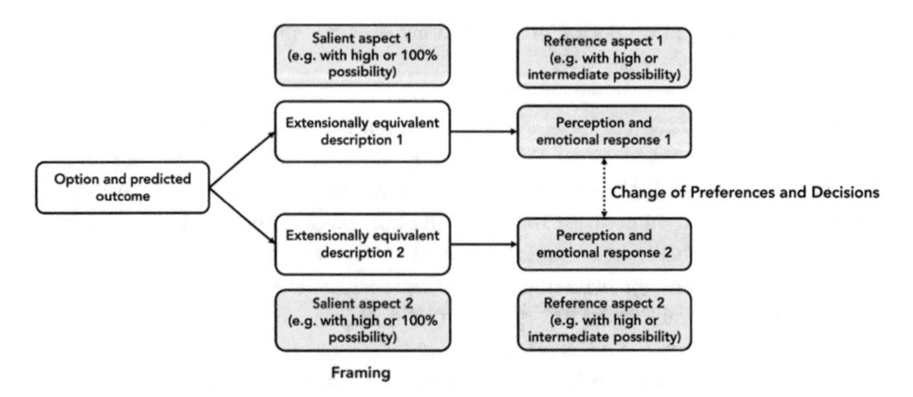

Fig. 4.6 Framing effect

Studies discussed above demonstrate the basic principle of framing effect: people often passively accept the formulation given and are easily influenced by the highlighted salient aspects of problem, without carefully examining the presented extensionally equivalent descriptions of the problem (Kahneman, 2003). This framing effect, which could lead to suboptimal and boundedly rational decisions, is usually caused by the limit of cognitive resources. With a finite mind, decision makers cannot afford fully examining all possible options and differentiate different versions of extensionally equivalent descriptions. Thus, the assumption of invariance in individuals' preferences is not tenable in most cases. Researchers need to recognize the limited room within which people's cognitive systems operate and pursue good enough outcomes among accessible options (Kaufman, 1999).

Confirmation bias can be considered as an extension of reference dependence, where the reference is existing knowledge and beliefs, expectations (e.g., regarding content of the retrieved information objects), or hypotheses in mind. According to Nickerson (1998), the term confirmation bias characterizes the tendency or behavior of seeking or interpreting evidences in ways that support or confirm existing beliefs and expectations established beforehand. Confirmation bias is one of the most widely known problematic aspect of human reasoning and judgment (Evans, 1989). The behavioral impacts of confirmation bias have been observed and investigated in a broad range of experimental settings and real-world contexts. For example, based on the observation on US foreign policies, Tuchman (1984) argued that due to the effects of confirmation bias, once a policy has been established and implemented by a government, there would be a series of subsequent activities, from the same government, which try to justify the policy. During the justification process, decision makers often focus on reinforcing the justifications and insist on a rooted notion, regardless of contrary evidence coming up from multiple sources (Tuchman, 1984). Under the influence of confirmation bias, a policy or conclusion made by decision makers could be biased and become increasingly difficult to correct as more justifications and supporting evidences pile up over time.

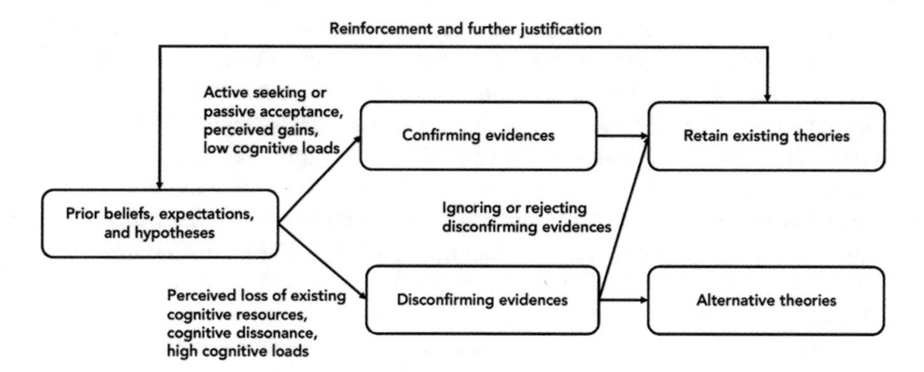

Fig. 4.7 Confirmation bias

Based on the research findings discussed above, Fig. 4.7 summarizes the underlying mechanism of confirmation bias. The confirmation bias also frequently occurs in scientific fields. according to Nickerson (1998), although the falsifiability principle has been widely accepted as part of the foundation by the scientific community, "one would look long and hard to find an example of a well-established theory that was discarded when the first bit of disconfirming evidence came to light" (p.206). Lehner et al. (2008) examined confirmation bias in experimental tasks where participants were asked to draw inferences from a small set of evidences. Researchers found that professional analysts as participants were also subject to the impact of confirmation biases in complex analysis tasks, such as law enforcement investigations, intelligent analysis, and financial decision analysis. Their findings also indicated that applying the *analysis of competing hypotheses* (ACH) can mitigate the confirmation bias in judgments. Kappes et al. (2020) investigated the hidden neural mechanism underlying confirmation biases by examining the utilization of others' opinion strength in judgments. Their results show that existing judgments as the established references can change the neural representation of information strengthen. Consequently, individuals become less likely to change their opinions when facing disagreements or disconfirming evidences.

The effect of confirmation bias could also be interpreted from loss aversion perspective. Specifically, when encountering disconfirming evidences or disagreements from others, a decision maker needs to choose between further reinforcing or justifying their existing beliefs or abandoning their existing beliefs or hypotheses and exploring alternatives. However, the establishment of existing beliefs often comes with certain costs or efforts (e.g., learning knowledge from reading books and papers, reaching a consensus or common hypothesis among a group of people). Thus, abandoning the beliefs could be perceived as a loss of "rewards" obtained through past efforts. Furthermore, it may also weaken or overturn other related beliefs, expectations, and hypotheses that individual decision makers have in mind, which thereby further increases the potential loss of accepting alternative opinions or conclusions. In the scientific community, the ubiquitous of confirmation bias may also contribute to *survivorship bias*: the statistically insignificant differences (or null hypothesis not being rejected) and results that disconfirm well-established theories may end up being rejected by researchers themselves at different stages of their studies (Liu, 2021). Consequently, the "successful confirmations" supported by empirical evidences may be overrepresented through publications and further reinforce related biases or even mistakes in scientific research.

Anchoring bias could be considered as a special type of reference dependence, where people's opinions and decisions are heavily influenced by the first piece of information encountered (Tversky & Kahneman, 1974; Caputo, 2014). For instance, when exploring an unfamiliar topic, people's opinions are often significantly affected by the initially collected information, which may not be relevant or useful for addressing the immediate information need. Similar to confirmation bias, anchoring bias could also come from prior experience and existing beliefs and affects the way in which people process newly encountered information on related problems (Lau & Coiera, 2007). To explore the quantitative form of anchoring, Chapman and Johnson (1994) conducted a controlled experiment where participants were asked to evaluated the value of monetary lotteries under the influence of several predesigned anchors. The study results demonstrate that anchoring bias has its boundaries: (1) people are less likely to be affected by implausibly extreme anchors that go way beyond the fair value ranges of the items being evaluated, and (2) anchor and preference judgment needs to be comparable and be represented on the same scale. Going beyond textual and numerical anchors, Wesslen et al. (2019) investigated the effect of visual anchors by examining people's interaction with a visual analytics system under different scenario videos as visual anchor conditions. Wesslen et al. (2019) found that manipulating the initial visual anchors can affect users' interaction activities, confidence, speed, and even accuracy in some cases. These studies explored anchoring biases over multiple aspects and demonstrate the ubiquitous and multidimensional effects of anchoring in human judgments.

Related to the anchoring bias explained above, people's judgments, especially in sequences of interactions and evaluations, are often affected by *priming effect*. Priming refers to the situations where an individual's early exposure to a certain type of stimulus affects their reactions and judgments on subsequent stimuli (Tipper, 1985; Kahneman, 2003). The stimulus could be initially encountered information or opinion, early response of a system to certain actions, as well as some other types of externally provided signals prior to the judgment and decision-making tasks. When encountering the initial stimulus, people may activate certain mental concepts or memories that affect their subsequent perceptions and associated actions.

Similar to anchoring, according the empirical findings from a series of behavioral and psychological experiments, priming could also happen at multiple aspects and dimensions, such as behavioral, cognitive, and affective dimensions (e.g., Dennis et al., 2020; Kreuter et al., 2000; Kristjánsson & Ásgeirsson, 2019; Spruyt et al., 2002). Methodologically, it is worth noting that the observed priming effects in experiments and participants' behaviors are also affected by experimenter belief and thus need to be examined under double-blind experiment designs (Gilder & Heerey, 2018). In the context of information seeking and retrieval, Scholer et al. (2013) investigated the effects of *threshold priming* in relevance evaluation sessions and found that the quality and relevance of initially encountered documents will shape people's relevance thresholds in mind and thereby affect their evaluation of subsequently presented documents under varying topics. Beyond controlled experimental settings, the threshold priming effects may also influence people's in situ search expectations and judgments of retrieved information in real-world information seeking and searching episodes over multiple evaluation dimensions, such as in situ relevance, usefulness, credibility, and informativeness.

In summary, based on the discussions above, we conclude that framing effect, confirmation bias, anchoring bias, and priming effect can affect people's judgments and choices in different ways and that the underlying mechanisms behind these biases can be interpreted from a reference dependence perspective. Incorporating the appropriate representations of these biases into formal user models would allow researchers to better characterize the individual differences in interactions with information systems and also predict people's interaction behaviors, perceived performance, and overall experience in a more accurate manner.

4.7 Decoy Effect

As shown in studies on reference dependence and framing effects, people's preferences could be influenced or even manipulated without any change in the nature of presented options or estimated outcomes (Kahneman, 2003; Tversky & Kahneman, 1985). In a wide range of decision-making scenarios, people's decision-making activities could be systematically changed with revised or newly introduced reference points. These reference points can be *explicit new options* that directly change people's perceptions regarding existing options and associated outcomes. They can also be *implicit changes in existing options*, such as the change in highlighted salient aspects of current choices. In many controlled experiments and simplified economic analyses, the change of references could be measurable and quantitatively presented to decision makers, such as changes in the reward amount associated with each choice and the related possibility, despite the fact that this information might be difficult to obtain in real-life scenarios, especially for individuals. However, in many cases, the change of reference points might be qualitative in nature and difficult to quantitatively compare, such as the establishment and changes of existing beliefs or the content of initially encountered information, which may trigger confirmation bias and anchoring bias in information evaluation.

Decoy effect in decision-making usually happens in situations where a new option as reference point is introduced. Specifically, according to studies on decoy effect (e.g., Highhouse, 1996; Kahneman, 2003; Wedell & Pettibone, 1996), individuals' preferences for options A and B may change from A to B, if a third option C is included in the decision-making conditions, where option C is clearly inferior to option B, and this significant difference is perceived by the decision maker. Particularly, decoy effects could also occur in situations where the presented options A and B are not really comparable as they may have their respective advantages and

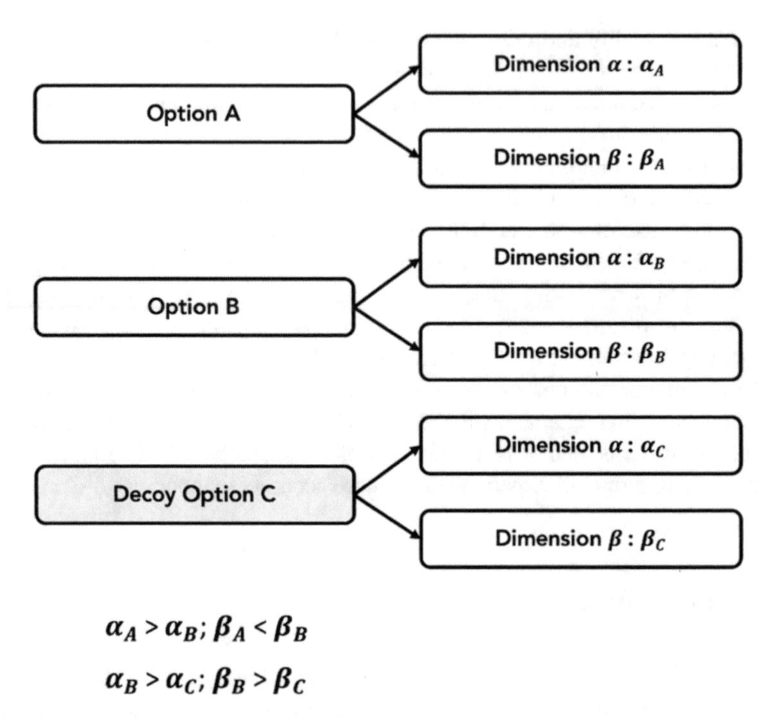

Fig. 4.8 Decoy effect

disadvantages on different dimensions. Under this circumstance, when an option C is introduced to the decision-making problem, which is inferior to option B over the same dimension(s), then option B may appear to be more attractive than not only option C, but also option A. By introducing a new reference point and creating the environment of asymmetric dominance, decoy option may lead to significant changes in individuals' perceptions and in situ preferences without introducing any change to existing options under consideration.

Figure 4.8 illustrates the structure and basic conditions of decoy effect. As it is shown in the Figure, the original decision-making scenario involves option A and option B. The assumption is that the two options can be evaluated over two dimensions, α and β. Option A and option B have their own respective advantages and disadvantages when comparing with each other, so it might be difficult for people to decide which choice to take, especially when the weights of each dimension is uncertain. However, when the decoy option C is added, it is clearly inferior to option B ($\alpha_B > \alpha_C$; $\beta_B > \beta_C$). This difference may make option B more attractive to individuals because if this option is taken, the decision maker will perceive a gain through the decision compared to the added reference point C.

Within the basic structure presented in Fig. 4.8, more concrete examples can be introduced. For instance, suppose Tom is deciding between a hamburger and an apple as his breakfast choice. This decision could be difficult to make as these two options have their respective advantages: apple is healthier and fresher, but hamburger tastes better (at least to some people). However, if we include a decoy option, a rotten apple, as a candidate option besides the original options, then it would make the apple option more attractive to Tom. Therefore, we can probably nudge Tom to the healthier option without changing the original options at all. When people are making judgments under the operations of System 1 and with limited cognitive resources, they could not fully examine the actual utility and risk associated with each option. Under this circumstance, evaluating options based on perceived gains relative to references would serve as a mental shortcut that allows individuals to save time and cognitive resources in decision-making activities.

Similar to other triggering factors behind boundedly rational decisions discussed above, the behavioral impact of decoy options has also been examined in a wide range of application scenarios, such as consumer purchase behavior (e.g., Gonzalez-Prieto et al., 2013; Wu & Cosguner, 2020; Zhang & Zhang, 2007), travel and tourism (e.g., Josiam & Hobson, 1995), medical decision-making (e.g., Stoffel et al., 2019), and food preferences (e.g., Wu et al., 2020). Hu and Yu (2014) went beyond behavioral level and examined the neural correlates of decoy effect in human decisions through fMRI analysis. The experimental results indicate that perceptual salience associated with anterior insula activation triggers heuristic decision-making under the presence of decoy option and that the activity in anterior cingulate cortex can reliably predict a decreased susceptibility to the decoy effect. This result suggests that actively rejecting the effect of decoy options and heuristics is cognitively taxing to decision makers.

Similar to framing effect, empirical evidences on the behavioral impacts and neural correlates of decoy options clearly contradict the "context invariance" axiom that underpins a wide range of individual decision-making models and evaluation metrics in economics studies and beyond. When examining users' evaluations and comparisons of multiple options, such as different systems and ranking algorithms, recommendations, and retrieved results of varying types, it would be critical to identify the potential decoy options and incorporate decoy effect into user representation and behavior prediction models.

4.8 Peak-End Rule, Recency Effect, and Remembered Utility

Apart from comparing individual, discrete options based on perceived gains and losses, people also need to evaluate *extended episodes* or sequences of actions and outcomes. During the evaluation, people's perceived or *remembered utility* may be inconsistent with the actual *experienced utility* during the episode being evaluated. Certain key points in the episodes may have a major impact on whole-session evaluation, such as peak value points (e.g., the action the brings in the highest amount of marginal gains), end value points (the in situ experience in the most recent round of iteration), and initial experience at the beginning of the episodes

(Kahneman, 2003). Therefore, using widely applied simple representations, such as the average value across the entire episode or total sum value in the episode, may not be able to accurately predict people's remembered utility and their subsequent actions or changes in current decision-making strategies. As it is represented in the preliminary framework in Chap. 3, this variation in remembered utility across different moments could be represented by a customized weight distribution function that assigns relatively higher weights to certain key points. The variations of in situ remembered utility could mostly be characterized by the theories on *peak-end rule* and *recency effect* in the evaluation of extended episodes.

One of the classic examples that best illustrate the peak-end rule is the colonoscopy experiment conducted by Redelmeier et al. (2003). In the experiment, patients who participated the study reported their perceived intensity of pain every 60 s during the colonoscopy procedure, so that researchers can track and calculate the in situ version of perceived pain. All patients went through roughly the same colonoscopy procedure. Thus, for the main procedure part where colonoscopy screenings were performed, patients experienced similar levels of total perceived pain. However, for half of the patients, physicians did not remove the colonoscopy instrument immediately after the clinical examination. Instead, they waited for a short period of time before removing the instrument. As a result, this half of patients experience an extra period of uncomfortable experience, for which the pain intensity was certainly lower than the actual clinical examination process.

After all procedures were completed, participants were asked to rate their overall experience with their colonoscopy procedures. The results indicate that although the participants who went through an extra period of waiting time have a higher amount of total perceived pain (calculated based on the data collected on in situ pain reports), they reported a higher rating for the overall experience than the group of patients who went through a regular colonoscopy process. This is because people's remembered experiences or utility regarding an extended episode are heavily influenced or determined by certain typical moments. Although the "extended procedure" includes an extra waiting period, it also significantly reduced the in situ pain intensity at the end of the episode. Thus, with the peak pain intensity level remaining roughly the same across all patients, the extended procedures offer a better ending for the overall experience, which leads to higher scores in retrospective evaluation from patients. This phenomenon can also be considered as a demonstration of *recency effect*, where people's memory of an episode is largely affected by the in situ experience from the most recent moment.

The peak-end rule and recency effects capture and characterize the implicit biases and intuitive process behind extended episode evaluation (Alaybek et al., 2022), which contradicts most simulated rational evaluation strategies but helps explain the seemingly counterintuitive scenarios where more (in situ) perceived pain is preferred to less as it is reflected in retrospective evaluations (Kahneman, 2003; Kahneman et al., 1993). Findings on peak-end rule also reveal the phenomenon of *duration neglect*: people's global retrospective evaluation of an extended episode is not closely associated with the duration of the episode (Fredrickson & Kahneman, 1993; Hands & Avons, 2001; Redelmeier & Kahneman, 1996). These biases and associated effects have also been empirically confirmed in other experimental contexts, such as the perceived loudness and duration of unpleasant sounds (Schreiber & Kahneman, 2000), evaluation of perceived water temperature in a prolonged session (Kahneman et al., 1993), and whole-session satisfaction evaluation of information retrieval (Liu & Han, 2020).

It is worth noting that the impacts of peak- and end-effects may vary across different dimensions of human perceptions and have their boundaries and conditions. For instance, Schneider et al. (2011) conducted a study on patients' daily recalls of pain and fatigue, which are often used as part of the basis in physicians' clinical decision-making. Researchers found that the actual impacts of peak and end moments on retrospective judgments varied significantly across individual patients and that the peak-end rule did not have a significant impact on the recall of fatigue. Similarly, Langer et al. (2005) examined the quality of retrospective evaluations of payment sequences and found that participants' evaluations did show the tendency of assigning relatively higher weights to peak and end moments of sequences. However, they also observed the empirical boundary of peak-end effect: the biased evaluation only happened when researchers link payments being evaluated to the performance in strenuous tasks that are strong enough to distract participants. For simple tasks without any distraction being introduced, participants' evaluations tended to be *normatively appropriate* and were less affected by the peak and end moments. Apart from enhancing the understanding of related human biases, studying the boundaries of peak-end effects may also help researchers identify the implicit boundaries of intuitive thinking and boundedly rational decision-making in general.

In information seeking and retrieval, evaluating whole-session human-information interaction process has been one of the central topics to the research community (Belkin et al., 2012). To facilitate the research on this topic, researchers can explore different representations and weight distributions that utilize the knowledge of peak-end rule, duration neglect, and recency effects and develop more realistic, human-centered evaluation models for both online and offline experiments. Also, as it is indicated in several behavioral studies, peak-end effects and recency biases have their boundaries and conditions and may not have a significant impact in some scenarios. Therefore, it would also be useful to explore the possible limits and conditions associated with these effects in the evaluation of information seeking, retrieval, and evaluation and investigate the ways in which they are connected to widely studied contextual factors, such as users' domain knowledge and search skills, perceived task difficulty, and task complexity.

4.9 Other Biases and Heuristics in Decision-Making Under Uncertainty

In addition to the human biases and heuristics explained above, people's decision-making processes under uncertainty are also affected by other types of biases that contradict with the fundamentals of various oversimplified normative models.

For instance, in contrast to the widely employed assumption of seeking maximized or optimal utility, people may actually search through the accessible solution space and alternatives until an acceptable, "good enough" option is located. According to Simon (1955), people usually rely on this mental shortcut, especially in the decision-making scenarios where the optimal solution is uncertain or may involve a series of complex, intellectually challenging, computation tasks that one cannot afford in real-life settings. Thus, instead of finding or formulating an optimal solution in a simulated oversimplified setting, people may satisfice through seeking for and finding satisfactory solutions that meet their aspiration levels in a more behaviorally realistic world. The *theory of satisficing* and associated bounded rational approach to decision-making analysis cast doubts on the assumption that people are perfectly rational and always seek for optimized outcome. Although satisficing decision-making events are ubiquitous across different problems and environments, it is worth noting that normative, maximizing behaviors also occur, and the optimization and satisficing strategies tend to co-exist in real-world decision-making practices (Simon, 1955; Schwartz et al., 2002).

Under the satisficing basis, it would be useful to explore the potential gaps between ideal or optimized outcomes and people's aspiration levels in specific settings and investigate the ways in which the satisficing thresholds and aspiration levels are related to the nature of presented options and the overall problematic situation within which the decisions are made by people. In particular, researchers may need to examine how people's implicit aspiration levels are connected to potential reference points (e.g., in situ expectations, prior experiences, existing beliefs and knowledge) and the operation of System 1 in ongoing decision-making processes.

Beyond individual cognitive factors and characteristics of available options, people's decisions are also affected by *group think* or *herd behavior*. Specifically, people may decide to take an option or make certain decisions without deliberate thinking or balanced evaluation of potential gains and losses. Instead, they may take a similar option or point of view simply because other people are doing so, even in situations where their own opinion is different from that of the majority. This effect is also referred to as *Bandwagon effect*. In marketing studies, researchers found that consumers' behaviors are often heavily influenced by the actions taken by other consumers on the same or similar products (Kessous & Valette-Florence, 2019). Bandwagon effect has been examined in a wide range of application fields, such as healthcare (e.g., Kaissi & Begun, 2008), e-commerce (e.g., Mainolfi, 2020), travel and tourism (e.g., Abd Mutalib et al., 2017), as well as consumer purchase on luxury (e.g., Kastanakis & Balabanis, 2012; Kessous & Valette-Florence, 2019). A more detailed review that reports on recent research progress on Bandwagon effects can be found in Bindra et al. (2022).

Regarding human-information interaction, in addition to the quality of collected information (e.g., relevance, usefulness, offline-evaluation-metric-based scores on SERPs) and individual characteristics, researchers may also need to incorporate popularity and other social factors (if available) into modeling and examine their impacts on people's opinions and preferences over different opinions, subtopics, and specific contents. Including and representing social factors (e.g., other users' comments and activities on the same systems, events, and activities) can help design effective *social nudging* tools that shape and improve users' interactions with new systems and programs, such as developing healthy diets, encouraging household recycling, and improving privacy protection practices (Czajkowski et al., 2019; Gonçalves et al., 2021; Wisniewski et al., 2017).

4.10 Summary

Continuing our exploration on developing a novel bounded rational approach to modeling users, this chapter focuses on the research on human behavior and cognition and discusses the research progress on the triggers and impacts of bounded rationality, especially on the widely examined human biases and heuristics that facilitate people's immediate, "automatic" decision-making and judgments. We first introduce Kahneman (2003)'s theory of two systems, which offers an overall theoretical umbrella under which we could investigate and explain two largely different logics and mechanisms of human decision-making processes.

Moreover, we further clarify the importance and potential of studying boundedly rational decisions, especially for enhancing formal user models and evaluation metrics (see Chap. 2). Specifically, this chapter expands our discussion on individual human biases that are briefly introduced in Chap. 3 where we identify the gaps between formal models and theories on human biases. To fully explain the role and impacts of the biases included in discussion, we illustrate their structures and associated factors based on previous studies, present concrete examples, and discuss empirical findings on both behavioral and neural levels. In addition, for some of the biases, based on relevant studies from multiple disciplines, we also explain the boundaries and conditions for them to generate behavioral impacts. To help readers better understand the relationships among different types of biases, this chapter also discusses the similarities and intrinsic connections among these biases, especially under the analytical framework of reference dependence. We hope that our discussion on the behavioral impacts of human biases and heuristics as well as the connections among them can help readers better understand and synthesize the knowledge regarding human biases and apply the integrated knowledge in their research agenda, both conceptually and empirically, on relevant topics.

The following chapters will build upon the discussion from current and previous chapters and introduce recent progress and existing challenges on human-bias-related research in information seeking, retrieval, and recommendation. In these chapters, we will also explain the specific implications and possible applications of the empirical evidences on bounded rationality in building more accurate, behaviorally realistic user models.

References

Abd Mutalib, N. S., Soh, Y. C., Wong, T. W., Yee, S. M., Yang, Q., Murugiah, M. K., & Ming, L. C. (2017). Online narratives about medical tourism in Malaysia and Thailand: A qualitative content analysis. *Journal of Travel & Tourism Marketing, 34*(6), 821–832. https://doi.org/10.1080/10548408.2016.1250697

Akerlof, G. A., & Dickens, W. T. (1982). The economic consequences of cognitive dissonance. *The American Economic Review, 72*(3), 307–319. http://www.jstor.org/stable/1831534

Alaybek, B., Dalal, R. S., Fyffe, S., Aitken, J. A., Zhou, Y., Qu, X., Roman, A., & Baines, J. I. (2022). All's well that ends (and peaks) well? A meta-analysis of the peak-end rule and duration neglect. *Organizational Behavior and Human Decision Processes, 170*, 104149. https://doi.org/10.1016/j.obhdp.2022.104149

Alesina, A., & Passarelli, F. (2019). Loss aversion in politics. *American Journal of Political Science, 63*(4), 936–947. https://doi.org/10.1111/ajps.12440

Apesteguia, J., & Ballester, M. A. (2009). A theory of reference-dependent behavior. *Economic Theory, 40*(3), 427–455. https://doi.org/10.1007/s00199-008-0387-z

Arguello, J. (2014). Predicting search task difficulty. In *European Conference on Information Retrieval* (pp. 88–99). Springer.

Azzopardi, L. (2014). Modelling interaction with economic models of search. In *Proceedings of the 37th ACM SIGIR Conference on Research & Development in Information Retrieval* (pp. 3–12). ACM. https://doi.org/10.1145/2600428.2609574

Azzopardi, L. (2021). Cognitive biases in search: A review and reflection of cognitive biases in information retrieval. In *Proceedings of the 2021 ACM SIGIR Conference on Human Information Interaction and Retrieval* (pp. 27–37). ACM. https://doi.org/10.1145/3406522.3446023

Barac-Cikoja, D., & Turvey, M. T. (1995). Does perceived size depend on perceived distance? An argument from extended haptic perception. *Perception & Psychophysics, 57*(2), 216–224. https://doi.org/10.3758/BF03206508

Bateman, I., Munro, A., Rhodes, B., Starmer, C., & Sugden, R. (1997). A test of the theory of reference-dependent preferences. *The Quarterly Journal of Economics, 112*(2), 479–505. https://doi.org/10.1162/003355397555262

Battaglio, R. P., Jr., Belardinelli, P., Bellé, N., & Cantarelli, P. (2019). Behavioral public administration ad fontes: A synthesis of research on bounded rationality, cognitive biases, and nudging in public organizations. *Public Administration Review, 79*(3), 304–320. https://doi.org/10.1111/puar.12994

Belkin, N. J., Dumais, S., Kando, N., & Sanderson, M. (2012). Whole-session evaluation of interactive information retrieval systems. In *NII Shonan Meeting Report* (Vol. 7).

Bem, D. J. (1967). Self-perception: An alternative interpretation of cognitive dissonance phenomena. *Psychological Review, 74*(3), 183–200. https://doi.org/10.1037/h0024835

Benson, B. (2016). *Cognitive bias cheat sheet.* https://betterhumans.pub/cognitive-bias-cheat-sheet-55a472476b18.

Bhattacherjee, A. (2001). Understanding information systems continuance: An expectation-confirmation model. *MIS Quarterly, 25*(3), 351–370. https://doi.org/10.2307/3250921

Bindra, S., Sharma, D., Parameswar, N., Dhir, S., & Paul, J. (2022). Bandwagon effect revisited: A systematic review to develop future research agenda. *Journal of Business Research, 143*, 305–317. https://doi.org/10.1016/j.jbusres.2022.01.085

Bonnichsen, O. L. E., & Ladenburg, J. (2015). Reducing status quo bias in choice experiments. *Nordic Journal of Health Economics, 3*(1), 47–67. https://doi.org/10.5617/njhe.645

Canessa, N., Crespi, C., Motterlini, M., Baud-Bovy, G., Chierchia, G., Pantaleo, G., Tettamanti, M., & Cappa, S. F. (2013). The functional and structural neural basis of individual differences in loss aversion. *Journal of Neuroscience, 33*(36), 14307–14317. https://doi.org/10.1523/JNEUROSCI.0497-13.2013

Capra, R., Arguello, J., O'Brien, H., Li, Y., & Choi, B. (2018). The effects of manipulating task determinability on search behaviors and outcomes. In *Proceedings of the 41st International ACM SIGIR Conference on Research & Development in Information Retrieval* (pp. 445–454). ACM. https://doi.org/10.1145/3209978.3210047

Caputo, A. (2014). Relevant information, personality traits and anchoring effect. *International Journal of Management and Decision Making, 13*(1), 62–76. http://eprints.lincoln.ac.uk/id/eprint/18553/

Chapman, G. B., & Johnson, E. J. (1994). The limits of anchoring. *Journal of Behavioral Decision Making, 7*(4), 223–242. https://doi.org/10.1002/bdm.3960070402

Choi, B., Ward, A., Li, Y., Arguello, J., & Capra, R. (2019). The effects of task complexity on the use of different types of information in a search assistance tool. *ACM Transactions on Information Systems (TOIS), 38*(1), 1–28. https://doi.org/10.1145/3371707

Cooper, J. (2019). Cognitive dissonance: Where we've been and where we're going. *International Review of Social Psychology, 32*(1), 7. https://doi.org/10.5334/irsp.277

Croskerry, P. (2003). The importance of cognitive errors in diagnosis and strategies to minimize them. *Academic Medicine, 78*(8), 775–780. https://doi.org/10.1097/00001888-200308000-00003

Czajkowski, M., Zagórska, K., & Hanley, N. (2019). Social norm nudging and preferences for household recycling. *Resource and Energy Economics, 58*, 101110. https://doi.org/10.1016/j.reseneeco.2019.07.004

Dennis, A. R., Yuan, L., Feng, X., Webb, E., & Hsieh, C. J. (2020). Digital nudging: Numeric and semantic priming in e-commerce. *Journal of Management Information Systems, 37*(1), 39–65. https://doi.org/10.1080/07421222.2019.1705505

Draws, T., Rieger, A., Inel, O., Gadiraju, U., & Tintarev, N. (2021). A checklist to combat cognitive biases in crowdsourcing. In *Proceedings of the AAAI Conference on Human Computation and Crowdsourcing* (Vol. 9, pp. 48–59). https://ojs.aaai.org/index.php/HCOMP/article/view/18939

Eickhoff, C. (2018). Cognitive biases in crowdsourcing. In *Proceedings of the Eleventh ACM International Conference on Web Search and Data Mining* (pp. 162–170). ACM. https://doi.org/10.1145/3159652.3159654

Erev, I., Ert, E., & Yechiam, E. (2008). Loss aversion, diminishing sensitivity, and the effect of experience on repeated decisions. *Journal of Behavioral Decision Making, 21*(5), 575–597. https://doi.org/10.1002/bdm.602

Evans, J. S. B. (1989). *Bias in human reasoning: Causes and consequences*. Erlbaum.

Evans, J. S. B. (2003). In two minds: Dual-process accounts of reasoning. *Trends in Cognitive Sciences, 7*(10), 454–459. https://doi.org/10.1016/j.tics.2003.08.012

Fadel, K. J., Meservy, T. O., & Kirwan, C. B. (2022). Information filtering in electronic networks of practice: An fMRI investigation of expectation (dis) confirmation. *Journal of the Association for Information Systems, 23*(2), 491–520. https://doi.org/10.17705/1jais.00731

Fleming, S. M., Thomas, C. L., & Dolan, R. J. (2010). Overcoming status quo bias in the human brain. *Proceedings of the national Academy of Sciences, 107*(13), 6005–6009. https://doi.org/10.1073/pnas.0910380107

Frederick, S. F., & Fischhoff, B. (1998). Scope (in) sensitivity in elicited valuations. *Risk Decision and Policy, 3*(2), 109–123.

Fredrickson, B. L., & Kahneman, D. (1993). Duration neglect in retrospective evaluations of affective episodes. *Journal of Personality and social Psychology, 65*(1), 45–55. https://doi.org/10.1037/0022-3514.65.1.45

Gächter, S., Johnson, E. J., & Herrmann, A. (2022). Individual-level loss aversion in riskless and risky choices. *Theory and Decision, 92*(3), 599–624. https://doi.org/10.1007/s11238-021-09839-8

Gilder, T. S., & Heerey, E. A. (2018). The role of experimenter belief in social priming. *Psychological Science, 29*(3), 403–417. https://doi.org/10.1177/0956797617737128

Gonçalves, D., Coelho, P., Martinez, L. F., & Monteiro, P. (2021). Nudging consumers toward healthier food choices: A field study on the effect of social norms. *Sustainability, 13*(4), 1660. https://doi.org/10.3390/su13041660

Goswami, I., & Urminsky, O. (2016). When should the ask be a nudge? The effect of default amounts on charitable donations. *Journal of Marketing Research, 53*(5), 829–846. https://doi.org/10.1509/jmr.15.0001

Gonzalez-Prieto, D., Sallan, J. M., Simo, P., & Carrion, R. (2013). Effects of the addition of simple and double decoys on the purchasing process of airline tickets. *Journal of Air Transport Management, 29*, 39–45. https://doi.org/10.1016/j.jairtraman.2013.02.002

Hands, D. S., & Avons, S. E. (2001). Recency and duration neglect in subjective assessment of television picture quality. *Applied Cognitive Psychology: The Official Journal of the Society for Applied Research in Memory and Cognition, 15*(6), 639–657. https://doi.org/10.1002/acp.731

Harris, L. R., & Mander, C. (2014). Perceived distance depends on the orientation of both the body and the visual environment. *Journal of Vision, 14*(12), 17–17. https://doi.org/10.1167/14.12.17

Harrison, G. W. (1994). Expected utility theory and the experimentalists. In *Experimental economics* (pp. 43–73). Physica.

He, Y., & Cunha, M., Jr. (2020). Love leads to action: Short-term mating mindset mitigates the status-quo bias by enhancing promotion focus. *Journal of Consumer Psychology, 30*(4), 631–651. https://doi.org/10.1002/jcpy.1174

Highhouse, S. (1996). Context-dependent selection: The effects of decoy and phantom job candidates. *Organizational Behavior and Human Decision Processes, 65*(1), 68–76. https://doi.org/10.1006/obhd.1996.0006

Holt, C. A., & Laury, S. K. (2002). Risk aversion and incentive effects. *American Economic Review, 92*(5), 1644–1655. https://doi.org/10.1257/000282802762024700

Hu, J., & Yu, R. (2014). The neural correlates of the decoy effect in decisions. *Frontiers in Behavioral Neuroscience, 8*, 271. https://doi.org/10.3389/fnbeh.2014.00271

Hubbeling, D. (2020). Rationing decisions and the endowment effect. *Journal of the Royal Society of Medicine, 113*(3), 98–100. https://doi.org/10.1177/0141076819893541

Johnson, E. J., & Goldstein, D. (2003). Do defaults save lives? *Science, 302*(5649), 1338–1339. https://doi.org/10.1126/science.1091721

Josiam, B. M., & Hobson, J. P. (1995). Consumer choice in context: The decoy effect in travel and tourism. *Journal of Travel Research, 34*(1), 45–50. https://doi.org/10.1177/004728759503400106

Jung, A. K., Stieglitz, S., Kissmer, T., Mirbabaie, M., & Kroll, T. (2022). Click me...! The influence of clickbait on user engagement in social media and the role of digital nudging. *PLoS One, 17*(6), e0266743. https://doi.org/10.1371/journal.pone.0266743

Kahneman, D., Fredrickson, B. L., Schreiber, C. A., & Redelmeier, D. A. (1993). When more pain is preferred to less: Adding a better end. *Psychological Science, 4*(6), 401–405. https://doi.org/10.1111/j.1467-9280.1993.tb00589.x

Kahneman, D. (2003). Maps of bounded rationality: Psychology for behavioral economics. *American Economic Review, 93*(5), 1449–1475. https://doi.org/10.1257/000282803322655392

Kahneman, D. (2011). *Thinking, fast and slow*. Farrar, Straus and Giroux.

Kahneman, D., Knetsch, J. L., & Thaler, R. (1986). Fairness as a constraint on profit seeking: Entitlements in the market. *American Economic Review*, 728–741. https://www.jstor.org/stable/1806070

Kahneman, D., & Tversky, A. (2013). Prospect theory: An analysis of decision under risk. In *Handbook of the Fundamentals of Financial Decision Making: Part I* (pp. 99–127).

Kaissi, A. A., & Begun, J. W. (2008). Fads, fashions, and bandwagons in health care strategy. *Health Care Management Review, 33*(2), 94–102. https://doi.org/10.1097/01.HMR.0000304498.97308.40

Kappes, A., Harvey, A. H., Lohrenz, T., Montague, P. R., & Sharot, T. (2020). Confirmation bias in the utilization of others' opinion strength. *Nature Neuroscience, 23*(1), 130–137. https://doi.org/10.1038/s41593-019-0549-2

Kastanakis, M. N., & Balabanis, G. (2012). Between the mass and the class: Antecedents of the "bandwagon" luxury consumption behavior. *Journal of Business Research, 65*(10), 1399–1407. https://doi.org/10.1016/j.jbusres.2011.10.005

Kaufman, B. E. (1999). Emotional arousal as a source of bounded rationality. *Journal of Economic Behavior & Organization, 38*(2), 135–144. https://doi.org/10.1016/S0167-2681(99)00002-5

Kessous, A., & Valette-Florence, P. (2019). "From Prada to Nada": Consumers and their luxury products: A contrast between second-hand and first-hand luxury products. *Journal of Business Research, 102*, 313–327. https://doi.org/10.1016/j.jbusres.2019.02.033

Kim, H. W., & Kankanhalli, A. (2009). Investigating user resistance to information systems implementation: A status quo bias perspective. *MIS Quarterly, 33*(3), 567–582. https://doi.org/10.2307/20650309

Knetsch, J. L., & Wong, W. K. (2009). The endowment effect and the reference state: Evidence and manipulations. *Journal of Economic Behavior & Organization, 71*(2), 407–413. https://doi.org/10.1016/j.jebo.2009.04.015

Knutson, B., Wimmer, G. E., Rick, S., Hollon, N. G., Prelec, D., & Loewenstein, G. (2008). Neural antecedents of the endowment effect. *Neuron, 58*(5), 814–822. https://doi.org/10.1016/j.neuron.2008.05.018

Kőszegi, B., & Rabin, M. (2006). A model of reference-dependent preferences. *The Quarterly Journal of Economics, 121*(4), 1133–1165. https://doi.org/10.1093/qje/121.4.1133

Kreuter, M. W., Chheda, S. G., & Bull, F. C. (2000). How does physician advice influence patient behavior? Evidence for a priming effect. *Archives of Family Medicine, 9*(5), 426–433.

Kristjánsson, Á., & Ásgeirsson, Á. G. (2019). Attentional priming: Recent insights and current controversies. *Current Opinion in Psychology, 29*, 71–75. https://doi.org/10.1016/j.copsyc.2018.11.013

Langer, T., Sarin, R., & Weber, M. (2005). The retrospective evaluation of payment sequences: Duration neglect and peak-and-end effects. *Journal of Economic Behavior & Organization, 58*(1), 157–175. https://doi.org/10.1016/j.jebo.2004.01.001

Lankton, N. K., & McKnight, H. D. (2012). Examining two expectation disconfirmation theory models: Assimilation and asymmetry effects. *Journal of the Association for Information Systems, 13*(2), 88–115. https://doi.org/10.17705/1jais.00285

Lau, A. Y., & Coiera, E. W. (2007). Do people experience cognitive biases while searching for information? *Journal of the American Medical Informatics Association, 14*(5), 599–608. https://doi.org/10.1197/jamia.M2411

Lehner, P. E., Adelman, L., Cheikes, B. A., & Brown, M. J. (2008). Confirmation bias in complex analyses. *IEEE Transactions on Systems, Man, and Cybernetics-Part A: Systems and Humans, 38*(3), 584–592. https://doi.org/10.1109/TSMCA.2008.918634

Liu, C., Liu, J., & Belkin, N. J. (2014). Predicting search task difficulty at different search stages. In *Proceedings of the 23rd ACM International Conference on Conference on Information and Knowledge Management* (pp. 569–578). ACM. https://doi.org/10.1145/2661829.2661939

Liu, J. (2021). Deconstructing search tasks in interactive information retrieval: A systematic review of task dimensions and predictors. *Information Processing & Management, 58*(3), 102522. https://doi.org/10.1016/j.ipm.2021.102522

Liu, J., & Han, F. (2020). Investigating reference dependence effects on user search interaction and satisfaction: A behavioral economics perspective. In *Proceedings of the 43rd International ACM SIGIR Conference on Research and Development in Information Retrieval* (pp. 1141–1150). ACM. https://doi.org/10.1145/3397271.3401085

Liu, J., & Shah, C. (2019). Investigating the impacts of expectation disconfirmation on web search. In *Proceedings of the 2019 ACM SIGIR Conference on Human Information Interaction and Retrieval* (pp. 319–323). ACM. https://doi.org/10.1145/3295750.3298959

Ludolph, R., & Schulz, P. J. (2018). Debiasing health-related judgments and decision making: A systematic review. *Medical Decision Making, 38*(1), 3–13. https://doi.org/10.1177/0272989X17716672

Mainolfi, G. (2020). Exploring materialistic bandwagon behaviour in online fashion consumption: A survey of Chinese luxury consumers. *Journal of Business Research, 120*, 286–293. https://doi.org/10.1016/j.jbusres.2019.11.038

Mankiw, N. G. (2014). *Principles of economics*. Cengage Learning.

McGrath, A. (2017). Dealing with dissonance: A review of cognitive dissonance reduction. *Social and Personality Psychology Compass, 11*(12), e12362. https://doi.org/10.1111/spc3.12362

McKinney, V., Yoon, K., & Zahedi, F. M. (2002). The measurement of web-customer satisfaction: An expectation and disconfirmation approach. *Information Systems Research, 13*(3), 296–315. https://doi.org/10.1287/isre.13.3.296.76

Molyneux, L., & Coddington, M. (2020). Aggregation, clickbait and their effect on perceptions of journalistic credibility and quality. *Journalism Practice, 14*(4), 429–446. https://doi.org/10.1080/17512786.2019.1628658

Morewedge, C. K., & Giblin, C. E. (2015). Explanations of the endowment effect: An integrative review. *Trends in Cognitive Sciences, 19*(6), 339–348. https://doi.org/10.1016/j.tics.2015.04.004

Neys, W. D. (2006). Dual processing in reasoning: Two systems but one reasoner. *Psychological Science, 17*(5), 428–433. https://doi.org/10.1111/j.1467-9280.2006.01723.x

Nickerson, R. S. (1998). Confirmation bias: A ubiquitous phenomenon in many guises. *Review of General Psychology, 2*(2), 175–220. https://doi.org/10.1037/1089-2680.2.2.175

O'Brien, H. L., Arguello, J., & Capra, R. (2020). An empirical study of interest, task complexity, and search behaviour on user engagement. *Information Processing & Management, 57*(3), 102226. https://doi.org/10.1016/j.ipm.2020.102226

Oliver, R. L. (1980). A cognitive model of the antecedents and consequences of satisfaction decisions. *Journal of Marketing Research, 17*(4), 460–469. https://doi.org/10.1177/002224378001700405

O'Sullivan, E. D., & Schofield, S. J. (2018). Cognitive bias in clinical medicine. *Journal of the Royal College of Physicians of Edinburgh, 48*(3), 225–232. https://doi.org/10.4997/jrcpe.2018.306

Pirolli, P., & Card, S. (1999). Information foraging. *Psychological Review, 106*(4), 643–675. https://doi.org/10.1037/0033-295X.106.4.643

Redelmeier, D. A., & Kahneman, D. (1996). Patients' memories of painful medical treatments: Real-time and retrospective evaluations of two minimally invasive procedures. *Pain, 66*(1), 3–8. https://doi.org/10.1016/0304-3959(96)02994-6

Redelmeier, D. A., Katz, J., & Kahneman, D. (2003). Memories of colonoscopy: A randomized trial. *Pain, 104*(1–2), 187–194. https://doi.org/10.1016/S0304-3959(03)00003-4

Saab, F., Elhajj, I. H., Kayssi, A., & Chehab, A. (2019). Modelling cognitive bias in crowdsourcing systems. *Cognitive Systems Research, 58*, 1–18. https://doi.org/10.1016/j.cogsys.2019.04.004

Samuelson, W., & Zeckhauser, R. (1988). Status quo bias in decision making. *Journal of Risk and Uncertainty, 1*(1), 7–59. https://doi.org/10.1007/BF00055564

Schneider, S., Stone, A. A., Schwartz, J. E., & Broderick, J. E. (2011). Peak and end effects in patients' daily recall of pain and fatigue: A within-subjects analysis. *The Journal of Pain, 12*(2), 228–235. https://doi.org/10.1016/j.jpain.2010.07.001

Scholer, F., Kelly, D., Wu, W. C., Lee, H. S., & Webber, W. (2013). The effect of threshold priming and need for cognition on relevance calibration and assessment. In *Proceedings of the 36th International ACM SIGIR Conference on Research and Development in Information Retrieval* (pp. 623–632). ACM. https://doi.org/10.1145/2484028.2484090

Schreiber, C. A., & Kahneman, D. (2000). Determinants of the remembered utility of aversive sounds. *Journal of Experimental Psychology: General, 129*(1), 27–42. https://doi.org/10.1037/0096-3445.129.1.27

Schumm, G. F. (1987). Transitivity, preference and indifference. *Philosophical Studies: An International Journal for Philosophy in the Analytic Tradition, 52*(3), 435–437. https://www.jstor.org/stable/4319930

Schwartz, B., Ward, A., Monterosso, J., Lyubomirsky, S., White, K., & Lehman, D. R. (2002). Maximizing versus satisficing: Happiness is a matter of choice. *Journal of Personality and Social Psychology, 83*(5), 1178. https://doi.org/10.1037/0022-3514.83.5.1178

Simon, H. A. (1955). A behavioral model of rational choice. *The Quarterly Journal of Economics, 69*(1), 99–118. https://doi.org/10.2307/1884852

Sloman, S. A. (1996). The empirical case for two systems of reasoning. *Psychological Bulletin, 119*(1), 3–22. https://doi.org/10.1037/0033-2909.119.1.3

Sprenger, C. (2015). An endowment effect for risk: Experimental tests of stochastic reference points. *Journal of Political Economy, 123*(6), 1456–1499. https://doi.org/10.1086/683836

Spruyt, A., Hermans, D., Houwer, J. D., & Eelen, P. (2002). On the nature of the affective priming effect: Affective priming of naming responses. *Social Cognition, 20*(3), 227–256.

Stoffel, S. T., Yang, J., Vlaev, I., & von Wagner, C. (2019). Testing the decoy effect to increase interest in colorectal cancer screening. *PLoS One, 14*(3), e0213668. https://doi.org/10.1371/journal.pone.0213668

Thaler, R. H. (2016). Behavioral economics: Past, present, and future. *American Economic Review, 106*(7), 1577–1600. https://doi.org/10.1257/aer.106.7.1577

Tipper, S. P. (1985). The negative priming effect: Inhibitory priming by ignored objects. *The Quarterly Journal of Experimental Psychology, 37*(4), 571–590. https://doi.org/10.1080/14640748508400920

Tom, S. M., Fox, C. R., Trepel, C., & Poldrack, R. A. (2007). The neural basis of loss aversion in decision-making under risk. *Science, 315*(5811), 515–518. https://doi.org/10.1126/science.1134239

Tuchman, B. W. (1984). *The march of folly: From Troy to Vietnam*. Ballantine Books.

Tversky, A., & Kahneman, D. (1974). Judgment under uncertainty: Heuristics and biases: Biases in judgments reveal some heuristics of thinking under uncertainty. *Science, 185*(4157), 1124–1131. https://doi.org/10.1126/science.185.4157.1124

Tversky, A., & Kahneman, D. (1985). The framing of decisions and the psychology of choice. In *Behavioral Decision Making* (pp. 25–41). Springer.

Tversky, A., & Kahneman, D. (1986). The framing of decisions and the evaluation of prospects. *Studies in Logic and the Foundations of Mathematics, 114*, 503–520.

Tversky, A., & Kahneman, D. (1991). Loss aversion in riskless choice: A reference-dependent model. *The Quarterly Journal of Economics, 106*(4), 1039–1061. https://doi.org/10.2307/2937956

Tversky, A., & Kahneman, D. (1992). Advances in prospect theory: Cumulative representation of uncertainty. *Journal of Risk and Uncertainty, 5*(4), 297–323. https://doi.org/10.1007/BF00122574

Venkatesh, V., & Davis, F. D. (2000). A theoretical extension of the technology acceptance model: Four longitudinal field studies. *Management Science, 46*(2), 186–204. https://doi.org/10.1287/mnsc.46.2.186.11926

Venkatesh, V., & Goyal, S. (2010). Expectation disconfirmation and technology adoption: Polynomial modeling and response surface analysis. *MIS Quarterly, 34*(2), 281–303. https://doi.org/10.2307/20721428

Wang, W., Feng, F., He, X., Zhang, H., & Chua, T. S. (2021). Clicks can be cheating: Counterfactual recommendation for mitigating clickbait issue. In *Proceedings of the 44th International ACM SIGIR Conference on Research and Development in Information Retrieval* (pp. 1288–1297). ACM. https://doi.org/10.1145/3404835.3462962

Wedell, D. H., & Pettibone, J. C. (1996). Using judgments to understand decoy effects in choice. *Organizational Behavior and Human Decision Processes, 67*(3), 326–344. https://doi.org/10.1006/obhd.1996.0083

Wesslen, R., Santhanam, S., Karduni, A., Cho, I., Shaikh, S., & Dou, W. (2019). Investigating effects of visual anchors on decision-making about misinformation. In *Computer Graphics Forum* (Vol. 38, No. 3, pp. 161–171). https://doi.org/10.1111/cgf.13679

Wisniewski, P. J., Knijnenburg, B. P., & Lipford, H. R. (2017). Making privacy personal: Profiling social network users to inform privacy education and nudging. *International Journal of Human-Computer Studies, 98*, 95–108. https://doi.org/10.1016/j.ijhcs.2016.09.006

Wu, C., & Cosguner, K. (2020). Profiting from the decoy effect: A case study of an online diamond retailer. *Marketing Science, 39*(5), 974–995. https://doi.org/10.1287/mksc.2020.1231

Wu, L., Liu, P., Chen, X., Hu, W., Fan, X., & Chen, Y. (2020). Decoy effect in food appearance, traceability, and price: Case of consumer preference for pork hindquarters. *Journal of Behavioral and Experimental Economics, 87*, 101553. https://doi.org/10.1016/j.socec.2020.101553

Yu, R., Mobbs, D., Seymour, B., & Calder, A. J. (2010). Insula and striatum mediate the default bias. *Journal of Neuroscience, 30*(44), 14702–14707. https://doi.org/10.1523/JNEUROSCI.3772-10.2010

Zhang, Y., Liu, X., & Zhai, C. (2017). Information retrieval evaluation as search simulation: A general formal framework for IR evaluation. In *Proceedings of the ACM SIGIR International Conference on Theory of Information Retrieval* (pp. 193–200). ACM. https://doi.org/10.1145/3121050.3121070

Zhang, T., & Zhang, D. (2007). Agent-based simulation of consumer purchase decision-making and the decoy effect. *Journal of Business Research, 60*(8), 912–922. https://doi.org/10.1016/j.jbusres.2007.02.006

Chapter 5
Back to the Fundamentals: Extend the Rational Assumptions

Abstract In this chapter, we revisit the fundamental formal models of IR and associated simplified assumptions, with the goal of exploring and introducing actionable directions toward which the assumptions can be extended to at least partially cover the triggers and characteristics of bounded rationality. To this end, we first categorize different types of explicit and implicit assumptions into three groups, pre-search, within-search, and post-search, and discuss their conflicts with empirical findings on bounded rationality. Within each group, we discuss possible ways to extend and revise existing rational assumptions, as a key preparation for enhancing formal user models and IR evaluation techniques. When explaining the methods for extending rational assumptions, we also discuss related boundaries and explain the implications for user modeling and evaluation and how these potential boundaries are related to IIR-specific factors.

5.1 Introduction

The main goal of our book is to develop a behavioral economics framework that can characterize the role of human biases and boundedly rational decisions, especially in the context of search interaction and user-centered system evaluation. Also, we hope that the knowledge shared in our work can motivate students and future researchers to broadly explore critical, understudied research problems and hidden research paths that would enhance bounded rational or bias-aware user modeling and evaluation. In this chapter, we revisit the fundamental formal models of IR and associated simplified assumptions, with the goal of exploring and introducing actionable directions toward which the assumptions can be extended to at least partially cover the triggers and characteristics of bounded rationality. Our analysis is built upon the in-depth reviews on formal models (e.g., click models, user models of offline metrics, formal models of search sessions) and human biases offered in Chaps. 2 and 4, respectively. This chapter also takes a step forward from the identified gaps and preliminary framework introduced in Chap. 3 by discussing ways to extend rational assumptions and the components of ideal models (e.g., static costs and

J. Liu, *A Behavioral Economics Approach to Interactive Information Retrieval*, The Information Retrieval Series 48, https://doi.org/10.1007/978-3-031-23229-9_5

rewards, optimization functions, unbiased judgments) based on relevant concepts, theories, and empirical evidences prepared in previous chapters.

Although researchers could keep adding new parameters, representations, and components to accommodate the impacts of various cognitive and perceptual factors in user models, the increasingly complex models may not be practically applicable, especially for model training and testing purposes. Also, as discussed in Chap. 4, different human biases may operate within their respective boundaries and limits and may involve significant individual differences in actual behavioral impacts. Therefore, when explaining possible approaches to extending rational assumptions, we will also discuss related boundaries and explain the implications for user modeling and evaluation and how these potential boundaries are related to IIR-specific factors, such as dimensions of search tasks, labels from document judgments (e.g., query-document relevance, or *qrel*), as well as the characteristics of individual searchers (Liu, 2021).

Specifically, this chapter will categorize different types of explicit and implicit assumptions into three groups, pre-search, within-search and post-search, and discuss their conflicts with empirical findings on bounded rationality (e.g., Azzopardi, 2021; Kahneman, 2003; Simon, 1955; Thaler, 2016). Most of the existing formal models and assumptions are proposed to characterize and simulate the activities during search, especially in ad hoc retrieval scenarios, so that each search iteration and query-based retrieval evaluation be analyzed and evaluated individually. However, as indicated in Chap. 4, there are factors associated with bounded rationality that could affect people's in situ preferences, expectations, and retrospective evaluations in pre-search estimation and post-search stages as well.

Based on the identified gaps and conflicts, we will discuss possible ways to extend and revise existing rational assumptions, as a key preparation for enhancing formal user models and IR evaluation tools and methods. This chapter will be built upon the gaps and three main problems introduced in Chap. 3 and discuss more details regarding each category or phase of search modeling and the implications of research progresses on human biases and bounded rationality for updating rational assumptions. We believe that extending and revising existing assumptions based on rich theoretical and empirical basis would be an appropriate initial step toward building an actionable research agenda on bias-aware IR modeling and implementing next-generation intelligent search systems that can mitigate the negative effects of human biases.

5.2 Pre-search Stage

In most formal models of search and implicit assumptions underpinning evaluation metrics, factors emerging in *pre-search* stage, such as existing beliefs, initial preferences, pre-search expectations, and motivating tasks, are not represented or examined. Although there are offline evaluation metrics that include individual characteristics in underlying user models (e.g., patient and impatient users in rank-biased precision measure; Moffat & Zobel, 2008), there are still a wide range of user features and contextual factors, especially the ones involving human biases and bounded rationality, that are not considered in user simulation and system evaluation. The implicit assumption behind this general model setup is that users' search behavior and strategies of search evaluation are not affected by the factors beyond topics, queries (and associated search intents), and characteristics of retrieved documents (e.g., relevance, rank position).

A straightforward approach to revising the general assumption and enhancing existing user models is incorporating representations of the key pre-search factors and their associations with search interactions into models and metrics. For instance, instead of starting with no prior preferences or expectations, different users may have different in situ search expectations and search strategies due to their varying past experiences under similar *cases*, especially in situations where the solution space of current task is complex and uncertain. According to case-based decision theory (CBDT) (Gilboa & Schmeidler, 1995), the extent to which past search experience and actions affect current behaviors of decision makers depends on the perceived *similarity* of the past case(s) to the current task. In addition, this basic setup of CBDT also naturally connects to the principle of satisficing and aspiration levels in boundedly rational decision-making processes (cf. Schwartz et al., 2002; Simon, 1955).

From the reference-dependence perspective introduced in Chap. 4 (Kahneman, 2003; Tversky & Kahneman, 1991), the effects of past similar cases on current decision-making strategies and thresholds in judgments can also be framed as a type of reference effects. Under this circumstance, a representation of *pre-search reference* in user-related assumptions may need to crystallize one case or a set of multiple similar and recent cases that are *mentally accessible* to the decision maker at the moment. The case, in this context, can be considered as a motivating task that happens or is assigned to a person within a particular problematic situation. Different task facets and characteristics of problematic situations (e.g., available social and technical support, urgency of the problem) may have varying impacts or weights in similarity assessment. For instance, a past task (and the associated information search experience) of learning Python data analytics may be considered as similar to the current task of studying Python text analysis. However, a past task of learning a deep learning package for completing a self-designed project and the current task of learning deep learning functions for preparing a computer science final exam might be considered as separate cases with low level of similarity, due to the difference in underlying motivations and requirements in information seeking and use. In addition, people's judgments on case similarity may also be affected by users' familiarity with the involved topics and domains (Liu et al., 2019; White et al., 2009). Higher levels of knowledge and familiarity on involved tasks, topics, or cases may increase the accuracy of similarity estimation and enable users to bring truly relevant past experiences into current decision-making scenarios.

Figure 5.1 summarizes the structure of pre-search user preferences and expectations under the CBDT framework. The pre-search factors are affected by the cases, actions, and outcomes a user experienced before, and their respective weights in

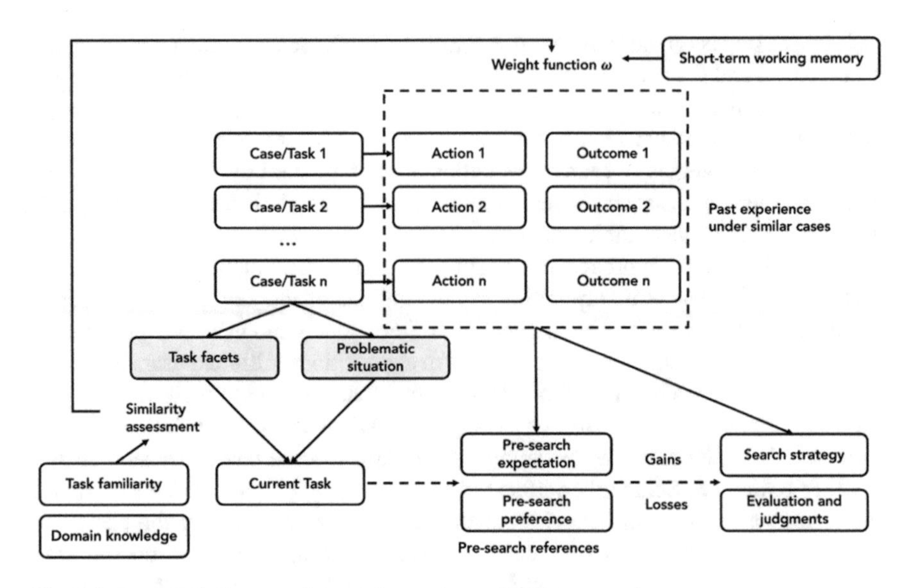

Fig. 5.1 Pre-search factors and search interaction: a CBDT perspective

current search strategies are affected by the implicit similarity assessment. These pre-search factors, from reference-dependence perspective, could serve as initial references based on which users evaluate their current information gains and search efforts. For example, based on past search experience on similar factual tasks, a user who is working on the task of "finding the Asian supermarket near me" may expect to see the most relevant results ranked on the top of the first SERP and would be dissatisfied or perceive a loss if this was not the case. In particular, from the expectation disconfirmation perspective (Oliver, 1980; Venkatesh & Goyal, 2010), people may have initial expectations and preferences regarding multiple aspects of search interactions, such as quality of retrieved results, effectiveness of search recommendations, and interface layouts. The ways in which these expectations are confirmed or disconfirmed may affect users' in situ search tactics, especially query reformulation types, and the thresholds for evaluating retrieved documents. For instance, a previous frustrating search experience under similar task (e.g., poor search results, irrelevant recommendations) may lower the user's expectation regarding document quality under their current similar task, which may result in a relatively lower threshold for relevance judgment and overestimation of document relevance.

As discussed above, estimating pre-search preferences and expectations from a traditional reference-dependence or CBDT perspective can enrich the pre-search component of user models and may facilitate subsequent search behavior predictions. At application level, however, achieving this representation and conducting model training would be challenging, as it would require sufficient information and knowledge about the individual users and their past relevant experiences beforehand. It might also be difficult to infer or simulate these pre-search factors merely based on previous search logs or document features. In addition, regarding possible perceptual biases, we need to take into consideration the gap between actual set of similar cases and mentally accessible set of similar cases at the moment. This gap can be traced back to even broader problems of investigating perception-outcome differences (under the influence of in situ relative gains and losses) and examining the limits of individuals' divergent limits in working memory. We will discuss more details regarding these problems and their implications at the *within-search* stage. Overall, although it is challenging to represent and estimate the impacts of all components discussed above, it would be helpful to utilize the framework illustrated in Fig. 5.1 to locate the progresses and limitations of our current models on related research problems and identify potential research themes for future efforts.

Compared to modeling the full structure of pre-search factors presented in Fig. 5.1 and estimating all initial references, it might be more feasible in most cases for researchers to estimate people's initial beliefs and preferences from a *confirmation bias* perspective (cf. Nickerson, 1998). Specifically, for instance, although it would be difficult to infer all accessible past cases, researchers might be able to infer users' preferences over different subtopics, opinions, and sentiments based on their past search logs and initial couple of queries and the associated search interactions with the SERPs and social media contents (e.g., examination and clicking, dwell time on content pages that covering certain opinions) (Knobloch-Westerwick et al., 2015; Rieger et al., 2021; Workman, 2018). Retrieved results that disconfirm these initial opinions and beliefs may receive less attention and underestimated relevance score (even though they may actually be topically relevant to the queries).

Thus, when developing user models for simulation and evaluation purposes, it would be reasonable to assume that individual users have one or multiple initial beliefs over a set of subtopics, opinions, and sentiments before the search session starts, and the search result snippets and documents that confirm the belief(s) would receive more attention from users and might also reinforce users' existing beliefs and biases. From the *loss aversion* perspective (cf. Tversky & Kahneman, 1991), examining and accepting the results that confirm existing beliefs and expectations could be perceived of a gain or at least an avoidance of possible loss, as the user would not need to give up the existing beliefs that cost previous cognitive resources to establish. At the implementation level, the initial beliefs and preferences can be considered as variables affecting browsing patterns and relevance judgments, apart from several widely examined factors, such as queries, rank positions, and externally labelled relevance scores. Identifying the implicit initial preferences and beliefs waiting to be confirmed can help researchers better predict users' clicking and evaluation behaviors and design effective low-cost search interventions for mitigating the potential negative impacts of confirmation bias and algorithmically debiasing relevance and credibility judgments (Draws et al., 2021; Rieger et al., 2021).

Apart from pre-search references, users' behaviors are also affected by human biases and heuristics that operate *within* search sessions. In the following section, we will discuss the ways in which we could extend the components of assumptions regarding people's actions and decision-making during information search processes.

5.3 Within-Search Stage

Compared to pre-search stage, within-search stage is more complicated as it involves multiple aspects of ongoing search interactions and changing user experience. Meanwhile, however, researchers can collect more diverse signals based on which user models and evaluation metrics can be constructed. In this section, we discuss a series of widely discussed intuitive assumptions applied in a broad range of formal user models and explain the ways in which we can (and should) revise and extend them to better predict real-world user behaviors and explain why they search and evaluate in such ways.

The first set of assumptions is related to the *Problem 1* discussed in the Chap. 3. When modeling users and search interactions, building pre-defined rules and assumptions based on actual *costs* and *rewards* tend to be a natural starting point for developing user models and evaluating system performances in a simulated environment. In simulation-based experiments, cost and reward measures are usually linked to user behavior and relevance-based scores, respectively. Based on these measures, researchers often assume the following:

1) Users' behaviors and implicit optimization goals are defined based on the actual experienced costs and rewards during search processes.
2) The costs associated with different actions (e.g., query formulation, search result snippet examination, clicks, dwell time on content pages) and the *relevance-based* reward functions remain the same across different queries, topics, and task types.

Based upon these two main assumptions, researchers can model user behavior and optimize retrieval algorithms on the same ground across different search states and problematic situations. In IR experiments, the two assumptions and their similar variants about costs and rewards have been widely applied in various formal models of search interactions (e.g., Moffat et al., 2012; Zhang et al., 2017; Zhang & Zhai, 2016), including the models that integrate economic theories into search cost modeling (e.g., Azzopardi, 2011, 2014). These assumptions largely simplify the process of estimating costs and rewards associated with different components of searching. They also allow researchers to turn the complex problem of improving search interactions and experiences into straightforward, mathematically solvable optimization problems that involve minimizing behavior-based costs and maximizing rewards and utilities measured by relevance or other judgment labels. In addition, from replicability and reproducibility perspective, assuming fixed connections between action types and costs also facilitates more flexible reuse and replication of user models and IR evaluation experiments. With these assumptions as the basis, many of the potential challenges related to changes of task nature, individual differences, and within-session cognitive variations in IR evaluations (cf. Gäde et al., 2021; Liu, 2022) could be at least temporarily bypassed in standardized experiments. In sum, before we bring in the behavioral economics perspective for extending the assumptions, we believe that it is almost equally important to acknowledge the value and contribution of the simplified assumptions to the field of IR and computing in general.

As discussed in Chap. 4, when users perceive and evaluate costs and rewards, their perceptions and search decisions are usually developed based on *gains* and *losses* relative to certain reference points, rather than the actual absolute values. This reference dependence perspective casts doubt on the fundamentals of a broad range of formal models and user-oriented evaluation techniques. When the reference points change before or during search sessions, it would lead to the variations in perceived costs and rewards associated with the same type of actions. In addition, depending on the nature of perceived changes (i.e., as gains or losses), the same size of changes in search behavior and result quality across queries and sessions may have different impacts on subsequent search interactions and retrospective evaluations within search sessions (i.e., *loss aversion*, Tversky & Kahneman, 1992). Perceived losses, such as increased dwell time or search actions, less relevant search result snippets or documents, lower readability of retrieved documents, and higher difficulty in formulating effective search queries, could generate larger impacts on users' following search tactics and levels of satisfaction, compared to the same or similar sizes of perceived search gains.

Therefore, to extend the original cost-reward analytical framework from a bounded rationality perspective, researchers need to identify the reference points in effect and compute the in situ perceived gains and losses relative to the reference points. Previous behavioral economics research introduced in Chap. 4 on related topics (e.g., reference dependence and prospect theory, confirmation bias, anchoring bias) have demonstrated that people's decision-making under uncertainty could be influenced by varying types of potential references that emerge at varying stages and are associated with different internal and external factors (Caputo, 2014; Gneezy et al., 2017; Kahneman, 2003; Nickerson, 1998; Tversky & Kahneman, 1991). In the context of information seeking and retrieval, different dimensions of search interactions may have different reference levels and are associated with divergent contextual factors, such as different task facets, user characteristics, as well as in situ search dynamics. Also, the co-exist references may also interact with each other and jointly affect users' in situ search evaluations.

Based on the discussion above, the users' references in search can be written as:

$$R = f_R(\omega_1 r_1, \omega_1 r_2, \ldots \omega_n r_n) \tag{5.1}$$

where R represents the *integrated reference point* for a certain dimension of current search session (e.g., cost of query reformulation and SERP browsing, gain from ranked result list). The integrated reference point is formulated based on a variety of active potential reference points that may have different weights in the user's search decision-making and evaluation. For instance, if a user is at *m-th* query segment, the user's reference point in terms of the cost of browsing may be affected by the pre-search expectations, beliefs, and preferences. These pre-search references may emerge from past search experience under similar motivating tasks or cases or other people's search interactions that the user observed. In addition to pre-search references, according to the studies on *anchoring bias* (e.g., Tversky & Kahneman, 1974; Caputo, 2014), the user's reference point could also be significantly affected by the initially encountered information objects (e.g., top ranked results presented on the SERPs under first or second queries). The content and quality of the first set of examined documents may heavily influence the user's understanding and threshold of document relevance (Scholer et al., 2013) and thereby affect the perceived gains and losses in following search iterations. The weight distribution on different original reference points, $W = \{\omega_1, \omega_2, \omega_3 \ldots \omega_n\}$, may vary significantly across different dimensions of search interactions and thus may need to be estimated separately. In addition, changes in reference points and their associated weights may also be associated with the transitions of local information seeking intentions and task states (Jansen et al., 2007; Liu et al., 2020). Under different intentions, users often search and evaluate documents differently and may also be affected by distinct reference points.

Based on the identified reference points, the perceived gains or losses for each dimension can be written as:

$$C = \sum_{i=1}^{m} f_c(c_i, R_{c_i}) * \mid c_i - R_{c_i} \mid \quad (5.2)$$

$$Re = \sum_{i=1}^{n} f_{Re}(Re_i, R_{Re_i}) * \mid Re_i - R_{Re_i} \mid \quad (5.3)$$

$$U = u(C, Re) \quad (5.4)$$

where C and Re measure the total *perceived gains* and *losses* in terms of search cost and search reward, respectively. Both *Cost* and *Reward* are multidimensional search components and could be deconstructed into m and n dimensions, respectively. R represents the in situ reference point corresponding to each specific dimension. U refers to the overall perceived utility, which is a function of C and Re. Depending on the nature of perceived changes (as gains or losses), the corresponding weights $f_c(c_i, R_{c_i})$ and $f_{Re}(Re_i, R_{Re_i})$ may vary. Users' search tactics and evaluation are more sensitive to perceived losses than to gains. Also, the dimensions where relative losses are perceived are more likely to attract users' attentions and thus receive higher weights in decisions. Figure 5.2 summarizes the process of gain- and loss-based search decision-making in sessions.

As presented, users' current search interactions and outcomes could be evaluated based upon a diverse set of potential reference points. The perceived losses relative to the integrated reference point, such as lower levels of relevance and usefulness of the retrieved SERP and increased dwell time on retrieved pages, may lead to significant changes in following query reformulation behaviors (e.g., formulating a

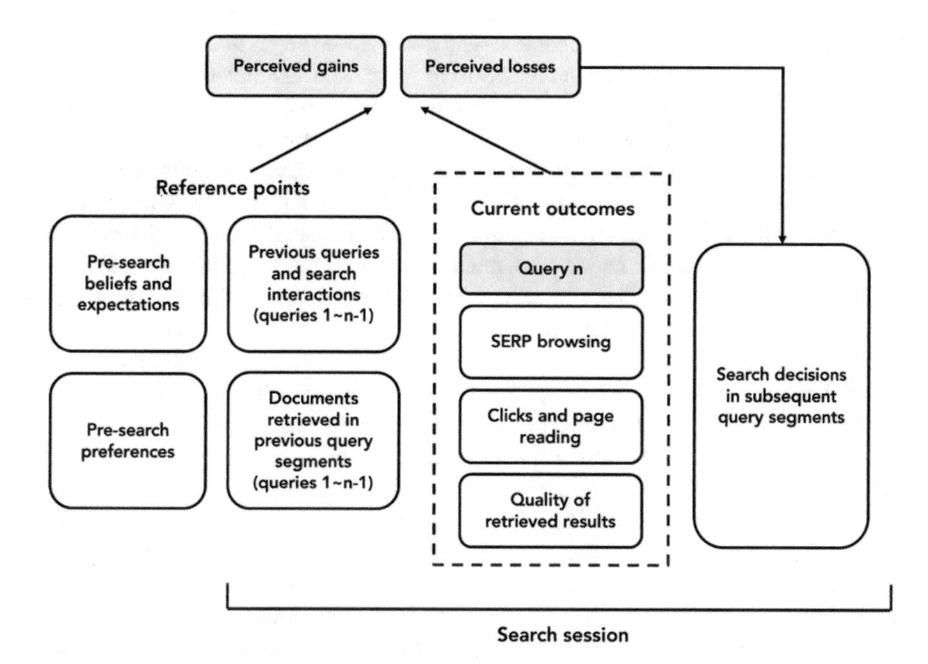

Fig. 5.2 Gain- and loss-based search decision-making process

new exploratory query, instead of slightly adjusting current query) and in situ search expectations. These changes of search outcomes and experiences in ongoing sessions may also lead to minor or major changes to the reference points in the user's mind, especially for subsequent query segments under similar search intentions.

Apart from the explicit, observable aspects of search behaviors and costs, many of the implicit components of search introduced in Chap. 2 may also be affected by reference dependence effects. Regarding clicking behavior, the perceived *attractiveness* and *probability of examination* on retrieved documents may also be affected by the user's previous experience (e.g., similar documents or subtopics encountered on similar rank positions). Previous examinations of search result snippets, clicking on documents, and click depth on SERPs as potential reference points may affect the thresholds of attractiveness and examination decisions for the documents encountered in following search iterations. When users examine result snippets on current SERP, the search result snippet that have a clearly lower quality than the previously encountered ones (e.g., lower perceived relevance or readability, higher level of ambiguity) may receive significantly less attention from the user. However, if the users start the session with encountering a set of poor-quality search results and documents, the relatively low thresholds or reference points may increase the attractiveness and probability of examination on subsequently retrieved documents that have an intermediate level of quality and are ranked at similar rank positions.

Note that some of the relative, reference-dependence aspects may be partially captured and characterized by some of the existing click models (e.g., graph-based session click models that take document- and query-based edges into account, cf. Lin et al., 2021; click model that includes users' click and examination preferences, cf. Xing et al., 2013). However, it would still be useful to explicitly investigate the relative changes in search result features and incorporate gain- and loss-based parameters into the estimation of the attractiveness, examination probability, and in situ preferences on clicking. Our multidimensional reference-dependence approach, which also considers the impacts of other related biases and heuristics (e.g., loss aversion, confirmation bias, anchoring bias), could also better explain the individual differences in click actions and extend existing personalized click models (PCMs) that seek to integrate user factors into click prediction and relevance estimation algorithms (e.g., Cheng & Cantú-Paz, 2010; Shen et al., 2012).

With respect to search browsing, apart from the explicit observable dimensions, such as dwell time on different pages and SERP components, scrolling patterns, and eye movements, users' implicit *cost budgets* in evaluation (cf. Zhang et al., 2017), if any, may also be affected by previously established reference points. Thus, the existing fixed cost budget setup or assumption in evaluation metrics could be extended by including the reference points extracted from or simulated based on empirical evidences. For instance, a lower in situ search expectation or threshold of relevance may result in higher tolerance of irrelevant documents and extended browsing sessions. Although these actual interactions can lead to linear increases of search costs as it is assumed in classic cost-reward models, due to the influence of relatively low references, users' perceived costs may increase slowly (e.g., as characterized by a logarithmic function). As a result, the perceived cost and subject cost budget may systematically deviate from the actual or simulated cost budgets. On the contrary, users may perceive a relative quick accumulation of costs under a high reference point (e.g., high-quality SERPs and documents encountered in previous query segments and sessions). Once the perceived costs hit the cost budget in mind, users may become increasingly sensitive to the relative changes in search due to the effect of loss aversion. Apart from quantifiable references, users' cost budgets may also vary across different search intentions and task states. For example, under exploratory search states, users may be more open to examine more search results and click deeper results on SERPs. In contrast, under factual known-item searches, users may have a very limited cost budgets in mind and expect to see the correct answers being ranked on the top positions of the SERPs.

Regarding search result evaluation, similar to other dimensions of search sessions, users' perceived gains and rewards obtained from each clicked relevant document are not fixed. Also, the thresholds of relevance and usefulness judgment may not be static or predefined as it is often implicitly assumed in user models, underpinning a variety of offline evaluation metrics. Instead, the in situ gains and underlying thresholds of relevance and usefulness evaluation could be affected by threshold priming effects (cf. Scholer et al., 2013) and are related to the document evaluation experience under previous queries or other similar search tasks. The threshold priming effects may also be moderated by other user characteristics, such as topic and task familiarity, domain knowledge, and search skills, in real-life search scenarios. Compared to topical relevance, document usefulness tends to be more subjective and diverse as documents and results could be useful in different ways during search sessions. From a behavioral economics perspective, estimating and simulating the reference points of usefulness judgment might be more challenging and involve a broader range of situational factors, such as search intentions, task progresses, distractions on SERPs, and information encountering and serendipity events (e.g., André et al., 2009; Mao et al., 2017; Mitsui et al., 2017; Rahman & Wilson, 2015).

Related to the idea and assumptions regarding cost budget and evaluation thresholds, users' *stopping rate* and utility *discounting factor* in browsing and evaluation (e.g., Chapelle et al., 2009; Zhang et al., 2017) may also be gain- and loss-based and be affected by both pre-search and in situ references. Specifically, a higher perceived gain (e.g., increased number of relevant documents ranked on top positions; reduced amount of dwell time needed before collecting useful information from clicked documents) may result in lower stopping rate and discounting rate in current SERP browsing. However, if an in situ search loss is encountered (e.g., dropping in search result quality, increased dwell time), the user's stopping rate in following rank positions may increase quickly and result in early search stopping or even query abandonment behavior. Thus, in the context of interactive search sessions, the assumptions of fixed or rank-based stopping rate and discounting factor by ranks could be extended by including reference dependence features or parameters and connecting to previously encountered search results and search costs within the same session. For instance, following the stopping rate function adapted from cascade model and expected reciprocal rank (ERR) measure (Chapelle et al., 2009), a bounded rational stopping rate function can be written as follows:

$$R_i = \frac{2^{r_i - Re_{i-1}} - 1}{2^{r_{max}}} \tag{5.5}$$

$$P_j = \prod_{i=1}^{j} (1 - R_i) R_j \tag{5.6}$$

where r_i measures the graded relevance score of the current document i. Re_{i-1} refers to the total perceived reward or accumulated gains up to the rank position $i - 1$. During SERP browsing and document examination, a document satisfies the user with the probability R_i. P_j represents the probability that the user is satisfied and stops at document j. In this simple initial setup, we change the absolute graded relevance score to the relative gain-based score as the basis for calculating the probability that the user is satisfied with the current document i. Note that in ERR measure, it is assumed that users will stop searching once they find the one document that satisfies their information needs. However, in exploratory searches, people may not stop at just one satisfactory document and be open to broader explorations and deeper clicking behavior. Under this circumstance, it is critical to extend evaluation metrics and consider the systematic impacts of perceived gains and losses at different levels. Incorporating potential reference points and biases into the estimation and simulation of stopping rate and discounting factor may be a viable approach to extending user-centered IR metrics, especially in the context of whole-session IR evaluation.

Regarding within-SERP examination and evaluation, the interdependence between different search results may also affect the user's overall perception of the SERP and the associated examination behavior. In existing research, *Document interdependence* has been examined in a series of offline IR evaluation studies as a factor or constraint in document relevance estimation (e.g., Montazeralghaem et al., 2018; Radlinski et al., 2009; Zhai et al., 2015). Taking *decoy effect* into consideration would offer a new perspective for examining different aspects and forms of document interdependence (Kahneman, 2003; Tversky & Kahneman, 1985; Wedell & Pettibone, 1996; Wu et al., 2020). Specifically, for example, under a short exploratory search query, the SERP may present documents involving different opinions, information sources, and subtopics, for which users may not have prior preferences. However, a potential decoy search result associated with a subtopic may increase the user's examination and clickthrough probability on results with relatively higher quality or level of informativeness under the same subtopic. Therefore, in information searches that involve a diverse set of results, users' in situ preferences over different types of contents may be shaped by implicit decoy options.

This decoy effect may also interact with the existing impacts of search snippet features and rank position biases and could be included and represented in both click models for attractiveness and examination probability estimation and offline evaluation metrics. Note that the decoy effect could happen at multiple dimensions, such as relevance and informativeness of search result snippets, document readability (e.g., Collins-Thompson et al., 2011), and perceived credibility of the search results (e.g., Hilligoss & Rieh, 2008), which may cause different reactions from users.

$$\alpha_i = \frac{d(sr_1, sr_2 \ldots sr_n)}{d(i,\ t)} \tag{5.7}$$

$$d(sr_1, sr_2 \ldots sr_n) = \sum_{r=1}^{n} w_r \mid Sr_{ri} - Sr_{rt} \mid \tag{5.8}$$

$$P(C_t = 1 | d_{ipresent} = 1) - P(C_t = 1 | d_{ipresent} = 0) = \alpha_i + \delta * max\,(i, t) \tag{5.9}$$

At the implementation level, researchers may need to start with identifying potential decoy options at multiple levels among the retrieved results and estimate possible decoy effects based on the distance between decoy options and the search results associated with similar subtopics, opinions, and information sources. This distance measure should consider both the superficial-level distance (i.e., distance in rank positions on SERPs) and the distance or difference in search result quality and presentation. As shown in Formula (5.7), α_i measures the potential decoy effect generated by the decoy option ranked at the rank position i. In Formula (5.8), the function d measures the aggregated differences between the regular/target result and decoy result, which plays an essential role in triggering potential decoy effect. As presented in Formula (5.9), the decoy effect can be represented by the probability

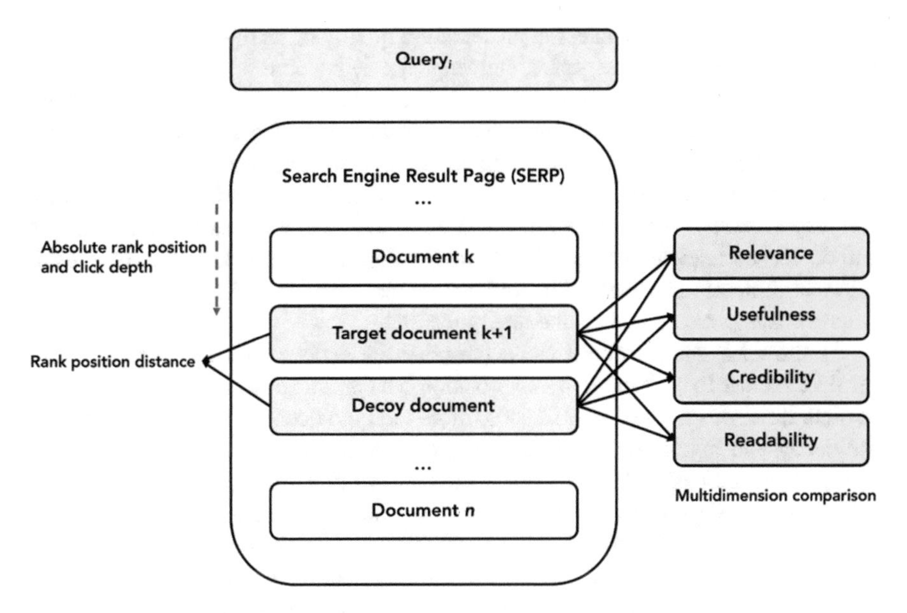

Fig. 5.3 The structure of decoy effect in IR evaluation

difference in user's clickthrough rate on the target document (with similar subtopics, opinions, themes, or sentiments) ranked at position t between two scenarios: (1) the decoy result is present, and (2) the decoy result is absent. sr_n represents different dimensions of search result snippets and corresponding documents, which may cause perceived quality difference and trigger decoy effect in user judgments.

δ measures the potential discounts on decoy impacts due to rank positions. Based on previous research on the effects of *rank position bias* (e.g., Agarwal et al., 2019; Wang et al., 2018), we assume that with all other conditions remaining the same, the decoy effect is more likely to occur when the decoy and target results are ranked higher as they would be more likely to receive the user's attention during browsing in top rank positions. In contrast, if both results are ranked in relatively low position, users may be less sensitive to the potential differences between the two results and thus are less likely to be influenced by the decoy result in evaluation. Also, given the potential effect of *diminishing sensitivity* (Trautmann & Kuilen, 2012; Tversky & Kahneman, 1991; Wakker & Tversky, 1993), users are less likely to completely change their click preferences at lower ranked results, especially in situations where the corresponding level of click depth is already way beyond their expected cost or in situ cost budget.

Figure 5.3 illustrates the structure of decoy effect discussed above and highlights the factors that may influence the effect size of decoy results, such as absolute rank position (where the target search result and decoy result are ranked on the SERP), rank position distance between target result and decoy result, and, more importantly, the multidimensional differences *perceived* by users. Note that different dimensions involved in comparison may have significantly different levels of saliency to users in

SERP browsing. For instance, the presentation quality of search result snippet (e.g., readability, informativeness, color, and length) may be more salient than some other implicit factors (e.g., overall usefulness and credibility of the documents) that are difficult to judge at the first glance, especially for users who are not quite familiar with the topic and domain involved. In addition, users may be more sensitive to the dimensions where a clear relative loss is perceived in the comparison between decoy and target results, such as a significant drop in the quality of search result snippets and decreased relevance or quality of images (i.e., loss aversion bias). As a result, different dimensions perceived in comparison may contribute differently to the final behavioral impacts caused by the decoy result.

As shown in the formulas, when the potential decoy result and regular search results are close to each other in rank position but significantly differ from each other in other dimensions, the decoy effect is more likely to occur as the contrast between the decoy and regular results would be more noticeable to the user. Investigating decoy effect in SERP evaluation can extend the implicit assumption of document or search result independence in a wide range of click models and evaluation metrics, especially in terms of estimating the probability of examination, predicting clicks, and modeling users' perceptions of SERP utility. Studying decoy effect in IR can also pave the path toward a new layer of document interdependence studies. The structure of decoy effect presented in Fig. 5.3 can serve as a theoretical framework for characterizing the behavioral impacts of decoy results in information seeking and retrieval and may also inform the design of controlled user studies (e.g., SERP-based crowdsourcing evaluation study), focusing on decoy options in SERPs across different information-intensive decision-making scenarios.

The following section will move on to the *post-search* stage and discuss the possible extensions of user model assumptions in light of the knowledge regarding bounded rationality, especially in terms of whole-session retrospective evaluation.

5.4 Post-search Stage

In addition to modeling user behaviors and system performance during search sessions, how users retrospectively evaluate the performance of search systems and their overall search experiences, especially in whole-session IR, is also one of the central themes in IR research. In post-search retrospective evaluation, researchers usually evaluate search system performances based on the average value and total value of each measure or dimension (e.g., sum dwell time on SERPs, average number of clicks and pages visited, average precision, reciprocal rank and nDCG scores of SERPs) (e.g., Chen et al., 2017; Liu et al., 2012). In offline Cranfield experiments, a series of average-value-based evaluation metrics have also been proposed to evaluate search systems in a set of diverse queries and topics (Voorhees, 2001). Differing from common average-value- and total-value-based metrics, *session-based* DCG (sDCG) metric takes query order into consideration when evaluating search sessions and discounts relevant search results retrieved from later queries within a session (Järvelin et al., 2008). Compared to other retrospective evaluation metrics, sDCG takes a step forward by simulating the discounted weights of each search iteration based on the linear query order in the session.

Estimating the weight distribution of different query segments is a critical aspect of whole-session search evaluation. In light of the empirical findings on *peak-end rule* and *recency effects* (Kahneman, 2003; Redelmeier et al., 2003), researchers can adjust the average-value-based metrics and linear query weight functions and assign higher weights on peak experience and most recent search iterations. As discussed in related behavioral economic experiments, people's in situ peak experience and most recent experience could generate relatively higher impacts on the retrospective remembered utility. This *remembered utility*, rather than actual *experienced utility*, serves as the basis for people's intuitive judgments and subsequent decision-making, especially under the operations of System 1 (Kahneman, 2003). Researchers also found that when retrospectively evaluating an extended episode, people are not sensitive to the actual duration of the entire session (i.e., *duration neglect*, Fredrickson & Kahneman, 1993; Hands & Avons, 2001). In addition, the initial queries in a session may also be associated with relatively higher weights compared to other following queries as they may serve the anchoring points in evaluation (i.e., anchoring bias, cf. Nickerson, 1998). Also, at the application level, extracting the anchoring references from initial queries may also facilitate early prediction of whole-session search effectiveness and thereby offer opportunities for proactive search intervention and recommendation (e.g., Koskela et al., 2018; Mitsui et al., 2018; Shah, 2018), especially in cases where the current user is on a potentially poor-performing or high-loss search path predicted by the search system.

The user biases and heuristics discussed above can help extend the implicit assumptions regarding the extent to which average-value-based and total-value-based metrics can approximate whole-session experience. Specifically, knowledge regarding these biases highlight several key moments in search sessions and can inform the design of a more behaviorally realistic weight distribution for connecting query-level evaluation to whole-session-based evaluation of system performance. In constructing session-level evaluation models and metrics, researchers should consider assigning relatively higher weights to these key points and examining their respective impacts on user evaluation under different tasks and search scenarios. In addition, given the impact of *duration neglect*, researchers may not be able to rely on session duration time as a main predictor in estimating a user's *remembered* whole-session experience.

Figure 5.4 illustrates and contrasts the key factors involved in the whole-session evaluations characterized by classical rational approach and boundedly rational approach, respectively. This figure highlights the difference in weight distributions of different factors and query positions and explains the role of each related human bias and heuristics in different aspects of the session evaluation process. Future researchers can use the framework presented here as a guideline in variable and model design for predicting whole-session search experience (e.g., levels of search satisfaction and cognitive loads) and evaluating the performance of bounded rational prediction models against that of the classic rational models as baselines. In addition

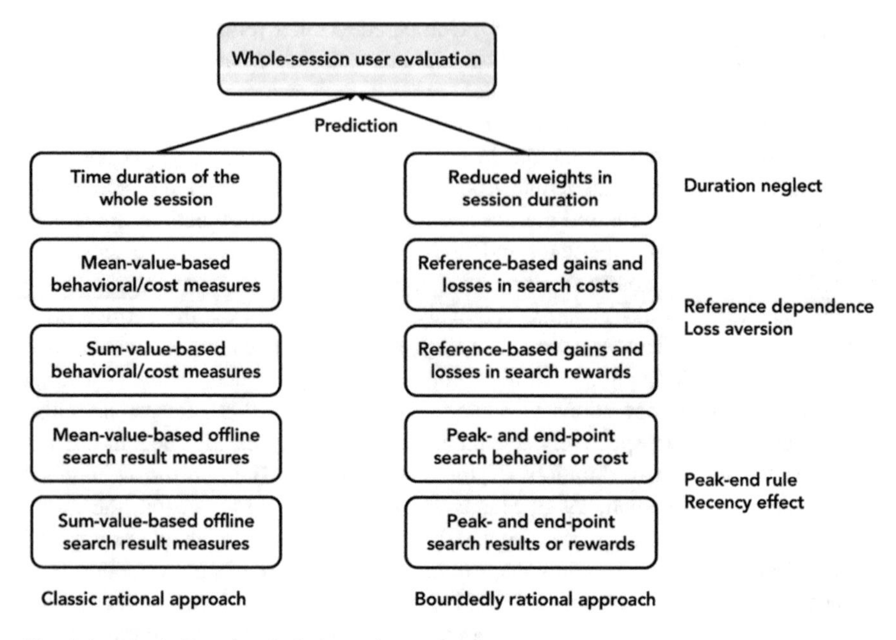

Fig. 5.4 Boundedly rational whole-session evaluation

to the findings from behavioral experiments introduced in the Chap. 4, in the following chapter, we will introduce empirical evidences from IR research that confirms the impacts of peak-end rule on retrospective evaluations and discuss how we can leverage the knowledge regarding related biases in better answering critical research questions in information seeking and retrieval communities.

It is also worth noting that peak-end effect usually has its boundaries and limits across different dimensions of decision-making problems (Langer et al., 2005; Schneider et al., 2011). The extent to which peak-end rule affects whole-session evaluation may vary significantly across different facets of search interactions and thus may have different weights and limits in affecting overall search interaction experience and judgments of the search system, such as levels of user engagement, task and cognitive loads, as well as perceived levels of success and satisfaction. Therefore, the actual weight distributions across different search dimensions may need be estimated individually based on corresponding search interaction signals. Given existing research on the divergent effects of peak-end rule across varying behaviors and decision-making sessions, IR researchers may also find similar variations in weight distributions and effect sizes of different query moments (particularly the initial, peak, and end queries that may trigger boundedly rational search decisions) in retrospective session evaluation across different behavioral measures, offline evaluation metrics, as well as types of search tasks.

In addition to the findings on peak-end rule and recency effects, behavioral economics research also casts doubt on the fundamental assumption regarding users' intents of *always pursuing maximized utility*. In contrast to the assumption of optimization, behavioral science and decision-making researchers found that people's decision-making often follows the principle of *satisficing* and aims for satisfactory or adequate options in all accessible options, rather than the optimal solution predicted by normative models (Simon, 1955). The satisficing strategy can by triggered by different reasons. For instance, people may find it difficult to deliberately compare and calculate the possible utility from different options as they are often restricted by limited time, cognitive resources, and computing capability. Also, although the optimal option can be identified through rational mathematical analysis and simulations, it may not always be actually accessible to users or decision makers due to the individual differences in varying aspects (e.g., domain knowledge, information search skills, existing beliefs, and cognitive biases) and situational limits. Moreover, the threshold of satisficing in each specific decision-making scenario may be linked to a prior reference point, perceived gains or losses that a person has in mind before current search iteration or session, and thus may vary significantly across different individuals and problematic situations (Kahneman, 2003; Schwartz et al., 2002).

In IR evaluation, the satisficing strategy in decision-making may be partially captured by some of the existing offline metrics, assuming that users will stop searches once they find the *first relevant document* that satisfies their information needs (e.g., reciprocal rank, expected reciprocal rank). However, current relevance-based metrics may not be able to fully characterize the nature of in situ satisficing moment or threshold. The threshold may also involve other features and dimensions of search results, such as usefulness for completing the task, topical diversity, interestingness, as well as unexpectedness (or information serendipity). Also, the evaluation of relevance itself may also be affected by other related human biases. For instance, the first couple of documents encountered in a session are often considered as relevant ones and may significantly affect users' evaluations of subsequently retrieved documents. Thus, focusing on available relevance labels in test collections only may lead to biased search ranking and inaccurate estimation of levels of user satisfaction. Consequently, it might be difficult for researchers and system designers to adaptively optimize ranking and search recommendation algorithms toward the goal of satisficing in real-world information seeking and search settings.

5.5 Summary

This chapter brings together the insights regarding formal IR models and human bounded rationality discussed in previous chapters and discusses the ways in which we can extend several widely adopted (explicitly or implicitly) assumptions in user modeling and make them more behaviorally realistic. Specifically, based on the nature of human biases and heuristics discussed in Chap. 4, we explain their possible impacts on users' search interaction and evaluation at pre-search, within-search, and post-search retrospective evaluation stages and suggest revised forms of existing assumptions that can incorporate the knowledge about human biases into formal user models and system evaluation metrics.

Nevertheless, it is worth noting that we as a research community still has a long way to go before achieving reliable, intelligent bias-aware user modeling and personalized recommendation. Extending rational assumptions and discussing potential research problems is the first step toward reaching the ultimate goal of bias-aware IR that addresses both human biases and algorithmic biases. Beyond this initial step, researchers also need to develop and further enhance bias-aware user models and incorporate the knowledge regarding bounded rationality into search and ranking algorithms, evaluation metrics, and standardized IR evaluation experiments (Liu, 2022). In addition to the open research problems discussed above, methodologically, how to accurately capture and estimate the real impacts of human biases and heuristics in naturalistic complex information seeking and retrieval settings, rather than the (over)simplified decision-making experiments employed in a series of classic behavioral economics research, also remains an open challenge to the research community. Also, given the high cost of user studies in both lab and naturalistic environments, we also need to develop and evaluate the methods through which we can reliably reuse the study materials (e.g., study design and instruments, collected data, statistical and machine learning models built and tested) and replicate the completed experiments in different settings. Researchers may need to both explore existing user study designs and techniques (e.g., Kelly, 2009; Kelly & Sugimoto, 2013; Liu & Shah, 2019) and also employ additional signals and design new study settings where boundedly rational decision-making processes could be better observed and identified.

In the following chapters, we will discuss the recent research progress on modeling and simulating human biases in information seeking, retrieval, and recommendation and identify more specific research questions, directions, as well as challenges that may require more attention and research efforts from future studies.

References

Agarwal, A., Zaitsev, I., Wang, X., Li, C., Najork, M., & Joachims, T. (2019). Estimating position bias without intrusive interventions. In *Proceedings of the Twelfth ACM International Conference on Web Search and Data Mining* (pp. 474–482). ACM. https://doi.org/10.1145/3289600.3291017

André, P., Teevan, J., & Dumais, S. T. (2009). From x-rays to silly putty via Uranus: serendipity and its role in web search. In *Proceedings of the SIGCHI Conference on Human Factors in Computing Systems* (pp. 2033–2036). ACM. https://doi.org/10.1145/1518701.1519009

Azzopardi, L. (2011). The economics in interactive information retrieval. In *Proceedings of the 34th International ACM SIGIR Conference on Research and Development in Information Retrieval* (pp. 15–24). ACM. https://doi.org/10.1145/2009916.2009923

Azzopardi, L. (2014). Modelling interaction with economic models of search. In *Proceedings of the 37th ACM SIGIR Conference on Research & Development in Information Retrieval* (pp. 3–12). ACM. https://doi.org/10.1145/2600428.2609574

Azzopardi, L. (2021). Cognitive biases in search: A review and reflection of cognitive biases in information retrieval. In *Proceedings of the 2021 ACM SIGIR Conference on Human Information Interaction and Retrieval* (pp. 27–37). ACM. https://doi.org/10.1145/3406522.3446023

Caputo, A. (2014). Relevant information, personality traits and anchoring effect. *International Journal of Management and Decision Making, 13*(1), 62–76.

Chapelle, O., Metlzer, D., Zhang, Y., & Grinspan, P. (2009). Expected reciprocal rank for graded relevance. In *Proceedings of the 18th ACM Conference on Information and Knowledge Management* (pp. 621–630). ACM. https://doi.org/10.1145/1645953.1646033

Chen, Y., Zhou, K., Liu, Y., Zhang, M., & Ma, S. (2017). Meta-evaluation of online and offline web search evaluation metrics. In *Proceedings of the 40th International ACM SIGIR Conference on Research and Development in Information Retrieval* (pp. 15–24). ACM. https://doi.org/10.1145/3077136.3080804

Cheng, H., & Cantú-Paz, E. (2010). Personalized click prediction in sponsored search. In *Proceedings of the Third ACM International Conference on Web Search and Data Mining* (pp. 351–360). ACM. https://doi.org/10.1145/1718487.1718531

Collins-Thompson, K., Bennett, P. N., White, R. W., De La Chica, S., & Sontag, D. (2011). Personalizing web search results by reading level. In *Proceedings of the 20th ACM International Conference on Information and Knowledge Management* (pp. 403–412). ACM. https://doi.org/10.1145/2063576.2063639

Draws, T., Rieger, A., Inel, O., Gadiraju, U., & Tintarev, N. (2021). A checklist to combat cognitive biases in crowdsourcing. In *Proceedings of the AAAI Conference on Human Computation and Crowdsourcing* (Vol. 9, pp. 48–59). https://ojs.aaai.org/index.php/HCOMP/article/view/18939

Fredrickson, B. L., & Kahneman, D. (1993). Duration neglect in retrospective evaluations of affective episodes. *Journal of Personality and Social Psychology, 65*(1), 45–55. https://doi.org/10.1037/0022-3514.65.1.45

Gäde, M., Koolen, M., Hall, M., Bogers, T., & Petras, V. (2021). A manifesto on resource re-use in interactive information retrieval. In *Proceedings of the 2021 International ACM SIGIR Conference on Human Information Interaction and Retrieval* (pp. 141–149). ACM. https://doi.org/10.1145/3406522.3446056

Gilboa, I., & Schmeidler, D. (1995). Case-based decision theory. *The Quarterly Journal of Economics, 110*(3), 605–639. https://doi.org/10.2307/2946694

Gneezy, U., Goette, L., Sprenger, C., & Zimmermann, F. (2017). The limits of expectations-based reference dependence. *Journal of the European Economic Association, 15*(4), 861–876. https://doi.org/10.1093/jeea/jvw020

Hands, D. S., & Avons, S. E. (2001). Recency and duration neglect in subjective assessment of television picture quality. *Applied Cognitive Psychology: The Official Journal of the Society for Applied Research in Memory and Cognition, 15*(6), 639–657. https://doi.org/10.1002/acp.731

Hilligoss, B., & Rieh, S. Y. (2008). Developing a unifying framework of credibility assessment: Construct, heuristics, and interaction in context. *Information Processing & Management, 44*(4), 1467–1484. https://doi.org/10.1016/j.ipm.2007.10.001

Jansen, B. J., Booth, D. L., & Spink, A. (2007). Determining the user intent of web search engine queries. In *Proceedings of the 16th International Conference on World Wide Web* (pp. 1149–1150). https://doi.org/10.1145/1242572.1242739

Järvelin, K., Price, S. L., Delcambre, L. M., & Nielsen, M. L. (2008). Discounted cumulated gain based evaluation of multiple-query IR sessions. In *European Conference on Information Retrieval* (pp. 4–15). Springer.

Kahneman, D. (2003). Maps of bounded rationality: Psychology for behavioral economics. *American Economic Review, 93*(5), 1449–1475. https://doi.org/10.1257/000282803322655392

Kelly, D. (2009). Methods for evaluating interactive information retrieval systems with users. *Foundations and Trends in Information Retrieval, 3*(1–2), 1–224. https://doi.org/10.1561/1500000012

Kelly, D., & Sugimoto, C. R. (2013). A systematic review of interactive information retrieval evaluation studies, 1967–2006. *Journal of the American Society for Information Science and Technology, 64*(4), 745–770. https://doi.org/10.1002/asi.22799

Knobloch-Westerwick, S., Johnson, B. K., & Westerwick, A. (2015). Confirmation bias in online searches: Impacts of selective exposure before an election on political attitude strength and shifts. *Journal of Computer-Mediated Communication, 20*(2), 171–187. https://doi.org/10.1111/jcc4.12105

Koskela, M., Luukkonen, P., Ruotsalo, T., Sjöberg, M., & Floréen, P. (2018). Proactive information retrieval by capturing search intent from primary task context. *ACM Transactions on Interactive Intelligent Systems (TiiS), 8*(3), 1–25. https://doi.org/10.1145/3150975

Langer, T., Sarin, R., & Weber, M. (2005). The retrospective evaluation of payment sequences: Duration neglect and peak-and-end effects. *Journal of Economic Behavior & Organization, 58*(1), 157–175. https://doi.org/10.1016/j.jebo.2004.01.001

Lin, J., Liu, W., Dai, X., Zhang, W., Li, S., Tang, R., He, X., Hao, J., & Yu, Y. (2021). A graph-enhanced click model for web search. In *Proceedings of the 44th International ACM SIGIR Conference on Research and Development in Information Retrieval* (pp. 1259–1268). ACM. https://doi.org/10.1145/3404835.3462895

Liu, J. (2021). Deconstructing search tasks in interactive information retrieval: A systematic review of task dimensions and predictors. *Information Processing & Management, 58*(3), 102522. https://doi.org/10.1016/j.ipm.2021.102522

Liu, J. (2022). Toward Cranfield-inspired reusability assessment in interactive information retrieval evaluation. *Information Processing & Management, 59*(5), 103007. https://doi.org/10.1016/j.ipm.2022.103007

Liu, C., Belkin, N. J., & Cole, M. J. (2012). Personalization of search results using interaction behaviors in search sessions. In *Proceedings of the 35th International ACM SIGIR Conference on Research and Development in Information Retrieval* (pp. 205–214). ACM. https://doi.org/10.1145/2348283.2348314

Liu, J., Mitsui, M., Belkin, N. J., & Shah, C. (2019). Task, information seeking intentions, and user behavior: Toward a multi-level understanding of Web search. In *Proceedings of the 2019 ACM SIGIR Conference on Human Information Interaction and Retrieval* (pp. 123–132). ACM. https://doi.org/10.1145/3295750.3298922

Liu, J., Sarkar, S., & Shah, C. (2020). Identifying and predicting the states of complex search tasks. In *Proceedings of the 2020 ACM SIGIR Conference on Human Information Interaction and Retrieval* (pp. 193–202). ACM. https://doi.org/10.1145/3343413.3377976

Liu, J., & Shah, C. (2019). Interactive IR user study design, evaluation, and reporting. *Synthesis Lectures on Information Concepts, Retrieval, and Services, 11*(2), i–93. https://doi.org/10.2200/S00923ED1V01Y201905ICR067

Mao, J., Liu, Y., Luan, H., Zhang, M., Ma, S., Luo, H., & Zhang, Y. (2017). Understanding and predicting usefulness judgment in web search. In *Proceedings of the 40th International ACM SIGIR Conference on Research and Development in Information Retrieval* (pp. 1169–1172). ACM. https://doi.org/10.1145/3077136.3080750

Mitsui, M., Liu, J., Belkin, N. J., & Shah, C. (2017). Predicting information seeking intentions from search behaviors. In *Proceedings of the 40th International ACM SIGIR Conference on Research and Development in Information Retrieval* (pp. 1121–1124). ACM. https://doi.org/10.1145/3077136.3080737

Mitsui, M., Liu, J., & Shah, C. (2018). How much is too much? Whole session vs. first query behaviors in task type prediction. In *Proceedings of the 41st International ACM SIGIR Conference on Research & Development in Information Retrieval* (pp. 1141–1144). ACM. https://doi.org/10.1145/3209978.3210105

Moffat, A., Scholer, F., & Thomas, P. (2012). Models and metrics: IR evaluation as a user process. In *Proceedings of the Seventeenth Australasian Document Computing Symposium* (pp. 47–54). https://doi.org/10.1145/2407085.2407092

Moffat, A., & Zobel, J. (2008). Rank-biased precision for measurement of retrieval effectiveness. *ACM Transactions on Information Systems (TOIS), 27*(1), 1–27. https://doi.org/10.1145/1416950.1416952

Montazeralghaem, A., Zamani, H., & Shakery, A. (2018). Theoretical analysis of interdependent constraints in pseudo-relevance feedback. In *Proceedings of the 41st International ACM SIGIR Conference on Research & Development in Information Retrieval* (pp. 1249–1252). ACM. https://doi.org/10.1145/3209978.3210156

Nickerson, R. S. (1998). Confirmation bias: A ubiquitous phenomenon in many guises. *Review of General Psychology, 2*(2), 175–220. https://doi.org/10.1037/1089-2680.2.2.175

Oliver, R. L. (1980). A cognitive model of the antecedents and consequences of satisfaction decisions. *Journal of Marketing Research, 17*(4), 460–469. https://doi.org/10.1177/002224378001700405

Radlinski, F., Bennett, P. N., Carterette, B., & Joachims, T. (2009). Redundancy, diversity and interdependent document relevance. In *ACM SIGIR Forum* (Vol. 43, No. 2, pp. 46–52). ACM. https://doi.org/10.1145/1670564.1670572

Rahman, A., & Wilson, M. L. (2015). Exploring opportunities to facilitate serendipity in search. In *Proceedings of the 38th International ACM SIGIR Conference on Research and Development in Information Retrieval* (pp. 939–942). ACM. https://doi.org/10.1145/2766462.2767783

Redelmeier, D. A., Katz, J., & Kahneman, D. (2003). Memories of colonoscopy: A randomized trial. *Pain, 104*(1–2), 187–194. https://doi.org/10.1016/S0304-3959(03)00003-4

Rieger, A., Draws, T., Theune, M., & Tintarev, N. (2021). This item might reinforce your opinion: Obfuscation and labeling of search results to mitigate confirmation bias. In *Proceedings of the 32nd ACM Conference on Hypertext and Social Media* (pp. 189–199). ACM. https://doi.org/10.1145/3465336.3475101

Schneider, S., Stone, A. A., Schwartz, J. E., & Broderick, J. E. (2011). Peak and end effects in patients' daily recall of pain and fatigue: A within-subjects analysis. *The Journal of Pain, 12*(2), 228–235. https://doi.org/10.1016/j.jpain.2010.07.001

Scholer, F., Kelly, D., Wu, W. C., Lee, H. S., & Webber, W. (2013). The effect of threshold priming and need for cognition on relevance calibration and assessment. In *Proceedings of the 36th International ACM SIGIR Conference on Research and Development in Information Retrieval* (pp. 623–632). ACM. https://doi.org/10.1145/2484028.2484090

Schwartz, B., Ward, A., Monterosso, J., Lyubomirsky, S., White, K., & Lehman, D. R. (2002). Maximizing versus satisficing: Happiness is a matter of choice. *Journal of Personality and Social Psychology, 83*(5), 1178. https://doi.org/10.1037/0022-3514.83.5.1178

Shah, C. (2018). Information fostering-being proactive with information seeking and retrieval: Perspective paper. In *Proceedings of the 2018 International ACM SIGIR Conference on Human Information Interaction & Retrieval* (pp. 62–71). ACM. https://doi.org/10.1145/3176349.3176389

Shen, S., Hu, B., Chen, W., & Yang, Q. (2012). Personalized click model through collaborative filtering. In *Proceedings of the Fifth ACM International Conference on Web Search and Data Mining* (pp. 323–332). ACM. https://doi.org/10.1145/2124295.2124336

Simon, H. A. (1955). A behavioral model of rational choice. *The Quarterly Journal of Economics, 69*(1), 99–118. https://doi.org/10.2307/1884852

Thaler, R. H. (2016). Behavioral economics: Past, present, and future. *American Economic Review, 106*(7), 1577–1600. https://doi.org/10.1257/aer.106.7.1577

Trautmann, S. T., & van de Kuilen, G. (2012). Prospect theory or construal level theory? Diminishing sensitivity vs. psychological distance in risky decisions. *Acta Psychologica, 139*(1), 254–260. https://doi.org/10.1016/j.actpsy.2011.08.006

Tversky, A., & Kahneman, D. (1974). Judgment under uncertainty: Heuristics and biases: Biases in judgments reveal some heuristics of thinking under uncertainty. *Science, 185*(4157), 1124–1131. https://doi.org/10.1126/science.185.4157.1124

Tversky, A., & Kahneman, D. (1985). The framing of decisions and the psychology of choice. In *Behavioral Decision Making* (pp. 25–41). Springer.

Tversky, A., & Kahneman, D. (1991). Loss aversion in riskless choice: A reference-dependent model. *The Quarterly Journal of Economics, 106*(4), 1039–1061. https://doi.org/10.2307/2937956

Tversky, A., & Kahneman, D. (1992). Advances in prospect theory: Cumulative representation of uncertainty. *Journal of Risk and Uncertainty, 5*(4), 297–323. https://doi.org/10.1007/BF00122574

Venkatesh, V., & Goyal, S. (2010). Expectation disconfirmation and technology adoption: Polynomial modeling and response surface analysis. *MIS Quarterly, 34*(2), 281–303. https://doi.org/10.2307/20721428

Voorhees, E. M. (2001). The philosophy of information retrieval evaluation. In *Workshop of the Cross-Language Evaluation Forum for European Languages* (pp. 355–370). Springer.

Wakker, P., & Tversky, A. (1993). An axiomatization of cumulative prospect theory. *Journal of Risk and Uncertainty, 7*(2), 147–175. https://doi.org/10.1007/BF01065812

Wang, X., Golbandi, N., Bendersky, M., Metzler, D., & Najork, M. (2018). Position bias estimation for unbiased learning to rank in personal search. In *Proceedings of the Eleventh ACM International Conference on Web Search and Data Mining* (pp. 610–618). ACM. https://doi.org/10.1145/3159652.3159732

Wedell, D. H., & Pettibone, J. C. (1996). Using judgments to understand decoy effects in choice. *Organizational Behavior and Human Decision Processes, 67*(3), 326–344. https://doi.org/10.1006/obhd.1996.0083

White, R. W., Dumais, S. T., & Teevan, J. (2009). Characterizing the influence of domain expertise on web search behavior. In *Proceedings of the second ACM International Conference on Web Search and Data Mining* (pp. 132–141). ACM. https://doi.org/10.1145/1498759.1498819

Workman, M. (2018). An empirical study of social media exchanges about a controversial topic: Confirmation bias and participant characteristics. *The Journal of Social Media in Society, 7*(1), 381–400.

Wu, L., Liu, P., Chen, X., Hu, W., Fan, X., & Chen, Y. (2020). Decoy effect in food appearance, traceability, and price: Case of consumer preference for pork hindquarters. *Journal of Behavioral and Experimental Economics, 87*, 101553. https://doi.org/10.1016/j.socec.2020.101553

Xing, Q., Liu, Y., Nie, J. Y., Zhang, M., Ma, S., & Zhang, K. (2013). Incorporating user preferences into click models. In *Proceedings of the 22nd ACM international Conference on Information & Knowledge Management* (pp. 1301–1310). ACM. https://doi.org/10.1145/2505515.2505704

Zhai, C., Cohen, W. W., & Lafferty, J. (2015). Beyond independent relevance: Methods and evaluation metrics for subtopic retrieval. In *ACM SIGIR Forum* (Vol. 49, No. 1, pp. 2–9). ACM. https://doi.org/10.1145/2795403.2795405

Zhang, Y., Liu, X., & Zhai, C. (2017). Information retrieval evaluation as search simulation: A general formal framework for IR evaluation. In *Proceedings of the ACM SIGIR International Conference on Theory of Information Retrieval* (pp. 193–200). ACM. https://doi.org/10.1145/3121050.3121070

Zhang, Y., & Zhai, C. (2016). A sequential decision formulation of the interface card model for interactive IR. In *Proceedings of the 39th International ACM SIGIR conference on Research and Development in Information Retrieval* (pp. 85–94). ACM. https://doi.org/10.1145/2911451.2911543

Part III
Toward a Behavioral Economics Approach

Chapter 6
Behavioral Economics in IR

Abstract Following previous discussions on extending rational assumptions and formal user models, this chapter introduces the research progress on factors associated with human bounded rationality, especially cognitive and perceptual biases, in IR and other closely related fields, including information seeking and recommender systems. By explaining and synthesizing the findings and methods extracted from empirical research on bounded rational IR, we hope to (1) clarify the existing progress and achievements that the research community has already made toward developing and applying intelligent bias-aware search support and, more importantly, (2) identify existing gaps, open challenges, and unsolved problems that may require further investigations. In addition, the knowledge learned from previous studies that leverage the theories from behavioral economics in user modeling, re-ranking, and simulation-based evaluation of algorithm performances can inform the development of our behavioral economics research agenda on bias-aware user modeling, search system design, and evaluation.

6.1 Introduction

In contrast to what most formal models assume, real-world users are susceptible to a variety of human biases and heuristics, which can lead to bounded rational decisions that systematically deviate from rational decisions and optimal outcomes (Agosto, 2002; Kahneman, 2003; Simon, 1955). Following the discussions on extending rational assumptions and formal user models in Chap. 5, Chap. 6 introduces the research progress on factors associated with human bounded rationality, especially cognitive and perceptual biases, in IR and other closely related fields (e.g., information seeking behavior, recommender systems). By explaining and synthesizing the methods, findings, and insights from empirical research on bounded rational IR, we hope to clarify the advances and progress that the research community has already made toward achieving intelligent bias-aware search support and, more importantly, identify existing gaps, open challenges, and unsolved problems that require further investigations. In addition, the information seeking, retrieval, and recommendation studies that leverage insights from behavioral economics in user modeling and

J. Liu, *A Behavioral Economics Approach to Interactive Information Retrieval*, The Information Retrieval Series 48, https://doi.org/10.1007/978-3-031-23229-9_6

search evaluation can inform the development of our behavioral economics approach or research agenda on bias-aware IR and the associated specific research questions (which speaks on the focus of Chap. 7).

This chapter adopts the classification scheme from the previous chapter (i.e., *pre-search* stage, *within-search* stage, *post-search* stage) to organize empirical studies and data-driven experiments on this topic and categorizes human biases and heuristics based on the stage where they are formed or generate their main behavioral impacts. For instance, we categorize confirmation bias into the pre-search stage group as it is often associated with existing beliefs, expectations, and preferences established before a decision-making process is initiated (e.g., Nickerson, 1998), despite the fact that this bias also affects users' in situ relevance judgments and perceptions of search interactions. Nevertheless, although the underlying mechanism of anchoring bias is similar to that of the confirmation bias in search interactions, we put it into the within-search group as it is usually related to the initially encountered information items and opinions at the beginning of search sessions (Caputo, 2014). Adopting this typology used in Chap. 5 can allow us to contrast the possible extensions of formal models and assumptions with existing research findings on bounded rationality in IR and thus further clarify the progress we have already made within the same problem space as well as the specific open research problems that we still need to investigate and resolve in future research.

In general, existing studies have examined different aspects of bias-aware information seeking and retrieval under divergent research goals, such as describing the characteristics of human biases and related contextual factors that trigger the biases, investigating the impacts of biases and heuristics on search behavior and search system evaluation, as well as implementing reasonable recommendations, interventions, and nudging techniques for mitigating the negative impacts caused by human biases on search effectiveness and search experiences (Draws et al., 2021; Rieger et al., 2021). In addition, researchers have also investigated the effects of human biases and heuristics in diverse search tasks and environments, such as health information seeking, sociopolitical information evaluation, as well as general Web search and document evaluation tasks (Azzopardi, 2021). Note that some of the biases and general frameworks identified in Chap. 4 (e.g., reference dependence, loss aversion bias, principle of satisficing) may cause "global impacts" on user decisions and judgments at multiple stages of search interactions. For instance, the effects of existing beliefs and previous experience under similar tasks as reference points can shape users' evaluations of the search costs and rewards in both *single-query-based* search iterations and *whole-session* retrospective evaluations. Human biases like this will be mentioned across multiple relevant stages and sections in Chap. 6.

Regarding the logical structure of this book, we hope that the discussions on the insights and empirical evidences from individual studies on bounded rational information seeking, IR, and recommendation can further enrich our preliminary discussions on the gaps between formal models and widely examined human biases reported in Chap. 3 and partially illustrate the possible extensions of formal model assumptions explained in Chap. 5. In addition, research advances synthesized and summarized in Chap. 3 will also shed light on the discussions on future research paths, available methods, and challenges in Chap. 7.

6.2 From Rational Agents to Boundedly Rational Decision Makers

Instead of being perfectly rational, users often engage in search interactions and document judgments with a series of pre-search beliefs, biases, and expectations (Azzopardi, 2021; White, 2013). The information seeking and search strategies are often triggered by and associated with overall information overload and biased exposure of information items that are from different sources or cover varying topics and opinions (Baeza-Yates, 2018). When facing information-intensive complex decision-making scenarios and uncertain solutions space, people usually develop and rely on mental shortcuts for information seeking and processing, which often lead to efficient searches and quick decisions without initiating slow effortful cognitive processes or exhausting all accessible actions. In general, when evaluating options and making decisions (including search decision-making) under the impacts of cognitive biases, heuristics, and the operations of System 1, people are more likely to make mistakes and miss out optimal outcomes. However, it is critical to acknowledge the positive effects of human biases and bounded rational decision-making strategies given the common constraints in cognitive resources and environments. Regarding this, researchers found that fast and frugal heuristics that people adopt often result in good decisions in a wide range of problematic situations, despite their potential negative impacts on the quality and accuracy of each specific decisions (Gigerenzer & Brighton, 2009). Part of the reason is that cognitive biases can simplify the overall process of decision-making and reduce the amount of risk and uncertainty that needs to be cognitively processed and computed during option comparisons (Todd & Gigerenzer, 2000).

The cognitively biased or boundedly rational decision-making strategies have also been examined and conceptualized from a rational perspective. For instance, Lieder and Griffiths (2020) sought to accommodate human biases and heuristics in existing decision-making framework and augment classic rational models developed in economics and behavioral science. They argue that the adoption of mental shortcuts and biased decisions reflects a smart strategy under situational constraints and is essentially consistent with the rational use of limited resources, which is an underlying unifying principle that governs diverse approaches and models of human decision-making. Within the unified framework, we could reconcile complex, rational, decision-making skills with diverse types of biases and irrationality under *resource-rational analysis* (Lieder & Griffiths, 2020). Similarly, Bhui et al. (2021) focused on an information-theoretic formalization of cognitive resources and utilized it in characterizing widespread cognitive biases, such as reference dependence and stochastic choice. The researchers argued that while human decisions governed by

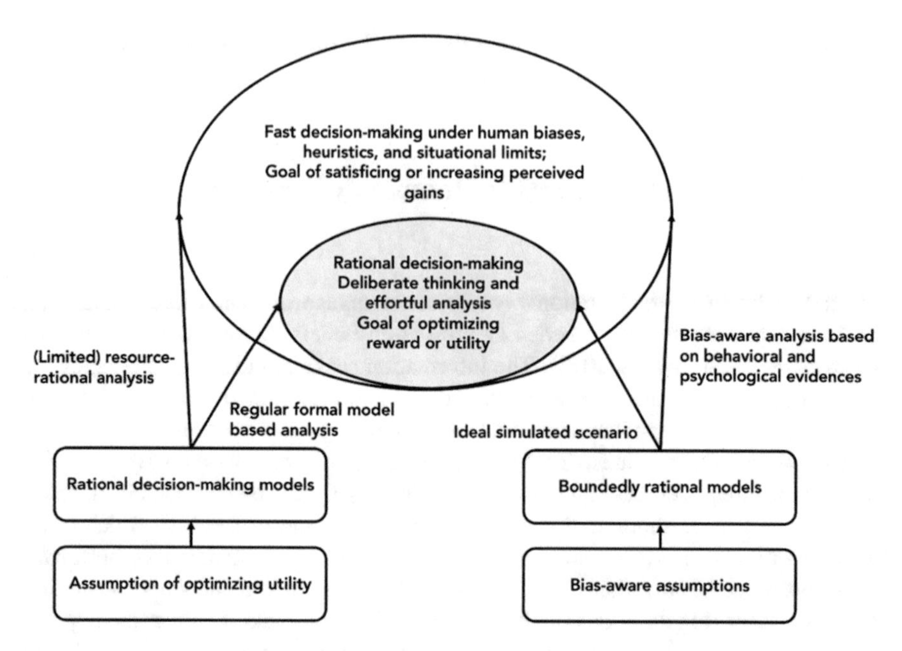

Fig. 6.1 Rational model and bounded rational approach

cognitive biases and heuristics seem to be irrational, they may be associated with an intrinsic rational solution to the problem of limited resources. Despite the fundamental differences in the analytical framework and perspective, Lieder and Griffiths (2020)'s resource-rational analysis approach is similar to the general behavioral economics approach (Kahneman, 2003; Tversky & Kahneman, 1992) in that they both highlight the underlying implicit connections between rational models and boundedly rational decisions under cognitive and perceptual constraints and speak to the possibility and importance of accommodating and reconciling these two largely different approaches under one extended, unified theoretical umbrella of human behavior and judgment. Apart from traditional human judgment and decision-making studies, research on information seeking, retrieval, and search evaluation would also benefit from the unified theoretical framework.

Figure 6.1 illustrates the difference and connections between general rational models and bounded rational approach to analyzing human decision-making. The rational assumptions behind formal user models and empirical evidences on decision-making activities under human biases are presented in Chaps. 2 and 4, respectively. In the context of information seeking and retrieval, while rational approach may consider users' search decision-making activities under the goal of optimizing reward is common and consistent with most real-world cases, the behavioral economics or bounded rational approach may bring more irrational decisions and biased choices to researchers' attention. Within the behavioral economics framework, the perfectly rational decision-making may be considered as an ideal simulated scenario that are rare in real-life settings and could be extended by incorporating more dynamic user characteristics, such as cognitive and perceptual biases, individual preferences, and situational limits. With respect to bounded rational decisions under the influence of human biases, although behavioral economics researchers would consider them as common scenarios and may analyze them under specific bias types and task scenarios, resource-rational analytical framework may frame them as special rational decision circumstances, where people try to maximize their accessible utility under the constraints of cognitive resources, time, and informational support from the search system and environment.

In light of the above discussions on the connection between rational agents and boundedly rational decision makers, we can better understand the possible rational roots of seemingly irrational decisions and also explain the potential research paths and approaches that could bring formal user models, system evaluation metrics, and optimization algorithms closer to real-world information searchers and their interaction experiences.

6.3 Pre-search Stage

Human biases could occur and be established internally before decision-making activities actually start. In information searching, pre-search biases and heuristics could be triggered by users' previous information seeking experiences (especially the ones under similar tasks and information needs), existing beliefs, as well as other people's opinions and actions. These biases are different from several widely examined external factors, such as rank positions, features of search result snippets, as well as query-document relevance, and can also affect users' in situ relevance judgments, search behaviors, and retrospective evaluation.

In IR, people often formulate queries and engage in search sessions with pre-search beliefs and hypotheses. During the process of search and document judgments, due to the impacts of confirmation bias, users may actively search for the results that confirm their existing beliefs and hypotheses and discount or disregard information that is not consistent with their beliefs (Klayman & Ha, 1987; Nickerson, 1998; White, 2013). As discussed in Chap. 4, retrieved documents that confirm a user's existing hypotheses can help the user avoid the anticipated loss associated with the *cognitive dissonance* in rejecting current hypotheses and the potential *efforts* in establishing new hypotheses and beliefs. Thus, users' rejection and discounts on disconfirming evidences and conflicting results in search interactions can also be considered as a reflection of loss aversion bias.

Investigating the role and impacts of confirmation bias is critical not only for characterizing boundedly rational decisions in information seeking but also for explaining the cultural and societal impacts of online information platforms. One of the key platforms on which polarization of views and confirmation bias often occur is social media sites (Bail et al., 2018; Cinelli et al., 2021). Modgil et al. (2021) studied the role of social media in polarizing users' views and the spreading of misinformation on climate change, politics, and the COVID-19 pandemic and examined the role of users' confirmation bias in *social media induced polarization* (SMIP). The researchers conducted a thematic analysis of data collected from 35 participants engaging in supply chain information processing tasks and found that users' choices of social media platforms, prior experiences, and algorithmic personalization on social media usually trigger and reinforce confirmation bias and contribute to the development of *echo chambers* in work tasks. Based on empirical findings, Modgil et al. (2021) argued that members of online communities need to actively reflect on and reexamine their preexisting beliefs and biases as a way to proactively address or mitigate the possible negative effects and investigate the reinforcement mechanism between their interactions with social media information and their deep-seated belief system.

Xu et al. (2022) examined information exposure effects and confirmation bias in the context of COVID-19 vaccination. Based on the results from three national surveys, researchers found that misinformation exposure, existing attitudes toward vaccination, and misperceptions reinforced each other over time. In particular, due to confirmation bias, people's attitudes toward the COVID-19 vaccine reinforced themselves through their misperceptions. Regarding users' interaction with political online information, Knobloch-Westerwick et al. (2020) examined the impact of confirmation bias from a cognitive dissonance perspective. They found that selective exposure in viewing political information is greater when the presented political messages were aligned with the user's preexisting political attitudes and that greater cognitive reflection, greater need for cognition, and worse affective state can strengthen a user's existing confirmation bias and lead to the phenomenon of echo chamber in information interaction.

White and Horvitz (2015) studied the ways in which beliefs about the efficacy of medical interventions are affected by searchers' exposure to information retrieved by Web search engines. They found that users' pre-search beliefs significantly affect people's examinations of search results and people tend to spend longer dwell time on Web contents that are consistent with their pre-search beliefs and expectations. Suzuki and Yamamoto (2020) investigated the interactions between confirmation bias and Web search behavior and found that participants under the influence of confirmation bias browsed the top ranked search results only, explicitly looked for information that supports their existing opinions, and completed assigned health search tasks quickly. On the system side, researchers also found that in online health information searching, users' pre-search biases and misbeliefs are usually confirmed and reinforced by the misinformation presented in search result snippets on SERPs (Bondarenko et al., 2021; Cacciatore, 2021; Hashavit et al., 2021; Meppelink et al., 2019).

The empirical research discussed above highlights the ubiquitous impacts of confirmation bias and demonstrates its dynamic connections to related cognitive phenomena (e.g., cognitive dissonance, echo chambers) and information biases generated by personalization algorithms. Based on these empirical findings, Fig. 6.2 presents the effects of users' confirmation bias in their interactions with search systems and illustrates the interaction between users' existing beliefs and retrieval algorithms. As the figure shows, users' confirmation biases motivate them

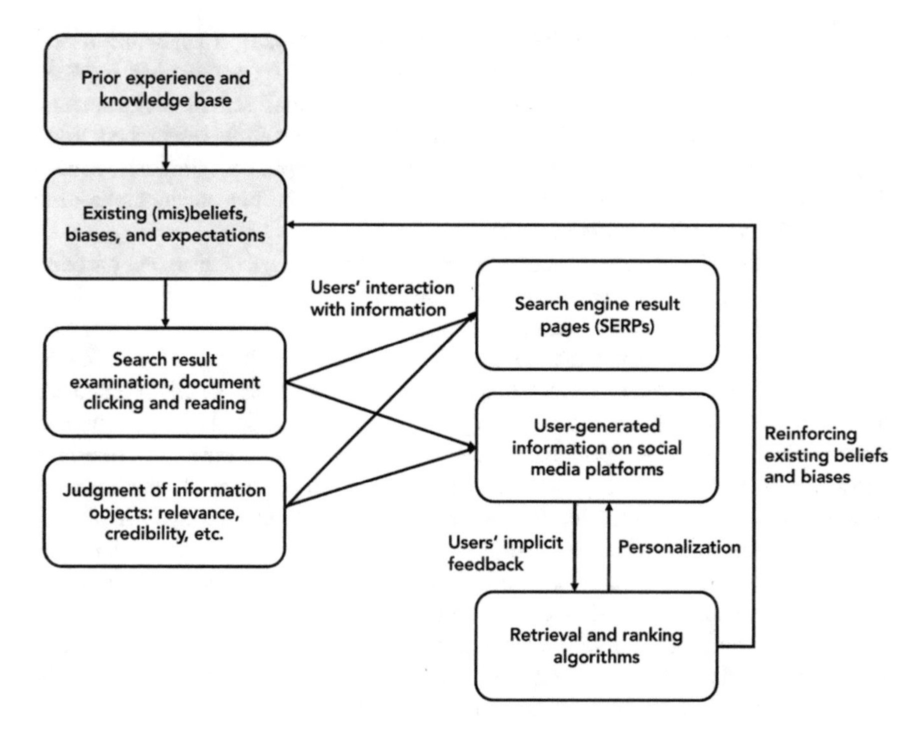

Fig. 6.2 Confirmation bias in user-information interactions

to actively search for and collect information that confirms existing beliefs and hypotheses. Meanwhile, users' actions on the confirming documents and pages (e.g., search engine snippet examination, document clicking and reading) are also employed by the personalization algorithms as implicit feedback in adjusting search ranking and recommendation strategies for the next search iteration. As a result, documents and Web pages that confirm users' existing beliefs may be considered as relevant and obtain more exposure on SERPs, which, in turn, cause the echo chamber effect and further reinforce users' pre-searching beliefs and expectations.

Similar to confirmation bias, status quo bias can also be considered as part of the pre-search stage cognitive factor and is established based on prior beliefs and experiences. In human-information interaction, the status quo could be an existing information system applied in the workplace, current information seeking and search strategies, as well as a specific set of sites and information sources that users frequently use for certain types of tasks. In information systems studies, researchers suggest that introducing the *status quo bias perspective* (SQBP) into empirical studies can provide unique insights into the implicit biases in users' decision-making and help system designers better overcome user resistance to new information systems, tools, and strategies (Fan et al., 2015; Lee & Joshi, 2017; Li et al., 2016; Nel & Boshoff, 2020). Although studies on status quo bias in information seeking and retrieval are not as common as they are in management information systems research, it might still be valuable to employ SQBP in analyzing users' search and evaluation behaviors, especially when they are transitioning between different retrieval systems, user search interfaces, and overall search environments. Studying users' status quo bias in different dimensions may allow researchers to go beyond existing cost-reward-based formal models and simplified optimization functions (e.g., Azzopardi, 2014; Zhang & Zhai, 2016) and further understanding the impacts of pre-search cognitive factors.

Besides, users' pre-search reference points and biases can also be partially characterized by *expectation disconfirmation theory* (EDT), which has also been widely adopted in explaining users' acceptance of new information systems and predicting their levels of satisfaction (Fan & Suh, 2014; Hsieh et al., 2010; Oliver, 1980; Venkatesh & Goyal, 2010). Compared to the existing beliefs and preferences behind confirmation biases (e.g., existing attitudes toward COVID-19 vaccine and climate change; previous political views before reviewing tweets on American politics), users' pre-search expectations regarding system performance and interface layout may be more dynamic, flexible, and sensitive to the changes in search intentions, search behaviors, and retrospective evaluations of search systems. A series of information systems research demonstrate that the disconfirmation of users' pre-adoption expectation, rather than the absolute final performance or outcome, significantly affects their acceptance and intention of continuance on new systems (e.g., Bhattacherjee, 2001; Lankton & McKnight, 2012; Oliver, 1980). The status of expectation disconfirmation involves both pre-adoption experiences and also in situ perceived performances influenced by users' gains and losses in interactions with information systems.

In the context of information seeking and retrieval, Liu and Shah (2019) revised the traditional user models built upon final search outcomes and post-search perceptions and investigated the role and impacts of expectation disconfirmation in Web search sessions. Specifically, the researchers studied task difficulty expectation disconfirmation, which is operationalized as the difference between pre-search estimated difficulty and post-search experienced or retrospectively evaluated task difficulty (Δ task difficulty). Based on the findings from a controlled user study, Liu and Shah (2019) demonstrated that unexpectedly difficult task can lead to significant decreases in users' perceived levels of search success and major increases in perceived time pressure in search sessions. Also, the size and direction of task difficulty expectation disconfirmation (e.g., surpass pre-search expectation or lower than expectation) significantly affect users' Web search behavior, such as dwell time on Web pages, query reformulation strategies, search result snippet examination, and clicking behavior.

Complex search tasks usually involve different task dimensions or facets (Li & Belkin, 2008; Liu, 2022), which may be associated with different aspects of users' in situ expectations regarding the search process, interface layout, and the system's retrieval performance. These different aspects of expectations and associated disconfirmation statuses may have varying impacts on users' search strategies, document judgment thresholds, as well as whole-session experience. Liu and Shah's research (2019) indicates the value and importance of integrating EDT into the study

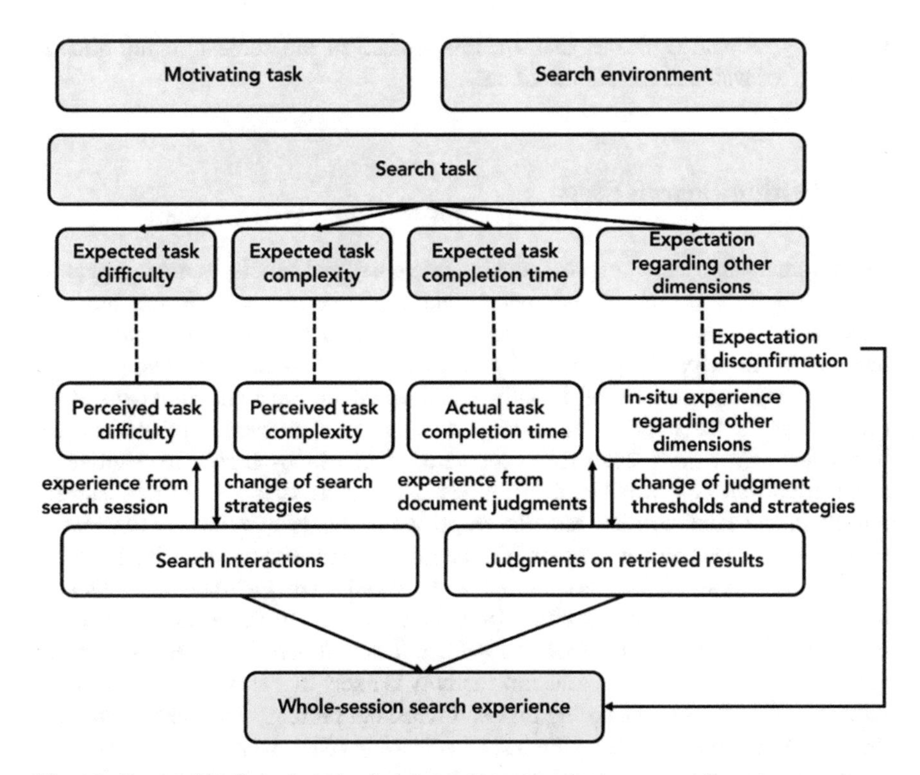

Fig. 6.3 Expectation disconfirmation in information retrieval

of Web search evaluation and serves as the initial step toward exploring other aspects (e.g., task complexity, perceived knowledge gain, ease of use) and broader impacts of expectation disconfirmation in IR (see Fig. 6.3). With the prediction models developed in the study, future IR systems could leverage the knowledge about users' in situ expectation disconfirmation status in developing proactive search support, especially when users encounter unexpected difficult and complex search tasks (Liu et al., 2020).

The human biases and heuristics identified at the pre-search stage highlight the initial reference points and biases that users may have in mind before engaging in interactive search sessions. Different types of references may generate different sizes and directions of impacts on users' search behavior and document judgments and overall interaction experiences. Also, different types of biases may have different levels of *sensitivity* to the changes (particularly the perceived losses and costs) in search interactions and the system-side biases in information exposure associated with retrieval and ranking algorithms. During search processes, some of the pre-search biases and preferences may also be reinforced by the personalized search result ranking and recommendations and affect users' search decision-making in subsequent query segments. In the following section, we will discuss the biases and boundedly rational decisions that are investigated in the context of information seeking, retrieval, and recommendation.

6.4 Within-Search Stage

Apart from the impacts from pre-searching references and beliefs, users' information search activities, document judgments, and whole-session experiences are also affected by a series of human biases and heuristics triggered by search result features, in situ reference points, and perceptions of search gains and losses.

Regarding the impacts of initially encountered information, Shokouhi et al. (2015) studied the implicit anchoring effect in users' relevance judgments and found that when the previously encountered document is highly relevant or to some extent relevant, it will affect the relevance labels assigned to the document ranked in the next position and the implicit thresholds of relevance judgment. Furthermore, based on natural search behavior data, researchers also found that the implicit relevance judgments inferred from dwell time measures can also be influenced by the anchoring effect (Shokouhi et al., 2015). Similarly, Thomas et al. (2022) investigated the role of cognitive factors in large-scale crowd labeling and found that a user's current labeling activity is likely to match the previous label, indicating the effect of anchoring bias and threshold priming. They also found that this anchoring effect in evaluation tasks tends to decrease over time as users make more judgments on example documents and better calibrate their own scales and thresholds. This impact of anchoring bias on human judgment and labeling has also been examined and empirically confirmed in other crowdsourcing-based experimental settings (e.g., Draws et al., 2021; Eickhoff, 2018).

Inspired by behavioral economics research on cognitive biases in human judgments, Chen et al. (2022) took a step forward by examining the extent to which users' judgments and search decisions are biased toward the initially encountered search results and also incorporating this anchoring bias into the design of new *anchoring-aware* evaluation metrics. Focusing on the widely studied problem of query-level search evaluation, Chen et al. (2022) integrate anchoring effect parameter into the user model behind evaluation metrics based on two assumptions regarding document utility: (1) the utility obtained from the first document on SERP only depends on the quality of the document per se, and (2) for the documents at rank 2 or below, the document utility perceived by a user not only depends on the quality of the document (e.g., relevance) but is also associated with the quality of the previously examined document. In this sense, the documents ranked above the current one being evaluated may serve as the anchoring point. According to Chen et al. (2022), this document utility model can be written as:

$$rel'_i(q) = \begin{cases} rel_i(q) & (i=1) \\ \partial \cdot rel_{i-1}(q) + rel_i(q) & (i>1) \end{cases} \tag{6.1}$$

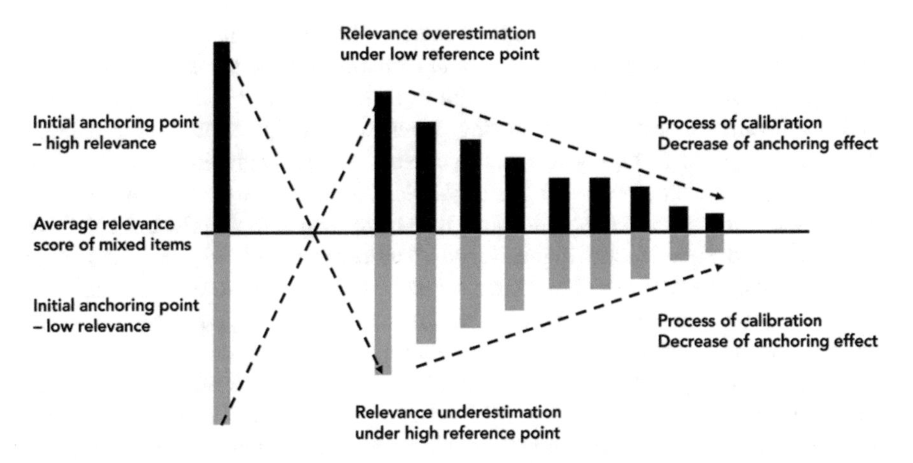

Fig. 6.4 Anchoring effect in a sequence of document judgments

where $rel_i(q)$ refers to the relevance level of the search result on i-th rank. Based on this anchoring-aware document utility model, the researchers proposed anchoring-aware metrics (AM) for a series of offline evaluation metrics, such as ERR, precision, RBP, and INST. They meta-evaluated the quality of these AM-based metrics against their corresponding original metrics with fine-tuned parameters in terms of the correlations with users' query-level search satisfaction. Based on the experimental results on a publicly available Web search dataset, researchers found that the AM-based measures outperformed all original offline evaluation metrics, indicating that taking anchoring effect into consideration can help researchers better understand users' own perceptions and evaluations of search experiences (Chen et al., 2022). Future studies could extend the anchoring-aware utility models and evaluation metrics to the session level and investigate the impacts of potential anchoring points developed at initial queries on users' retrospective whole-session evaluation. For this, the modeling and representation of anchoring points may need to consider both rank positions and query orders and examine the possible variations in their weight distributions across task types.

Based on the aforementioned empirical evidences on anchoring bias and anchoring-aware evaluation in IR, Fig. 6.4 illustrates the anchoring effect discussed above and the process of users' calibration and adjustment of relevance thresholds toward the average relevance score or expert assessment of document relevance. Similar patterns might also be found in users' judgments of other evaluation dimensions. Similar to the studies on anchoring effect introduced above, Scholer et al. (2013) studied the impact of reviewing different degrees of relevant documents on people's evaluation and calibration of relevance thresholds in mind. In the experiments, participants in different groups were presented documents of varying relevance as their respective initial reference points. Then, all of them were asked to evaluate a common set of documents of mixed relevance levels. The results demonstrate that due to the impact of *threshold priming*, participants who started their judgment sessions with only non-relevant documents tend to assign significantly higher relevance scores to the following documents, compared to the participants who were exposed to highly relevant documents at the beginning of evaluation. Moreover, researchers found that this threshold priming bias might be mitigated by the *need for cognition* as the participants who enjoy engaging in effortful cognitive tasks achieved significantly higher level of agreement with expert assessors in relevance judgment, indicating better calibrated relevance thresholds and less impacts from in situ cognitive biases. The advance in knowledge regarding anchoring bias, threshold priming, and need for cognition can enhance our understanding of users' document judgments and the implicit changing thresholds and enables researchers and system designers to debias users' judgments and improve the quality of implicit feedback for facilitating more balanced and accurate IR personalization.

In addition to the human biases and heuristics discussed above, users' query-level or within-SERP evaluations, especially their perceptions and judgments of search result snippets, are also affected by decoy effect and framing effect. Specifically, for example, Eickhoff (2018) indicates that users' preferences over two search results could be altered without changing the nature of the presented results. Instead, this change could happen merely with one additional information item being added to the SERP. When two non-relevant items were presented with a relevant result, but one of the non-relevant items was clearly inferior to the other one on a salient dimension, the assessor tends to overestimate the relevance of the dominant non-relevant document. Eickhoff's crowdsourcing study (2018) shares a similar experimental setup with many of the behavioral economics studies on decoy effect (e.g., Highhouse, 1996; Wedell & Pettibone, 1996; Wu & Cosguner, 2020) and confirms the behavioral impacts of decoy in relevance judgment. From a reference dependence perspective, the similarity between the two non-relevant items motivates the user to consider one of the items as a qualified reference point or similar case when evaluating the other information item or document. Then, since there is a clear dominant item among the two similar items, a relatively low reference point can easily generate a major perceived gain or overestimated level of relevance in the evaluation of the dominant non-relevant item, which in turn leads to the changes of the user's in situ document preference.

In Chap. 5, apart from the direct impacts of decoy effect on relevance labeling, we also discussed other possible dimensions on which users' judgments could be influenced by potential decoy items, such as document *usefulness* and *credibility*. Besides, the overall behavioral impacts of decoy may also be moderated by the *rank positions* of all items involved, as users tend to pay less attentions to lower ranked documents in general. This rank position bias may weaken the predicted decoy effect when the decoy and dominant items are ranked in relatively low positions. To enhance our understanding of decoy effect in search evaluation and interaction, future studies need to further explore the implicit dimensions of search result surrogates and documents that may trigger decoy effect and also investigate the potential moderating effects of rank positions, task nature, and user characteristics.

In addition to decoy effect, users may also make different search decisions on the same information due to the variations in the ways in which the information is framed and presented (i.e., framing effect). For instance, researchers found that in Web search, the genre in which diverse sources of information and documents are presented will affect the extent to which diverse perspectives and opinions are represented in the retrieval output under a query (Novin & Meyers, 2017a). Different genres and framing of search results may also lead to divergent perceptions of the same topic (Novin & Meyers, 2017b). Apart from the document genre, different forms of result presentations may also lead to different perceptions and user interaction patterns. For instance, in click model studies, researchers found that vertical blocks on SERPs usually appear to be more salient and attract more attention from users compared to the regular organic search results in SERP browsing processes (Chen et al., 2012; Chuklin et al., 2015). With the same or similar contents, results that are presented as verticals (e.g., videos, images, answer cards) may be more likely to be viewed and clicked and even receive a higher relevance score in document judgments. Also, the search results that are presented close to verticals should also be assigned higher weights in the estimation of examination and click probabilities (Liu et al., 2015). Capra et al. (2013) investigated the impacts of augmenting text-based search result surrogates with images extracted from related Web pages. Based on the results from two user studies on evaluating search results with images, researchers found that re-framing results with the support of good images can cause small, insignificant benefits in judgment quality and increased judgment time compared to the traditional framing (i.e., text-only surrogates). However, on the SERPs where search results had diverse and potentially confusing meaning, users achieved significantly higher click precision on surrogates with images. Similarly, Arguello and Capra (2012) examined users' search behaviors in aggregated search that involves different specialized search services or verticals. The study results demonstrate that the behavioral impacts of images on SERP depend on the topical relevance of the regular Web search results. When text-based search results are not relevant or merely marginally relevant to the task, the results that are framed as images have significant effects on users' search tactics. These results indicate that different ways of framing search results and surrogates in IR could lead to significant variations in users' perceptions, clicking behavior, quality of relevance judgments, and overall search performances.

Taking a step back from the specific biases and mental shortcuts introduced above, Liu and Han (2020) investigated the problem of search behavior and user satisfaction prediction from a general *reference-dependence* perspective. Specifically, inspired by the behavioral economics research and gain- and loss-based evaluations and decision-making (e.g., Kahneman, 2003; Tversky & Kahneman, 1991), Liu and Han (2020) simulated a series of reference points in search sessions. Then, for each traditional outcome-based evaluation metric, such as dwell time on Web pages, number of clicks, precision, and nDCG scores, the researchers developed the corresponding reference-dependent metrics using different simulated reference points, respectively. The simulated reference points for each behavior or evaluation metric, built upon behavioral economics experiments on reference dependence, peak-end rule, and recency effects in decision-making, include:

- *Reference 1*: peak value up to the current point of search (*Peak value*)
- *Reference 2*: end value (or the value from the most recent search iteration) up to the current point of search (*End value or recency effect*)
- *Reference 3*: average value up to the current point of search (*Common baseline*)
- *Reference 4*: (Reference 1 + Reference 2)/2 (*Combination of peak and end values*)

Based on the psychology-informed simulated reference points, researchers developed gain- and loss-based evaluation metrics based on the delta value between the current value or absolute outcome of an evaluation measure and one of the corresponding reference points. Therefore, for each evaluation metric, Liu and Han (2020) obtained four reference-dependent evaluation metrics. In statistical analysis and prediction modeling, the researchers found that the loss-based evaluation measures (e.g., when the delta value is negative) are associated with significantly larger changes in query-level user satisfaction, compared to the same size of gain-based evaluation measures. This result confirms the effect of *loss aversion* in Web search evaluation and highlights the asymmetric variations in search satisfaction sensitivity on the two sides of reference points. Furthermore, the researchers developed a set of experimental prediction models based on the reference-dependence measures and evaluate their performances against classic final outcome-based prediction models. The results demonstrate that applying the reference-dependence approach can significantly improve the performance in predicting several aspects of search interactions, such as click depth, dwell time in query segment, average relevance score of documents on SERP, and number of clicks in top five rank positions. Also, the study result indicates that the prediction performance of reference-dependence models varies across search tasks of different types. Thus, future research may need to further examine the hidden heterogeneity and boundaries in reference-dependence effects in complex search tasks.

Following Liu and Han's (2020) reference-dependence approach, Brown and Liu (2022) explored the problem of early predicting session-level search decisions and user satisfaction, with the ultimate goal of achieving early identification of whole-session search strategies and offering proactive search support when needed (Shah, 2018). Specifically, the researchers developed reference-dependent early prediction models based on a series of simulated reference points in first query segments of search sessions and evaluated the model performance against that of the non-reference traditional models. Based on the experimental results obtained from datasets of diverse types, this study demonstrated that the reference-dependent models, built upon simulated reference points, can achieve significantly high accuracy in predicting clicks in sessions, whole-session dwell time, as well as user satisfaction. Also, by testing a variety of simulated search time expectations, researchers found that most participants expected to complete their searches within 60 s. Once the actual dwell time surpassed the 60-s reference point, a relative loss (or extra cost) might be perceived by the participant, which led to a rapid rate of *search satisfaction decay* in a logarithmic fashion (Brown & Liu, 2022). The improvement in early prediction performances achieved with simulated user expectations indicates the importance of further investigating varying dimensions of reference dependence in search interactions and also highlights the value of incorporating in situ user expectation into IR user modeling and evaluation measures of search systems.

Taking a step forward from Brown and Liu's (2022) simulation of users' search expectations, one of our recent user studies investigated users' in situ search expectations regarding costs and gains by collecting their explicit response or label on query-level expectations. Specifically, in our study, participants were recruited and asked to conduct information searching on open Web for completing assigned complex search tasks from journalism domain. To control the potential impacts of task familiarity and topical knowledge, we recruited undergraduate students from outside the journalism discipline and designed two task topics that our participants are quite unlikely to be familiar with. The task and topic design were employed and empirically tested in our previous user studies, which achieved our goal for controlling the effects of task types and topics (e.g., Liu et al., 2019; Mitsui et al., 2017). Our study involved 48 participants, and each participant was asked to complete two predefined search tasks. To collect information regarding in situ expectations, we asked each participant to complete a short survey through interface pop-up window each time they issued a new query and before they could review the results presented on the related SERP. The survey questions on query-level search expectations include:

- [*Useful pages*]: How many useful pages do you expect to find (under the current query)? [Numeric]
- [*Clicks*]: How many results/pages do you expect to click before obtaining the expected number of useful pages? [Numeric]
- [*Spending/dwell time*]: How much time do you expect to spend on this current search? [Ordinal]
  - Less than 30 s
  - 30 s–1.5 min
  - 1.5–3 min
  - 3–5 min
  - More than 5 min

As presented above, our survey questions on search expectation cover both the information gain aspect and search cost aspect. Similar to relevance judgments, users' explicit feedback on in situ expectations can also serve as ground-truth labels for characterizing users' query-level search experience and facilitating user-oriented search evaluation. Based on the search expectation labels collected from different queries and task-based search sessions, we examined the distribution patterns of user expectation features across different search contexts.

As shown in Fig. 6.5, we examined the distribution of levels of user expectations mainly at three key search moments: first query, peak-value query, and end query. Overall, in a query segment, most users expected to obtain two to four useful search results. Users often expect to collect less useful search results toward the end of

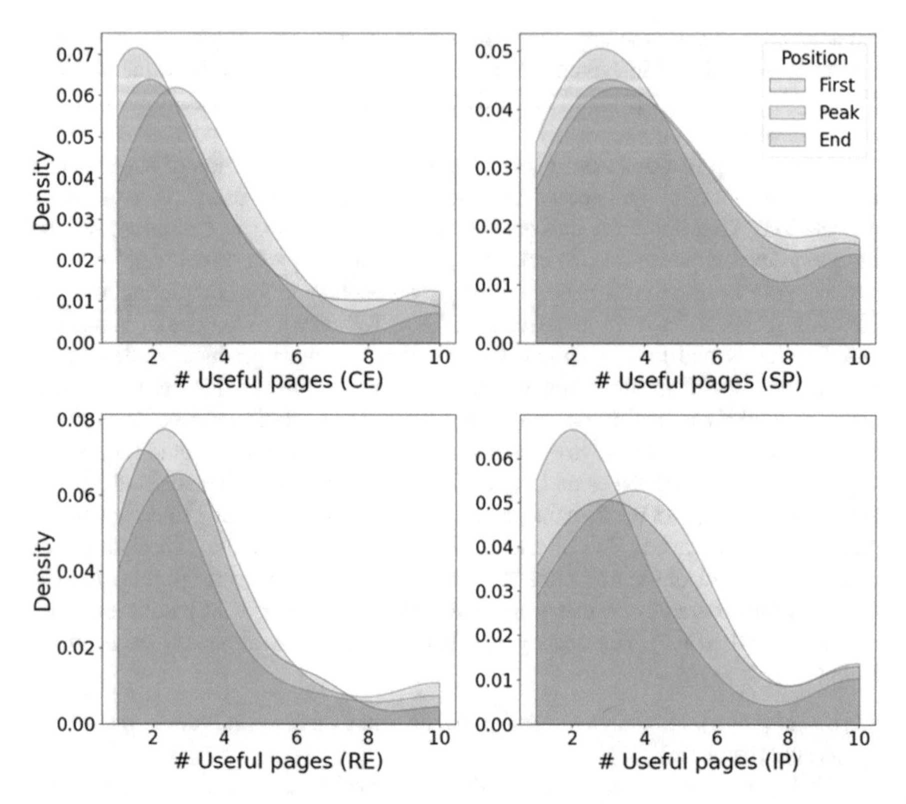

Fig. 6.5 In situ expectation regarding number of useful pages collected. *CE* copy editing task, *SP* story pitch task, *RE* understanding relationship (between different facts) task, *IP* interview preparation task

search sessions (the peak density point appears near the point where # useful pages = 2). Apart from the expectation variations across these three key moments associated with anchoring bias, peak-end rule, and recency effect (Kahneman, 2003), we also observed overall differences in expectation distributions across the four task types. In general, we found that compared to more open-ended tasks, the distributions of useful page expectations in the CE task tend to be more right-skewed compared to that of other task types. This result indicates that users expected or needed to collect less useful documents in relatively simple factual tasks (i.e., CE) compared to the intellectually more challenging search tasks (e.g., SP, IP) (Fig. 6.6).

Similarly, with respect to the expectations regarding the number of clicks needed before reaching the expected numbers of useful pages, we also observed significant variations in expectation distributions across different query moments and types of search tasks. Under the factual search tasks (CE and SP), the distributions are generally more right-skewed, suggesting that users expected to click less search results and documents for fulfilling the task requirements. In contrast, for the intellectual, open-ended search tasks (i.e., RE and IP), users generally expected to

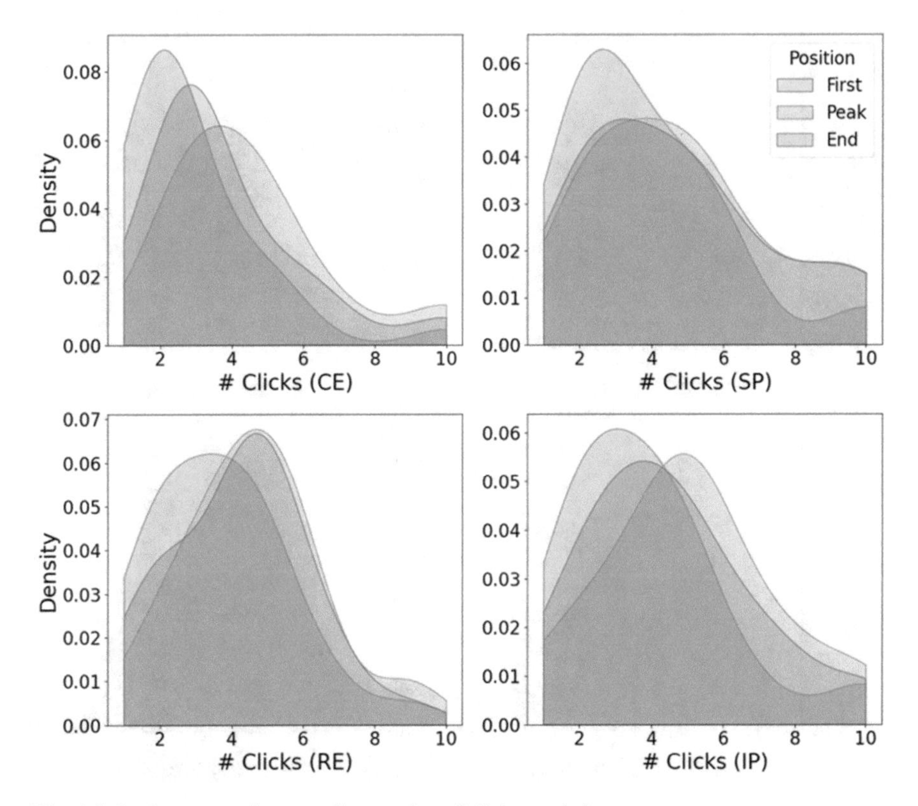

Fig. 6.6 In situ expectation regarding number of clicks needed

click and review more search results before the search tasks can be completed. Also, users were open to engage in more effortful searches (e.g., do more clicking) at the beginning of search sessions. However, at the end of search sessions, they generally expected to click less search results before achieving the query-level search goal, suggesting an implicitly increasing in situ expectation regarding search effectiveness and efficiency (Fig. 6.7).

Similar distribution patterns were also observed in terms of expected dwell/ spending time within query segments. In open-ended search tasks, the expectation distributions at the three selected query moments were more left-skewed compared to that of the factual search tasks. Based on the results above, we found that (1) users' in situ search expectations regarding information gains and search costs vary over time, which may lead to changes in perceived gains and losses when facing similar search results or levels of SERP quality, and (2) users' in situ search expectations vary significantly across different task types.

Our next-step studies following this line of research will focus on the interactions between users' in situ search expectations and Web search behaviors and explore ways in which the expectation labels could be utilized in building, training, and evaluating more solid expectation-aware user models and search evaluation metrics.

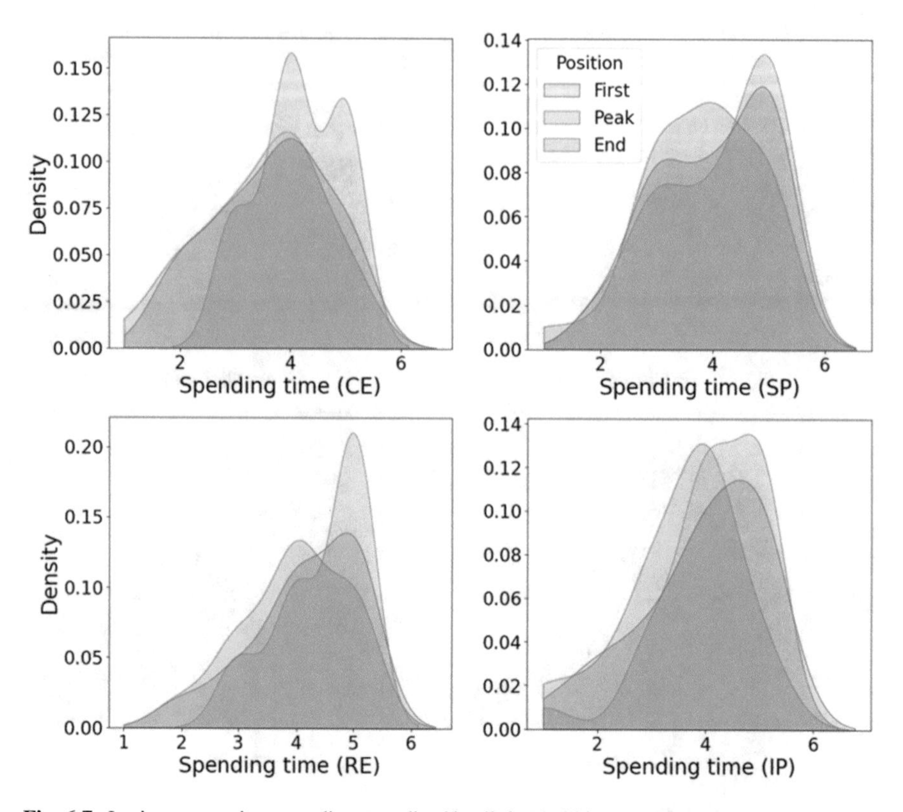

Fig. 6.7 In situ expectation regarding spending/dwell time within a query segment

In addition, we hope that the knowledge learned about user expectations on gains and costs from our research can contribute to the development of intelligent search systems that can automatically predict and better fulfill users' in situ expectations at different moments of search sessions.

Compared to query-level evaluation, modeling whole-session retrospective evaluation often tends to be more challenging as it involves more implicit variations at both cognitive and perceptual levels during search sessions (Belkin et al., 2012). In the following section, we will discuss existing information seeking and retrieval research that examines users' post-search retrospective evaluation of entire search session or online information seeking episodes.

6.5 Post-search Stage

In addition to developing and evaluating reference-dependent prediction models, Liu and Han (2020) also examined the role of *peak-end rule* and *recency effect* in whole-session retrospective evaluation. Specifically, the researchers ran ordered logit models to examine the effects of within-session peak and end query-level satisfaction (Q-SAT) scores on the final whole-session satisfaction score (S-SAT). The peak-end-based model was evaluated against the baseline model built upon whole-session average-value-based and sum-value-based measures. The results of regression analysis demonstrate that the peak-end-based prediction model can achieve significant improvement in predicting S-SAT compared to the widely used traditional model (adjusted R^2 increased from 0.21 to 0.45). In addition, researchers found that both peak Q-SAT and end Q-SAT have significant impacts on the final S-SAT. Meanwhile, the whole-session dwell time and total numbers of click counts do not have statistically significant effect on users' whole-session retrospective evaluation. This result empirically confirms the effect of *duration neglect* (cf. Alaybek et al., 2022; Fredrickson & Kahneman, 1993) in whole-session Web search evaluation and highlights the value of integrating peak-end rule into evaluation models. To further illustrate the peak-end effect and how it leads to the deviation of remembered utility from experienced utility (Kahneman, 2003), Liu and Han (2020) also identified several pairs of search sessions where users had very similar or the same levels of total Q-SAT scores but largely different distributions of Q-SAT scores and divergent values of peak and end Q-SAT scores. As a result, in each pair, the users assigned largely different S-SAT scores to the corresponding Web search sessions as an indicator of their (remembered) whole-session experience.

In online information seeking, Agosto (2002) adopted Simon (1955)'s behavioral decision-making theories of *bounded rationality* and investigated the *principle of satisficing* in young people's Web-based decisions. Based on the coded qualitative data collected from group interviews with 22 adolescent females, researchers found that when searching on open Web and utilizing the collected information in making decisions, young searchers did operate within the limits of their bounded rationality. In addition, Agosto (2002) also identified two main methods or forms of satisficing behaviors: *reduction* and *termination*. Reduction method is usually employed to reduce the amount of information and information sources that need to be examined and processed. Specifically, it includes a series of specific methods, such as returning to previously known sites, adopting indexing categories to remove sites from further consideration, and relying on site synopses. In addition, the researchers also found behavioral patterns under the termination category that contradict the original theory of bounded rationality and satisficing: although searchers sometimes use finding a satisficing search result as the search stop (or acceptance) rule, they also employed other events as stop rules, such as preset time limits, physical discomfort onset, and boredom onset. These occurrences may appear and stop searchers' sessions *before* a satisficing option is actually obtained, which could result in unsatisfactory and frustrating search experiences. These search-experience-related stop rules that are independent of aspiration levels echo related findings from search stopping studies at both query and whole-session/task levels (e.g., Browne et al., 2007; Wu & Kelly, 2014).

Similar satisficing search strategy discussed above was also confirmed in other empirical studies. Wirth et al. (2007) found that when exploring a new topic through

Web search, users tend to quickly scan the clicked search results and see if any relevant information is included and move on to the next page or query segment. During the SERP browsing process, users navigate quickly and do not apply much reflection and deliberate evaluation. Users seek to gather useful information that is sufficient for continuing the exploration, rather than achieving optimal information gains. This result echoes the finding on satisficing principle in Agosto (2002).

6.6 Behavioral Economics and Recommender Systems

In addition to information seeking and retrieval research, we also briefly discuss relevant studies in *Recommender Systems* (RecSys) where behavioral economics approach was adopted to model user behavior and improve recommendation performances measured by a series of offline evaluation metrics. The RecSys studies on human biases and bias-aware ranking and personalization may inspire further research on boundedly rational users' interactions with recommendations in Web search engine and social media sites and also inform the design, implementation, and evaluation of bias-aware intelligent search systems. We hope that our work can further strengthen the connections between IR and RecSys studies, especially in terms of modeling users' biases and heuristics in decision-making activities.

Ge et al. (2020) investigated the interactions between users' interests as anchoring point and the personalized recommendations from e-commerce recommender systems. Particularly, based on the clicks, purchases, and browsing logs collected from Alibaba Taobao transactions, the researchers sought to explore possible *self-reinforcement* effect on users' interests due to the narrowed exposure of product types. This mutual reinforcement between users' initial interests and preferences and the recommendations tailored according to users' behaviors may lead to the *echo chamber* effect. To measure the strength and temporal changes of the possible reinforcement on users' interests, the researchers employed *cluster validity* (Halkidi et al., 2008) to compare the user embeddings of two user groups and investigated the changes in clustering over several months. With respect to the reinforcement from users' behaviors on the narrowed scope of recommendations, Ge et al. (2020) measured the temporal changes of *content diversity* in recommendation lists based on the pairwise distance of item embeddings. The listwise diversity is represented by the average of the item distances. The experimental results indicate that the echo chamber effect does exist in user click behaviors. Users' initial interests on certain product or product types can be reinforced by the repeated exposure to similar recommended items. Knowledge regarding the mutual reinforcement process learned from Ge et al. (2020)'s simulation-based experiments may enable future real-world e-commerce systems to better predict the changes of users' interests and debias the iterative recommendation process in order to mitigate negative impacts of echo chamber.

Similarly, Xu et al. (2020) developed a weighted expected utility model in predicting users' clicks and adjusting product ranking and represented personalized risk attitude and psychological biases toward outcome probabilities in their models based on the empirical findings associated with *Prospect Theory* (Tversky & Kahneman, 1992). Specifically, within the rational expected utility function, the researchers introduced probability weight function (WEU), which characterizes people's tendencies of overestimating small-probability events and underestimating high-probability events. With respect to evaluation, the researchers randomly sampled 1000 negative items from the e-commerce datasets for each user and rank them with the ground-truth items extracted from the user's click and purchase logs. The experimental WEU models were evaluated against classic rational expected utility models. Based on the results from extensive re-ranking experiments, Xu et al. (2020) showed that the weighted EU framework achieved significant improvements in item ranking performances measured by Precision@10, Recall@10, F1@10, and nDCG@10 across different types of e-commerce settings. This study illustrates a viable approach to integrating the knowledge regarding risk attitudes and biased probability estimation into ranking algorithms and to enhancing human-bias-aware recommender systems. The insights, model design, and experimental setups from related RecSys studies could be adapted and reused in IR and other related fields to further investigate the effects of human biases and heuristics in information-intensive decision-making tasks.

6.7 Summary

This chapter introduces the user studies and simulated-based experiments that incorporate the knowledge of human biases, heuristics, and bounded rational decision-making into the models of IR, information seeking, and recommender systems. The research findings and insights discussed above jointly illustrate the existing advances and progresses we, as a research community, have made toward addressing the open questions presented in Chap. 5 and developing bias-aware intelligent information systems. The bias-aware user models, revised assumptions, and evaluation metrics proposed in existing studies can be leveraged in further exploring the impacts of a broader range of human biases and heuristics and constructing corresponding user behavior prediction, item re-ranking, and system evaluation models.

More broadly, the current and continuing research on bounded rationality can complement ongoing mainstream computing research on algorithmic bias and offer a more comprehensive research agenda and analytical framework for investigating the interaction between human biases and algorithmic biases in general human-information interactions. The mutual reinforcement between users' preferences and personalized biased recommendations is a good example to illustrate the interaction between the two-side biases (e.g., Modgil et al., 2021; Xu et al., 2020). Researchers still need to further explore other dimensions of both human and algorithmic biases and reflect on the bias-related concepts, such as diversity, fairness, and transparency, from a user-oriented perspective.

Existing IR studies that involve the knowledge of bounded rationality serve as an important initial step toward addressing the research challenges discussed in previous chapters and open new research paths within this problem space. Chapter 7 will continue our discussion on the behavioral economics approach and explain the implications, new directions, and perspectives that this new approach could bring to us in different sub-areas of IR theories, research, and practices.

Acknowledgment The in situ search expectation study discussed in this chapter (Sect. 6.4) is supported by the National Science Foundation (NSF) Award IIS-2106152. Any opinions, findings, and conclusions or recommendations expressed in this work are those of the author and do not necessarily reflect those of the sponsor.

References

Agosto, D. E. (2002). Bounded rationality and satisficing in young people's web-based decision making. *Journal of the American Society for Information Science and Technology, 53*(1), 16–27. https://doi.org/10.1002/asi.10024

Alaybek, B., Dalal, R. S., Fyffe, S., Aitken, J. A., Zhou, Y., Qu, X., Roman, A., & Baines, J. I. (2022). All's well that ends (and peaks) well? A meta-analysis of the peak-end rule and duration neglect. *Organizational Behavior and Human Decision Processes, 170*, 104149. https://doi.org/10.1016/j.obhdp.2022.104149

Arguello, J., & Capra, R. (2012). The effect of aggregated search coherence on search behavior. In *Proceedings of the 21st ACM international conference on information and knowledge management* (pp. 1293–1302). ACM. https://doi.org/10.1145/2396761.2398432

Azzopardi, L. (2014). Modelling interaction with economic models of search. In *Proceedings of the 37th international ACM SIGIR conference on research & development in information retrieval* (pp. 3–12). ACM. https://doi.org/10.1145/2600428.2609574

Azzopardi, L. (2021). Cognitive biases in search: A review and reflection of cognitive biases in information retrieval. In *Proceedings of the 2021 international ACM SIGIR conference on human information interaction and retrieval* (pp. 27–37). ACM. https://doi.org/10.1145/3406522.3446023

Baeza-Yates, R. (2018). Bias on the web. *Communications of the ACM, 61*(6), 54–61. https://doi.org/10.1145/3209581

Bail, C. A., Argyle, L. P., Brown, T. W., Bumpus, J. P., Chen, H., Hunzaker, M. F., Lee, J., Mann, M., Merhout, F., & Volfovsky, A. (2018). Exposure to opposing views on social media can increase political polarization. *Proceedings of the National Academy of Sciences, 115*(37), 9216–9221. https://doi.org/10.1073/pnas.1804840115

Belkin, N. J., Dumais, S., Kando, N., & Sanderson, M. (2012). Whole-session evaluation of interactive information retrieval systems. In *NII Shonan meeting report* (Vol. 7).

Bhattacherjee, A. (2001). Understanding information systems continuance: An expectation-confirmation model. *MIS Quarterly, 25*(3), 351–370. https://doi.org/10.2307/3250921

Bhui, R., Lai, L., & Gershman, S. J. (2021). Resource-rational decision making. *Current Opinion in Behavioral Sciences, 41*, 15–21. https://doi.org/10.1016/j.cobeha.2021.02.015

Bondarenko, A., Shirshakova, E., Driker, M., Hagen, M., & Braslavski, P. (2021). Misbeliefs and biases in health-related searches. In *Proceedings of the 30th ACM international conference on information & knowledge management* (pp. 2894–2899). ACM. https://doi.org/10.1145/3459637.3482141

Brown, T., & Liu, J. (2022). A reference dependence approach to enhancing early prediction of session behavior and satisfaction. In *Proceedings of the 22nd ACM/IEEE Joint Conference on Digital Libraries* (pp. 1–5).

Browne, G. J., Pitts, M. G., & Wetherbe, J. C. (2007). Cognitive stopping rules for terminating information search in online tasks. *MIS Quarterly, 31*(1), 89–104. https://doi.org/10.2307/25148782

Cacciatore, M. A. (2021). Misinformation and public opinion of science and health: Approaches, findings, and future directions. *Proceedings of the National Academy of Sciences, 118*(15), e1912437117. https://doi.org/10.1073/pnas.1912437117

Capra, R., Arguello, J., & Scholer, F. (2013). Augmenting web search surrogates with images. In *Proceedings of the 22nd ACM international conference on information & knowledge management* (pp. 399–408). ACM. https://doi.org/10.1145/2505515.2505714

Caputo, A. (2014). Relevant information, personality traits and anchoring effect. *International Journal of Management and Decision Making, 13*(1), 62–76.

Chen, D., Chen, W., Wang, H., Chen, Z., & Yang, Q. (2012). Beyond ten blue links: Enabling user click modeling in federated web search. In *Proceedings of the fifth ACM international conference on web search and data mining* (pp. 463–472). ACM. https://doi.org/10.1145/2124295.2124351

Chen, N., Zhang, F., & Sakai, T. (2022). Constructing better evaluation metrics by incorporating the anchoring effect into the user model. In *Proceedings of the 45th international ACM SIGIR conference on research and development in information retrieval* (pp. 2709–2714). ACM. https://doi.org/10.1145/3477495.3531953

Chuklin, A., Markov, I., & de Rijke, M. (2015). Click models for web search. *Synthesis Lectures on Information concepts, Retrieval, and Services, 7*(3), 1–115. https://doi.org/10.2200/S00654ED1V01Y201507ICR043

Cinelli, M., De Francisci Morales, G., Galeazzi, A., Quattrociocchi, W., & Starnini, M. (2021). The echo chamber effect on social media. *Proceedings of the National Academy of Sciences, 118*(9), e2023301118. https://doi.org/10.1073/pnas.2023301118

Draws, T., Rieger, A., Inel, O., Gadiraju, U., & Tintarev, N. (2021). A checklist to combat cognitive biases in crowdsourcing. In *Proceedings of the AAAI conference on human computation and crowdsourcing* (Vol. 9, pp. 48–59) https://ojs.aaai.org/index.php/HCOMP/article/view/18939

Eickhoff, C. (2018). Cognitive biases in crowdsourcing. In *Proceedings of the eleventh ACM international conference on web search and data mining* (pp. 162–170). ACM. https://doi.org/10.1145/3159652.3159654

Fan, L., & Suh, Y. H. (2014). Why do users switch to a disruptive technology? An empirical study based on expectation-disconfirmation theory. *Information & Management, 51*(2), 240–248. https://doi.org/10.1016/j.im.2013.12.004

Fan, Y. W., Chen, C. D., Wu, C. C., & Fang, Y. H. (2015). The effect of status quo bias on cloud system adoption. *Journal of Computer Information Systems, 55*(3), 55–64. https://doi.org/10.1080/08874417.2015.11645772

Fredrickson, B. L., & Kahneman, D. (1993). Duration neglect in retrospective evaluations of affective episodes. *Journal of Personality and Social Psychology, 65*(1), 45–55. https://doi.org/10.1037/0022-3514.65.1.45

Ge, Y., Zhao, S., Zhou, H., Pei, C., Sun, F., Ou, W., & Zhang, Y. (2020). Understanding echo chambers in e-commerce recommender systems. In *Proceedings of the 43rd international ACM SIGIR conference on research and development in information retrieval* (pp. 2261–2270). https://doi.org/10.1145/3397271.3401431

Gigerenzer, G., & Brighton, H. (2009). Homo heuristicus: Why biased minds make better inferences. *Topics in Cognitive Science, 1*(1), 107–143. https://doi.org/10.1111/j.1756-8765.2008.01006.x

Halkidi, M., Gunopulos, D., Vazirgiannis, M., Kumar, N., & Domeniconi, C. (2008). A clustering framework based on subjective and objective validity criteria. *ACM Transactions on Knowledge Discovery from Data (TKDD), 1*(4), 1–25. https://doi.org/10.1145/1324172.1324176

Hashavit, A., Wang, H., Lin, R., Stern, T., & Kraus, S. (2021). Understanding and mitigating bias in online health search. In *Proceedings of the 44th international ACM SIGIR conference on research and development in information retrieval* (pp. 265–274). ACM. https://doi.org/10.1145/3404835.3462930

Highhouse, S. (1996). Context-dependent selection: The effects of decoy and phantom job candidates. *Organizational Behavior and Human Decision Processes, 65*(1), 68–76. https://doi.org/10.1006/obhd.1996.0006

Hsieh, C. C., Kuo, P. L., Yang, S. C., & Lin, S. H. (2010). Assessing blog-user satisfaction using the expectation and disconfirmation approach. *Computers in Human Behavior, 26*(6), 1434–1444. https://doi.org/10.1016/j.chb.2010.04.022

Kahneman, D. (2003). Maps of bounded rationality: Psychology for behavioral economics. *American Economic Review, 93*(5), 1449–1475. https://doi.org/10.1257/000282803322655392

Klayman, J., & Ha, Y. W. (1987). Confirmation, disconfirmation, and information in hypothesis testing. *Psychological Review, 94*(2), 211–228. https://doi.org/10.1037/0033-295X.94.2.211

Knobloch-Westerwick, S., Mothes, C., & Polavin, N. (2020). Confirmation bias, ingroup bias, and negativity bias in selective exposure to political information. *Communication Research, 47*(1), 104–124. https://doi.org/10.1177/0093650217719596

Lankton, N. K., & McKnight, H. D. (2012). Examining two expectation disconfirmation theory models: Assimilation and asymmetry effects. *Journal of the Association for Information Systems, 13*(2), 88–115. https://doi.org/10.17705/1jais.00285

Lee, K., & Joshi, K. (2017). Examining the use of status quo bias perspective in IS research: Need for re-conceptualizing and incorporating biases. *Information Systems Journal, 27*(6), 733–752. https://doi.org/10.1111/isj.12118

Li, Y., & Belkin, N. J. (2008). A faceted approach to conceptualizing tasks in information seeking. *Information Processing & Management, 44*(6), 1822–1837. https://doi.org/10.1016/j.ipm.2008.07.005

Li, J., Liu, M., & Liu, X. (2016). Why do employees resist knowledge management systems? An empirical study from the status quo bias and inertia perspectives. *Computers in Human Behavior, 65*, 189–200. https://doi.org/10.1016/j.chb.2016.08.028

Lieder, F., & Griffiths, T. L. (2020). Resource-rational analysis: Understanding human cognition as the optimal use of limited computational resources. *Behavioral and Brain Sciences, 43*. https://doi.org/10.1017/S0140525X1900061X

Liu, J. (2022). Toward cranfield-inspired reusability assessment in interactive information retrieval evaluation. *Information Processing & Management, 59*(5), 103007. https://doi.org/10.1016/j.ipm.2022.103007

Liu, J., & Han, F. (2020). Investigating reference dependence effects on user search interaction and satisfaction: A behavioral economics perspective. In *Proceedings of the 43rd international ACM SIGIR conference on research and development in information retrieval* (pp. 1141–1150). ACM. https://doi.org/10.1145/3397271.3401085

Liu, J., & Shah, C. (2019). Investigating the impacts of expectation disconfirmation on web search. In *Proceedings of the 2019 international ACM SIGIR conference on human information interaction and retrieval* (pp. 319–323). ACM. https://doi.org/10.1145/3295750.3298959

Liu, Z., Liu, Y., Zhou, K., Zhang, M., & Ma, S. (2015). Influence of vertical result in web search examination. In *Proceedings of the 38th international ACM SIGIR conference on research and development in information retrieval* (pp. 193–202). ACM. https://doi.org/10.1145/2766462.2767714

Liu, J., Mitsui, M., Belkin, N. J., & Shah, C. (2019). Task, information seeking intentions, and user behavior: Toward a multi-level understanding of web search. In *Proceedings of the 2019 ACM SIGIR conference on human information interaction and retrieval* (pp. 123–132). ACM. https://doi.org/10.1145/3295750.3298922

Liu, J., Sarkar, S., & Shah, C. (2020). Identifying and predicting the states of complex search tasks. In *Proceedings of the 2020 ACM SIGIR conference on human information interaction and retrieval* (pp. 193–202). ACM. https://doi.org/10.1145/3343413.3377976

Meppelink, C. S., Smit, E. G., Fransen, M. L., & Diviani, N. (2019). “I was right about vaccination”: Confirmation bias and health literacy in online health information seeking. *Journal of Health Communication, 24*(2), 129–140. https://doi.org/10.1080/10810730.2019.1583701

Mitsui, M., Liu, J., Belkin, N. J., & Shah, C. (2017). Predicting information seeking intentions from search behaviors. In *Proceedings of the 40th international ACM SIGIR conference on research and development in information retrieval* (pp. 1121–1124). ACM. https://doi.org/10.1145/3077136.3080737

Modgil, S., Singh, R. K., Gupta, S., & Dennehy, D. (2021). A confirmation bias view on social media induced polarisation during Covid-19. *Information Systems Frontiers*, 1–25. https://doi.org/10.1007/s10796-021-10222-9

Nel, J., & Boshoff, C. (2020). Status quo bias and shoppers’ mobile website purchasing resistance. *European Journal of Marketing, 54*(6), 1433–1466. https://doi.org/10.1108/EJM-02-2018-0144

Nickerson, R. S. (1998). Confirmation bias: A ubiquitous phenomenon in many guises. *Review of General Psychology, 2*(2), 175–220. https://doi.org/10.1037/1089-2680.2.2.175

Novin, A., & Meyers, E. (2017a). Making sense of conflicting science information: Exploring bias in the search engine result page. In *Proceedings of the 2017 international ACM SIGIR conference on human information interaction and retrieval* (pp. 175–184). ACM. https://doi.org/10.1145/3020165.3020185

Novin, A., & Meyers, E. M. (2017b). Four biases in interface design interactions. In *International conference of design, user experience, and usability* (pp. 163–173). Springer.

Oliver, R. L. (1980). A cognitive model of the antecedents and consequences of satisfaction decisions. *Journal of Marketing Research, 17*(4), 460–469. https://doi.org/10.1177/002224378001700405

Rieger, A., Draws, T., Theune, M., & Tintarev, N. (2021). This item might reinforce your opinion: Obfuscation and labeling of search results to mitigate confirmation bias. In *Proceedings of the 32nd ACM conference on hypertext and social media* (pp. 189–199). ACM. https://doi.org/10.1145/3465336.3475101

Scholer, F., Kelly, D., Wu, W. C., Lee, H. S., & Webber, W. (2013). The effect of threshold priming and need for cognition on relevance calibration and assessment. In *Proceedings of the 36th international ACM SIGIR conference on research and development in information retrieval* (pp. 623–632). ACM. https://doi.org/10.1145/2484028.2484090

Shah, C. (2018). Information fostering-being proactive with information seeking and retrieval: Perspective paper. In *Proceedings of the 2018 international ACM SIGIR conference on human information interaction & retrieval* (pp. 62–71). ACM. https://doi.org/10.1145/3176349.3176389

Shokouhi, M., White, R., & Yilmaz, E. (2015). Anchoring and adjustment in relevance estimation. In *Proceedings of the 38th international ACM SIGIR conference on research and development in information retrieval* (pp. 963–966). ACM. https://doi.org/10.1145/2766462.2767841

Simon, H. A. (1955). A behavioral model of rational choice. *The Quarterly Journal of Economics, 69*(1), 99–118. https://doi.org/10.2307/1884852

Suzuki, M., & Yamamoto, Y. (2020). Analysis of relationship between confirmation bias and web search behavior. In *Proceedings of the 22nd international conference on information integration and web-based applications & services* (pp. 184–191). https://doi.org/10.1145/3428757.3429086

Thomas, P., Kazai, G., White, R., & Craswell, N. (2022). The crowd is made of people: Observations from large-scale crowd labelling. In *Proceedings of the international ACM SIGIR conference on human information interaction and retrieval* (pp. 25–35). ACM. https://doi.org/10.1145/3498366.3505815

Todd, P. M., & Gigerenzer, G. (2000). Précis of simple heuristics that make us smart. *Behavioral and Brain Sciences, 23*(5), 727–741. https://doi.org/10.1017/S0140525X00003447

Tversky, A., & Kahneman, D. (1991). Loss aversion in riskless choice: A reference-dependent model. *The Quarterly Journal of Economics, 106*(4), 1039–1061. https://doi.org/10.2307/2937956

Tversky, A., & Kahneman, D. (1992). Advances in prospect theory: Cumulative representation of uncertainty. *Journal of Risk and Uncertainty, 5*(4), 297–323. https://doi.org/10.1007/BF00122574

Venkatesh, V., & Goyal, S. (2010). Expectation disconfirmation and technology adoption: Polynomial modeling and response surface analysis. *MIS Quarterly, 34*(2), 281–303. https://doi.org/10.2307/20721428

Wedell, D. H., & Pettibone, J. C. (1996). Using judgments to understand decoy effects in choice. *Organizational Behavior and Human Decision Processes, 67*(3), 326–344. https://doi.org/10.1006/obhd.1996.0083

White, R. (2013). Beliefs and biases in web search. In *Proceedings of the 36th international ACM SIGIR conference on research and development in information retrieval* (pp. 3–12). ACM. https://doi.org/10.1145/2484028.2484053

White, R. W., & Horvitz, E. (2015). Belief dynamics and biases in web search. *ACM Transactions on Information Systems (TOIS), 33*(4), 1–46. https://doi.org/10.1145/2746229

Wirth, W., Böcking, T., Karnowski, V., & Von Pape, T. (2007). Heuristic and systematic use of search engines. *Journal of Computer-Mediated Communication, 12*(3), 778–800.

Wu, C., & Cosguner, K. (2020). Profiting from the decoy effect: A case study of an online diamond retailer. *Marketing Science, 39*(5), 974–995. https://doi.org/10.1287/mksc.2020.1231

Wu, W. C., & Kelly, D. (2014). Online search stopping behaviors: An investigation of query abandonment and task stopping. *Proceedings of the American Society for Information Science and Technology, 51*(1), 1–10. https://doi.org/10.1002/meet.2014.14505101030

Xu, Z., Han, Y., Zhang, Y., & Ai, Q. (2020). E-commerce recommendation with weighted expected utility. In *Proceedings of the 29th ACM international conference on information & knowledge management* (pp. 1695–1704). ACM. https://doi.org/10.1145/3340531.3411993

Xu, S., Coman, I. A., Yamamoto, M., & Najera, C. J. (2022). Exposure effects or confirmation bias? Examining reciprocal dynamics of misinformation, misperceptions, and attitudes toward Covid-19 vaccines. *Health Communication*, 1–11. https://doi.org/10.1080/10410236.2022.2059802

Zhang, Y., & Zhai, C. (2016). A sequential decision formulation of the interface card model for interactive IR. In *Proceedings of the 39th international ACM SIGIR conference on research and development in information retrieval* (pp. 85–94). ACM. https://doi.org/10.1145/2911451.2911543

Chapter 7
Implications and New Directions for IR Research and Practices

Abstract Previous chapters have thoroughly discussed recent advances and progresses in IR formal user models and behavioral economics research on human bounded rationality in decision-making. As presented in Chap. 6, some recent studies in IR, information seeking, and recommendation have empirically confirmed the impacts of human biases and heuristics on users' search interactions, judgments of information items, and reactions to personalized recommendations and partially incorporate the knowledge of bounded rationality into developing user behavior prediction models, system evaluation metrics, and bias-aware re-ranking algorithms. Taking a step forward from previous discussions, this chapter will introduce existing unresolved research gaps and open challenges from bounded rationality perspective and discuss the main research questions, practical implications, and new directions of our behavioral economics approach for various sub-areas of IR studies.

7.1 Background

Previous chapters have thoroughly discussed recent advances and progresses in IR formal user models and behavioral economics research on human bounded rationality in decision-making (with empirical evidences associated with both behavioral patterns and neural correlates). Contrasting the specific assumptions, model setups, and findings from these two areas of research clarify a series of gaps between simulated rational agents and real-world users engaging in search interactions under varying tasks. These gaps motivated us to reflect on the existing oversimplified assumptions and rational user models and encouraged us to explore ways in which we could extend the assumptions about user characteristics and behavioral patterns and also enhance existing formal models. As presented in Chap. 6, some recent studies in IR, information seeking, and recommendation have empirically confirmed the impacts of human biases and heuristics on users' search interactions, judgments of information items, and reactions to personalized recommendations and partially incorporate the knowledge of bounded rationality in developing user behavior prediction models, system evaluation metrics, and bias-aware re-ranking algorithms. Taking a step forward from previous discussions,

J. Liu, *A Behavioral Economics Approach to Interactive Information Retrieval*, The Information Retrieval Series 48, https://doi.org/10.1007/978-3-031-23229-9_7

Chap. 7 will introduce existing unresolved research gaps and open challenges from bounded rationality perspective and discuss the main research questions, practical implications, and new directions of our behavioral economics approach for various sub-areas of IR studies. We hope that our synthesis of the insights from related areas and new bias-aware research agenda can be of help for students and researchers who are interested in further investigating more specific human-bias-related IR problems and leveraging the learned knowledge in enhancing intelligent search systems.

7.2 Characterizing Bounded Rationality in IR

When making decisions under uncertainty, people are often boundedly rational due to a series of individual characteristics and situational limits, such as cognitive and perceptual biases, mental shortcuts, as well as limited resources and support (Simon, 1955; Kahneman, 2003). In the context of IR, previous studies have explored a set of the widely examined human cognitive biases and described their implicit connections to users' information search behaviors, document judgment thresholds, and whole-session evaluations (e.g., Azzopardi, 2021; Eickhoff, 2018; Liu & Han, 2020; Scholer et al., 2013). To further enhance our understanding of boundedly rational search decisions, researchers may need to address several general limitations.

First, it is worth noting that people's boundedly rational decisions and judgments usually involve perceived *multidimensional changes*, *gains*, and *losses* (Kahneman, 2003). Although existing IR research has examined several types of human biases and heuristics (see Chap. 6), many of them only focused on one or two dimensions associated with the impacts of biases. One of the widely examined dimensions is *relevance judgment* as a large body of user studies, and offline IR evaluation experiments include external relevance labeling as part of the standard experimental setup. However, users' biased perceptions and decisions could occur in other dimensions as well, such as the judgments of document credibility and usefulness, acceptance of different types of search recommendations, as well as the experience with certain search interfaces. For instance, the impact of decoy results and threshold priming could not only be triggered by the relevance labels of documents examined in sequence but also initiated by the difference in document presentation (e.g., text only or augmented with relevant images; presented as regular organic search results or vertical results) and perceived document credibility. In addition, users' search satisficing strategy and aspiration level may also be multidimensional in nature and are influenced by the perceived gains and losses on a variety of facets of search interactions, rather than depending on query-document relevance (*qrel*) only. More broadly, from the reference-dependence perspective (e.g., Tversky & Kahneman, 1991), users' pre-search and in situ preferences and expectations may also involve different dimensions, such as search interactions and costs, system effectiveness, and document quality, as well as overall search experience. These different dimensions of references could also change over time as a search session proceeds and may have different weights in users' search decision-making and whole-session remembered utility. It is difficult to characterize diverse references and associated temporal variations (e.g., changes of SERP quality across different queries; changes of users' preferences over diverse subtopics) with only one or two ground-truth labels.

Next, related to the first limitation, when characterizing the temporal changes along different dimensions and associated with varying human biases, researchers also need to explore the *interactions among different dimensions of search interactions and biases*. For instance, based on e-commerce click and purchase logs, Ge et al. (2020) identified the mutual reinforcements between individual users' interests and the biases in item exposure in recommender systems, which confirmed the echo chamber effect in personalized product recommendations. Azzopardi (2021) also discussed possible compounding effects caused by two or more cognitive biases on searchers. For example, individuals' decisions are often heavily influenced by the initial information available in a given sequence (*Primacy effect*; Jones et al., 1968). This primacy effect may couple with *anchoring bias*: when a user evaluates results in a SERP, the first item presented or examined may be considered as most relevant and used as an anchoring point for judging the relevance and credibility of following documents. Also, for each individual search decisions in a session, such as query reformulation, document clicking, and search stopping, the user may be influenced by both in situ reference points (e.g., search results with varying types of framing) and pre-search existing beliefs and preferences (*Confirmation bias*, Nickerson, 1998; White, 2013).

Although mutual reinforcement effect could occur among diverse human biases (Azzopardi, 2021), different biases may also compete with each other for people's attention and relatively higher weights in final decision-making. For instance, suppose a user has pre-search doubts about the effectiveness of a certain brand of vaccine. During the information search process, the user may be actively searching for results that confirm or is aligned with their pre-search beliefs. However, when the top ranked search results contradict with the pre-search expectations, the confirmation bias might be mitigated by the anchoring bias or in situ reference dependence as the user may consider the initially encountered or top ranked search results as most relevant. This impact of in situ reference may be weaker if the disconfirming results are ranked in lower positions on the SERP. Therefore, to comprehensively investigate the interaction between confirmation bias and anchoring bias (as well as the interplay of other human biases), researchers may also need to take into consideration the roles of several IR-specific factors, such as search query features, search result presentations (e.g., as organic search results or vertical blocks), and adaptive learning to rank algorithms.

With respect to the behavioral impacts of bounded rationality, researchers from multiple disciplines (including IR) have extensively studied the negative impact on search performance, document judgment quality, and overall experiences. As a result, a series of negative effects and biased decision strategies have been identified through the behavioral experiments where researchers start with assumed negative effect of human biases.[1] However, the potential *positive effects* of human biases remain understudied. For instance, cognitive biases and heuristics may reduce the complexity of decision-making processes (Azzopardi, 2021). Relying on a set of simple rules and mental shortcuts, individuals may be able to quickly obtain satisficing or good-enough outcomes without processing a large amount of new information (Kahneman, 2011). Also, people may be more likely to be affected by cognitive biases when facing conflicting information (which usually increases the uncertainty in option evaluation and decision-making). Thus, using certain mental shortcuts may help reduce the uncertainty and improve the efficiency in decision-making activities. This could be of high value to users, especially in scenarios where timeliness is more important than optimized accuracy. Future IR researchers should actively explore the positive effects of human biases and heuristics in making search decisions, judging information items, and performing information-intensive work tasks. More broadly, estimating the positive impact of bounded rationality may also enable researchers and system engineers to build more comprehensive computational models of real-time human decisions under bounded cognitive resources (Gershman et al., 2015).

Apart from the research gaps above, characterizing human biases and boundedly rational decisions in IR is also *methodologically challenging*. To capture the "pure effect" of human biases and heuristics, behavioral economics researchers often choose to observe human decisions within well-controlled, simplified, and sometimes unrealistic experimental settings (e.g., Kahneman, 2003; Thaler, 2016; Weber & Camerer, 2006), such as gambling with two options, selling or buying one item, or deciding the treatment plan with the complete knowledge of the probability of cure associated with each alternative. These simplified experimental settings allow researchers to extract one decision-making segment out of complex real-world settings and directly observe the phenomenon of bounded rationality with other contextual variables (e.g., work task characteristics, other people's opinions and actions, domain knowledge, and information seeking skills) being controlled. However, interactive search sessions often tend to be complex, dynamic, and involve contextual factors of multiple levels, such as action level, query level, search task level, as well as motivating task level. Even in controlled user study settings where users conduct search activities under a predefined search task, it is still difficult to redesign or deconstruct the complex search processes into a set of single-decision-based simplified experiments. In addition, to address the problem of observing and modeling the interactions between diverse human biases, researchers may not be able to restrict the decision-making experiment within an oversimplified setting.

As shown in Fig. 7.1, within a simplified representation of general methodological spectrum, researchers need to find the *scientifically reasonable* and *practically accessible* balance between the two directions or sides: On the one side, (over)-simplified task and study designs that are widely applied in behavioral economics

[1]This phenomenon may also confirm the existence of confirmation bias in IR research on bounded rationality.

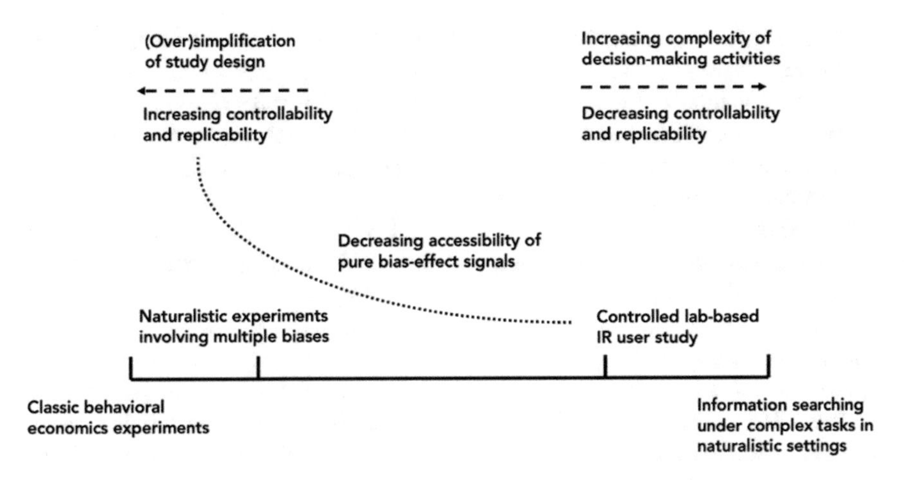

Fig. 7.1 Methodological challenges in IR research on bounded rationality

and cognitive psychology experiments can increase the chance of observing pure behavioral effects caused by human biases and heuristics. The well-controlled experimental settings can make the bias trigger for salient (e.g., a clear decoy option among different alternatives) and thus more likely to generate significant, testable behavioral variations. On the other side, however, we also need to consider the level of *realism* of the simulated tasks and decision-making settings. Although the simplified environments can better facilitate the investigation on human biases, it may affect the generalizability and practical value of the research findings. The behavioral effect measured in simple experiments may not be practically meaningful in complex IR settings where multilevel search decisions are mixed with each other. Also, it is worth noting that several types of biases are identified under artificially constructed experimental sessions; this may be because the study participants are not intrinsically motivated to find out the real credible information items (Azzopardi, 2021). For instance, a high school student participant may not have a clear motivation for learning about available retirement plans, except for the compensation payment for their participation. As a result, the participant may be more likely to stop searching at satisficing results, which present clear but overestimated signals of bounded rationality to the researchers who may be subject to *observer-expectancy effect* (Rosenthal, 1976). This issue of participants' motivations in task completion is a common issue in crowdsourcing studies (e.g., Law et al., 2016; Posch et al., 2019; Rogstadius et al., 2011) and may cause extra risk for user studies on human biases and heuristics. However, when completely departing from controlled lab experiment contexts and customized interventions, researchers may also find it difficult to identify and access reliable signals that indicate boundedly rational actions and capture the implicit deviation of biased decisions from mathematically optimal outcomes.

Crowdsourcing-based user experiments, especially the ones focusing on the judgment and labeling of information items (e.g., Eickhoff, 2018; Maddalena et al., 2016; Roitero et al., 2022), enable researchers to partially characterize users' evaluation decisions under the influence of cognitive biases that emerge from individuals' naturalistic settings. However, how to go beyond a single slice of search process and reasonably approximate whole-session search interaction experience that involves multistage decision-making still remains an open challenge. To address this challenge, researchers will need to both design effective tasks, interfaces, and interventions that can be naturally implemented in real-life settings and also identify new measures and signals for capturing the multidimensional effects of human biases, heuristics, and situational limits and depicting boundedly rational decisions.

This section summarizes the existing limitations and research gaps in terms of characterizing bounded rationality in IR. For each limitation, we have identified specific research problems to be addressed and suggested possible paths for future studies. The knowledge learned through exploring and characterizing users' bounded rationality can provide a solid behavioral and psychological basis for designing new search and ranking algorithms, user interface components, and recommendations, as well as bias-aware evaluation metrics.

7.3 Development of Bias-Aware Interactive Search Systems

The second part of our research agenda adopting the behavioral economics perspective focuses on the open challenges we need to address regarding the development of bias-aware interactive search systems. Our ultimate goal is that the bias-aware search algorithms and systems can take into account the impacts of both algorithmic biases and human biases and proactively address the potential negative effects from users' biased perceptions, judgments, and search decisions, especially in complex search tasks of varying types.

Taking a step forward from the discussions in the above section, researchers need to properly present diverse types of human biases, heuristics, as well as other situational factors that contribute to boundedly rational decisions and estimate corresponding parameters in updated formal user models with real-world search interaction data. As summarized in Chaps. 4 and 6, there are a large body of behavioral economics experiments and IR user studies that described and statistically tested the effects of various human biases on judgment and decision-making (Azzopardi, 2021; Kahneman, 2003). However, the knowledge of bounded rationality accumulated in a variety of disciplines has rarely been incorporated into the design of formal user models. This research gap can be considered as part of the broader, deeper disconnection between information seeking community and IR community: although a variety of online information seeking behavior models have been proposed in diverse specific settings, populations, and task scenarios, many of them have not been introduced or represented in formal, computational models of user behavior in IR experiments, partly because of the descriptive nature and significant individual differences embedded in information seeking models and practical limitations in available training datasets and ground truth labels (Liu, 2022).

The *enhancement of formal user models* under a bounded rational framework would start with the multifaceted extension of simplified rational assumptions discussed in Chap. 5. For instance, when estimating the attractiveness and probability of examination before clicking, researchers should consider not only the textual features of search result surrogates and the rank position of the document but also the past history of browsing, clicking, and judgments, especially the reference levels, anchoring points, and in situ preferences hidden in past search interactions. Also, due to the *threshold priming* effect (cf. Scholer et al., 2013), users may keep adjusting and calibrating their thresholds of relevance judgments during a sequence of query-driven search iterations. Regarding usefulness judgments, researchers will also need to examine search task facets (e.g., Li & Belkin, 2008; Liu, 2021) and monitor the distance between the current document and the overarching search tasks. Due to the subjective nature and since individual differences involved usefulness judgments, the calibrated thresholds may not regress to a relatively stable value as it is expected in relevance judgments (Thomas et al., 2022). Thus, researchers may need to design and empirically test different forms of customized *task-document distance* measures and see which one(s) best capture the user's in situ usefulness perceptions.

The dynamic nature of references, judgment thresholds, and information need often lead to unexpected deviations of users' examination and clicking behaviors from the predictions of traditional click models. Therefore, incorporating explicit representations of in situ references and implicit judgment thresholds into click models may improve the accuracy in both unbiased relevance estimation and click prediction. The connections between previous references extracted from actions, documents, and explicit feedback (if available) and current search actions could be represented by extra edges in the *session flow* of graph-based click models (Lin et al., 2021). Adopting a data-driven approach, the weights of hidden edges among pre-search and in situ references, implicit thresholds, and current document features could be learned through neural networks from search log data containing both intra-session and inter-session information. In addition to the graph-based method, researchers could also adopt a personalized click model (PCM) approach and incorporates users' reference points and cognitive biases into click models as part of the user factors. For instance, within Shen et al. (2012)'s PCM framework, user biases could be represented as elements of user matrix, which in turn shapes the Gaussian prior of the document attractiveness parameter in click modeling.

In addition to predicting clicking and characterizing within-SERP browsing, researchers have also developed a series of rational models for formally modeling interactive search sessions. One of the common modeling approaches is to deconstruct users' search sessions into the transitions of a fixed set of *phases* or *states*. The phases and states are either defined under a starting theoretical framework and a set of axioms in a top-down fashion (e.g., Dungs & Fuhr, 2017; Zhai, 2016) or empirically extracted from users' search logs and explicit annotations (e.g., Hendahewa & Shah, 2013; Liu et al., 2020; Liu & Yu, 2021). With the state-based framework, researchers have proposed a variety of optimization algorithms to iteratively maximize the search effectiveness or scores of evaluation metrics (e.g., nDCG, average precision, document usefulness) that measure ranking performances and SERP qualities (Luo et al., 2014; Liu & Shah, 2022; Zhang & Zhai, 2016). To enhance existing state transition models, researchers can incorporate bias-related factors into the models and estimate their impacts on state transitions. For instance, with the same local retrieval outcome, a relative change (perceived as a gain or loss) in the relevance of search result surrogate or page dwell time may significantly affect the probabilities of browsing continuation and transition to the stage of query reformulation. Also, encountering a document that confirms the user's existing beliefs and expectations may result in an unexpectedly high probability of clicking and relevance score that deviate from the average probability estimated based on past search behaviors and the textual features of current documents.

Another possible approach to integrate bounded rationality factors into session modeling is to add the hidden bias-aware states to the framework of observable behavioral states. Specifically, for example, in addition to the explicit transitions among query, search result snippet examination, and clicking, researchers can also characterize and monitor the reference-dependent state. With the knowledge of pre-search beliefs and preferences, researchers can estimate and label the (dis)-confirmation state of each document and also represent the query/SERP-level perceived utility based on the state associated with each document. In formal modeling, researchers can still focus on relevance-based scores as the main component of utility modeling and at the same time add factorized residuals and use latent confirmation-state factors to depict individuals' deviations from the "global model" built upon query-document relevance. Similarly, researchers could also model reference-dependent states with respect to the anchoring bias by investigating the anchoring effects of initially encountered documents, subtopics, and associated opinions from content generators and other users. In addition, based on the studies on user expectations in interactions with search and management information systems (e.g., Lankton & McKnight, 2012; Liu & Shah, 2019; Venkatesh & Goyal, 2010), researchers could estimate users' general multifaceted expectations regarding rewards and costs or efforts in search interactions and predict the *expectation (dis)confirmation* state at different moments of real-time search sessions. Behavioral and textual signals that indicate a negative expectation disconfirmation (i.e., search efficiency or SERP quality lower than pre-search expectations) may serve as useful features for predicting the changes of subsequent search tactics and users' in situ thresholds and criteria for usefulness judgment and search satisfaction.

On the system side, one of the central topics that connect multiple sub-areas of IR research is *learning to rank* (LTR). L2R refers to the research that applies machine learning (ML) techniques in training ranking models based on annotated relevance labels and implicit feedback (e.g., clicks) from users' search logs (Li, 2011). The goal of LTR research is to train a learning function that produces a ranking score $\pi_{\mu}(d)$ based on the feature vector of each document d so that the ranking result based on $\pi_{\mu}(d)$ would be the same as the result of ranking by the *intrinsic relevance* of documents. According to Ai et al. (2021), this ranking optimization goal can be formally written as:

$$\mu^* = arg_\mu \, min \, \mathcal{L}(\mu) = arg_\mu \, min \int_q^Q l(\pi_\mu, \boldsymbol{r}_q) \, dP(q) \tag{7.1}$$

where $\boldsymbol{r}_q$ refers to the perfect ranking generated based on the ground-truth intrinsic relevance of documents and Q refers to the set of all queries or topics q involved in ranking. $l(\pi_\mu, \boldsymbol{r}_q)$ represents the loss of local ranking computed based upon the ranked list of retrieved documents and their relevance levels. One of the key challenges is LTR experiments to improve the *unbiasedness* in ranking, especially in situations where the implicit feedback (in particular, clicking) is noisy and affected by different types of biases. To achieve unbiased learning to rank (ULTR), many IR researchers have designed and tested multiple click models and formal assumptions, based on features of query-document pairs, rank position information, and sequences of user actions, in order to facilitate the extraction of reliable relevance signals from noisy and biased click logs (e.g., Ai et al., 2018; Craswell et al., 2008; Joachims, 2002). Apart from the research efforts on reducing rank position bias, some recent studies focus on the behavioral side of LTR and have adopted inverse propensity weighting (IPW) (cf. Joachims et al., 2017) in addressing trust bias and recency effects (e.g., Agarwal et al., 2019; Chen et al., 2019; Vardasbi et al., 2021).

Following the line of research introduced above, researchers may be able to make further progress in ULTR research by taking a broader range of human biases into consideration. As discussed in previous chapters, apart from the widely examined rank position bias, knowledge of human biases and heuristics employed in search can enhance our understanding of the motivations behind clicking behavior. For instance, for documents being ranked at similar positions, users' examinations and clicks may be biased toward the documents that confirm their pre-search beliefs or are consistent with their initially encountered information in one or multiple aspects (e.g., subtopic, opinion, sentiment), due to the effects of confirmation bias and anchoring. Also, in addition to the document features that most ranking algorithms focus on, users' probability of clicking on certain documents may be affected by adjacent documents that may be perceived as a decoy option. In click modeling, identifying potential decoy search results along varying dimensions (e.g., relevance and presentation of search result surrogate, perceived credibility of documents) may be included as part of the modeling of local contextual factors. From a broader reference-dependence and CBDT perspective (e.g., Gilboa & Schmeidler, 1995; Tversky & Kahneman, 1991), the probability of clicking on a document may also be biased due to a recent experience of examining and reading similar documents under similar motivating tasks. This similarity could be represented with a vector containing multiple elements, such as the specific contents and involved subtopics, type of information sources, general opinion and sentiment, as well as other salient textual and graphical features. A past bad experience (e.g., a long reading session without much useful information obtained) accessible in the user's current short-term memory may result in a low estimated utility or predicted loss associated with the current document, which, in turn, leads to a fairly low probability of clicking (i.e., loss aversion bias). When evaluating search results under uncertainty (e.g., exploring an unfamiliar domain), users may tend to avoid potential risks and losses and click the search results that seem to be familiar and involve low risk of search failure to them (i.e., risk aversion bias). Actively debiasing noisy clicks based on the knowledge of human biases, heuristics, and search expectations could be useful for further improving the unbiasedness, generalizability, and reliability of ULTR algorithms.

In addition to predicting users' clicks, modeling search sessions, and improving LTR algorithms, researchers should also explore possible recommendation techniques and methods that can reactively or even proactively address the potential negative effects of bounded rationality. In the context of IR, query auto-completion and suggestion are two common and widely employed forms of search support. To stimulate critical thinking and careful decision-making, interactive IR researchers employed query recommendations to present search terms (e.g., survey, comparison, evidence) that could encourage critical thinking in search evaluation and query reformulation (Yamamoto & Yamamoto, 2018). Based on the results from crowdsourcing-based experiments, researchers found that the *query priming* with critical-thinking terms motivated users to issue more queries and revisited SERPs more frequently. Also, under the query priming condition, users were exposed to more Web pages that encourage evidence-based decision-making. From the bounded rationality perspective, the query priming techniques designed in Yamamoto and Yamamoto (2018) presented a positive anchoring point for users and motivated them to examine and click more search results that are aligned with the critical thinking terms advocated through recommended search terms. Similarly, Ong et al. (2017) manipulated the initial *information scent levels* for participants by changing the number and distribution of relevant documents on the first result page in a session. The results indicate that when improving the number and positioning of relevant results on the first result page, the participant's ability to locate relevant results were also improved in both desktop-based and mobile search environments. Therefore, in addition to passively react to biased implicit feedback (e.g., clicks) and search decisions (e.g., early abandonment of query), search systems could proactively adjust the initial query recommendations and the presentations of SERP items in order to mitigate possible negative effects of mental shortcuts and help users find the desired information items. Beside query priming and relevant documents, researchers can also explore other dimensions of SERP (Speicher et al., 2015), such as informativeness, information density, possible confusions and distractions, as well as the potential scrolling and interaction efforts, in order to estimate users' perceived costs in a more accurate manner (instead of assuming fixed equal costs of each action across all queries and topics) and address biased search decisions with more SERPs of higher levels of usability and accessibility.

Built upon the above discussions on different aspects of IR and bounded rationality, a broader vision we aim to pursue in future research is developing *bias-aware intelligent task support* (BITS) systems. The ultimate goal of this BITS system is to predict and proactively address the negative effects of *both* algorithmic biases and human biases in real-time information interactions and offer scalable, reliable, and unbiased informational support for users engaging in complex search and motivating tasks of varying types. As introduced and explained throughout this book, achieving the vision of BITS would require the completions of a series of interrelated research tasks, including:

- Reflecting on and redefining the basic unit of user and search session modeling and moving from absolute-outcome-based variables and measures to gain- and loss-based units and measures. A hidden challenge related to this is identifying potential reference points and estimating their weights in real-time search decision-making.
- Leveraging the knowledge of bounded rationality in extending simplified assumptions about users and their rules of decision-making and enhancing formal user models applied in predicting single search actions (e.g., examination of search result surrogates, clicking, and query reformulation), characterizing and simulating whole-session interaction processes, and building reusable evaluation metrics.
- Based on the predicted user behaviors and judgments within the limits of bounded rationality, adaptively adjusting the available tools and components for improving search support, such as query auto-completion and suggestion, learning to rank algorithms, and other usability dimensions of SERPs and overall search interface.
- Building new bias-aware evaluation framework that comprehensively assesses the performance of BITS system, at both single-iteration and whole-session levels, in terms of satisfying users' information needs and mitigating the negative impacts of both algorithmic biases and cognitive biases on users' search interaction, judgment of information items, as well as post-search information-intensive decision-making.

Based on the discussions above, Fig. 7.2 illustrates the basic structure and main components of the envisioned BITS system, which in real-time search sessions is evaluated in terms of both enhancing search effectiveness and addressing the effects of interrelated biases from both human and algorithm sides. In the third part of our research agenda, we will focus on the problem of *bias-aware evaluation* and discuss the ways in which we can leverage the knowledge of bounded rationality in better assessing the support that an intelligent search system offers for users engaging in complex tasks.

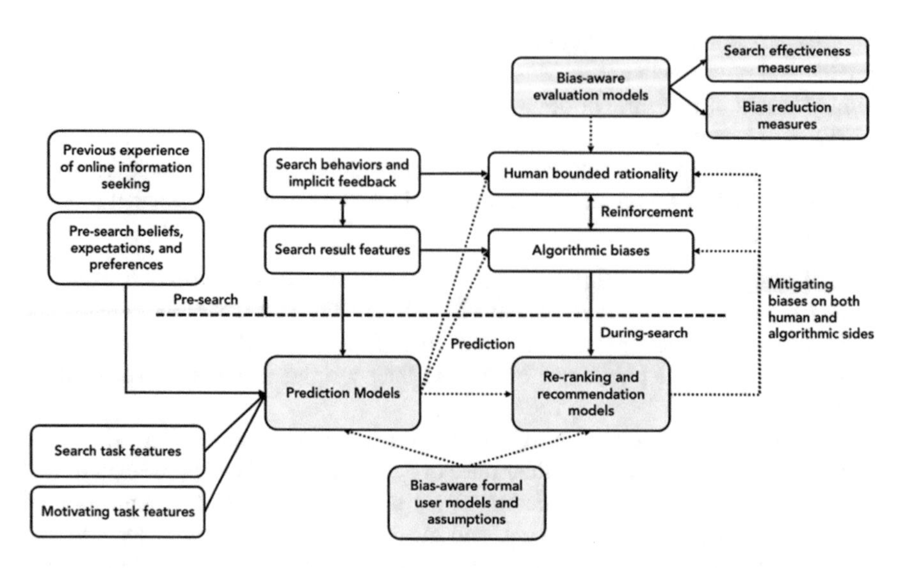

Fig. 7.2 The structure of BITS system. The main activities of the BITS system are denoted by dotted lines

7.4 Bias in Multiple Forms and Modalities of Search Interactions

As people increasingly rely on intelligent information systems for accessing information and making decisions, human biases could occur and operate in various modalities of information search interactions. Recent progress in automatic speech recognition (ASR), deep learning (DL), and natural language processing (NLP) opens new opportunities for research, applications, and technological innovations in *Conversational Information Seeking* (CIS) (Trippas et al., 2018; Yan et al., 2022). Instead of typing queries and studying logical operators in advanced search, users are enabled to simply speak natural language queries and receive visual or verbal respond from IR systems. Furthermore, systems can also help users refine their queries and better express their intentions by asking system-initiated clarifying questions (Sekulić et al., 2021; Zhang et al., 2018). Inspired by multimodal human conversations and interactions, IR researchers have developed models and techniques to go beyond standard SERP presentations, combine multiple channels of information interactions (e.g., spoken/voice-based, text-based, visual information), and facilitate the design, implementation, and evaluation of multimodal CIS (Deldjoo et al., 2021). Under the impact of human biases and *contextual triggers* (e.g., initially encountered information, existing beliefs and expectations, perceived gains and losses), users may change their inputs on multiple channels, such as queries and natural questions, conversational cues and intonations, eye movements, gestures, and facial expressions. Information communicated through these ways can be perceived as indicators of user preferences by search and recommendation systems and reinforce existing cognitive and algorithmic biases. Differing from traditional desktop searches, conversational search and retrieval systems are often used in in situ factual searches (e.g., looking for nearby convenience store and gas station), little-effort judgments, and intuitive quick decision-making (e.g., selecting an item to purchase among multiple similar items in online shopping sites, picking a restaurant for a quick meal, making subscription decisions for online services). Under these circumstances, people's behaviors are more likely to be affected by cognitive biases, mental shortcuts, as well as the rapid operation of System 1 (Kahneman, 2003). As many HCI researchers seek to build human-like features into conversational systems and treat them as social agents (Thomas et al., 2021), the cognitive and behavioral effect of human biases may occur more naturally and unconsciously in information interactions.

Given the challenges and opportunities associated with human biases in CIS, researchers need to first identify new signals and CIS-specific features that allow them to better identify and estimate the *risks* of human biases generating negative effects at the moment of interactions. The risk estimation will require the knowledge of both user characteristics (e.g., existing beliefs and expectations, prior experiences with search and CIS) and potential contextual triggers of biases (e.g., results that confirm certain misleading beliefs, biased presentation of varying perspectives). Furthermore, researchers need to develop bias-aware user models that predict users' judgments and decisions based on the signals from ongoing interactions and estimated risks of certain biases. The prediction results could be leveraged as part of the basis for developing and implementing adaptive and even proactive recommendations and interventions for effective debiasing. This process could be achieved through modifying the internal result ranking algorithms based on the predicted risks of biases, changing system-initiated questions to reminders of potential biases in mixed initiative CIS systems, and adaptively adjusting online evaluation metrics according to users' search intentions and the nature of predicted biases. Researchers can evaluate the performance of systems and the associated intervention techniques based on the extent to which they can predict and mitigate the risks of biased behaviors and judgments in search interactions.

In addition to CIS, the behavioral impact of user biases could also happen and need to be addressed in other modalities of search interactions, such as mobile search (Lagun et al., 2014; Mao et al., 2018), augmented-reality-based search (Büschel et al., 2018), and tangible IR (Leon et al., 2019; Jansen et al., 2010). Under varying modalities of interactions, researchers will need to identify different sets of signals, rebuild models to predict potential biases, and identify contextual triggers in system outputs and the problems that motivate users to interact with systems. With new signals collected, researchers can infer the perceived informational gains and search costs at different stages and under varying local intentions and utilize them as features in predicting users' search decisions (e.g., query/question reformulation or engaging with current responses, accepting or skipping system recommendations) and in situ experiences (e.g., search satisfaction, perceived cognitive load, overall level of engagement). Knowledge learned about human biases in multimodal information searching will allow researchers to better capture and address the impact of biases in real time.

7.5 Bias-Aware Evaluation and FATE in IR

To develop trustable AI-assisted intelligent systems (which include BITS and other types and modalities of intelligent search systems), researchers and system designers need to recognize the impacts of both algorithmic and human biases in AI and understand how and where they contribute to harms (Schwartz et al., 2022). In particular, users who are vulnerable to the negative effects of certain biases (e.g., due to prior beliefs, lack of domain knowledge and algorithmic awareness) should be protected from the recommendations and system interventions that leverage the knowledge about their biases for profits and engagements. Apart from formally modeling users and improving retrieval algorithms, the insights about bounded rationality discussed in previous chapters and sections can also be applied in enhancing multiple aspects of user-oriented IR evaluation. For example, in query-level or single-SERP evaluation, representing and estimating *anchoring effect* would be useful for improving the correlation between (anchoring-aware) evaluation metrics and users' levels of search satisfaction (Chen et al., 2022). Beyond Chen et al. (2022)'s work, in future evaluation experiments, researchers should go beyond relevance labels and explore other dimensions of initially encountered documents that may affect users' perceived utility. Based upon the identified anchoring point and other potential references, researchers can develop reference-aware evaluation metrics that assess the *perceived* performance of search systems based on the estimated search gains and losses.

In addition, at task level, researchers need to study pre-search existing beliefs, expectations, as well as their origins, such as past search experience under similar tasks, existing opinions and stereotypes, as well as other people's actions and opinions. Then, during search sessions, researchers can build and test expectation-aware evaluation metrics that consider both pre-search general expectations and in situ dynamic expectations and examine the impacts of expectation disconfirmation on users' search strategies and effectiveness, post-search decision-making, as well as the overall levels of satisfaction and engagement. Similar to query-level evaluation, the exploration of expectation disconfirmation states will also require researchers to investigate multiple facets of search tasks and system outputs (Liu & Shah, 2019), as different facets and dimensions may have significantly different impacts on users' decisions under uncertainty. Besides, in whole-session retrospective evaluation, researchers need to examine a series of key moments, such as initial experience, peak values, and last or most recent experience (Kahneman, 2003; Liu & Han, 2020; Liu et al., 2019) and examine their respective effects on users' remembered utility obtained from the session. Moving forward from the discrete reference points identified in studies on peak-end rule and recency effects, future research could design and implement a more generalizable and flexible *continuous weight distribution* that considers the varying impacts of all moments of search interactions. From this perspective, in evaluation analysis, different types of search tasks could be linked to different kinds of reference-aware weight distributions that partially characterize the associated search sessions.

More broadly, the behavioral economics research agenda presented in this chapter also motivates us to reflect on the problem of *fairness*, *accountability*, *transparency*, and *ethics* (FATE) in the context of IR evaluation. Although contemporary IR systems provide rapid ubiquitous access to information, they also encode and even amplify the biases, inequalities, and historical gaps through information presentation and recommendation. Addressing the limitations and inherited bias in algorithms would require a deep understanding of human bias as well. Specifically, for instance, when seeking to improve algorithmic fairness and avoid discrimination against different populations and communities, search systems need to take into consideration the specific thinking style and hidden cognitive biases associated with different task types, work environments, and cultural backgrounds (e.g., Ma-Kellams, 2020). Without proper regulation and intervention, the existing beliefs and preferences that people have may be leveraged and exploited by AI-assisted systems in promoting misinformation, obtaining unfair profits, and encouraging biased decision-making. Similarly, search systems need to be transparent to users in terms of why and how the search results are generated and make the search results scrutable to users. Systems should also inform users of the potential risks and biases associated with personalized search results, such as confirmation bias, framing effects and echo chamber effects, and offer proactive support to help users avoid or mitigate the negative effects of biases triggered by retrieved results, search recommendations, and users' own previous experiences. The ultimate goal is that users with different backgrounds, existing beliefs, and knowledge base should have equal chance of achieving desired or optimal outcomes, regardless of their individual vulnerability to varying cognitive and perceptual biases in search interactions.

Inspired by equal-odds fairness measures in machine learning (ML) research (cf. Hardt et al., 2016), we write the human-side debiasing or fairness goal as follows:

$$P(Y=Y^*|\,M=0,\ A=a)=P((Y=Y^*|\,M=1,\ \ A=a) \tag{7.2}$$

where Y^* refers to the desired or accessible optimal outcome of an individual or group, given the nature of search intentions and motivating task. A represents the set of general contextual attributes that are not directly related to human biases. M indicates if the individual is part of the protected group that is more vulnerable to certain user biases. Note that as it is introduced in previous chapters, different cognitive and perceptual biases may involve different contextual triggers and behavioral impacts. Thus, the associated risks may need to be assessed separately with individual functions. In contrast to algorithmic bias research in AI and ML, users' membership in high risk of human bias category (i.e., protected group) is less likely to be predefined and may need to be inferred from user traits and contextual triggers identified in real-time information seeking and search episodes.

In addition, IR and recommender systems need to be hold accountable when they are used in making automatic critical decisions about different aspects of human-information interaction and everyday life in general, such as approving home loans, generating clinical recommendations based on health records, making hiring decisions, and retrieving a family doctor. The accountability assessment on IR algorithms should include the real-time evaluation of the potential risks of triggering and exploiting factors associated with bounded rationality in making obscure and harmful decisions. This assessment should also cover the *explanations* that search systems provide for justifying recommendations. Systems need to provide explanations that are consistent with how the algorithms *actually* generate real-time recommendations and what features and user information were utilized in the process, rather than simply offering a plausible story that increases the user's acceptance and trust of recommendations by confirming their existing beliefs, biases, and expectations regarding the recommendation mechanism.

Compared to the observable impacts of problematic algorithms on discrimination and bias, the interaction between biased algorithms and boundedly rational users and the associated consequences are usually difficult to characterize, predict, and regulate. Extending the mainstream definition of algorithmic FATE in IR (e.g., Culpepper et al., 2018), we argue that the next-generation AI-assisted search systems should be designed and encouraged to not only monitor and address algorithmic biases (e.g., enhancing fair exposure of documents from different content generators and with different perspectives and political views) but also be transparent about and proactively address the existing problems and potential risks associated with human biases and heuristics in search interaction and judgments of information items. Under the effect of certain cognitive biases and mental shortcuts, users may make local satisficing decisions that may contradict with their goals and tasks behind whole-session interactions. With respect to evaluation, systems need to be assessed in terms of both enhancing algorithmic fairness and transparency and predicting and addressing the potential undesired outcomes caused by human biases and heuristics. Human bias mitigation could be carried out through re-adjusting query recommendations and learning to rank algorithms, or actively reminding users of the possible biases they might have, such as focusing on a narrowed scope of item types or only clicking documents that represent the one single perspective on a controversial topic. Achieving this extended version of FATE in IR will require the integration of insights from data-driven IR experiments, bounded rational research, as well as user interaction design. In practical applications and regulations, the extended FATE approach will go way beyond intelligent search systems and retrieval algorithms themselves and involve a *collective social practice* consisting of actors, forums and platforms, shared beliefs and norms, performativity, as well as regulations and sanctions in broad sociotechnical systems (Johnson, 2021; König, 2020).

7.6 Summary

Chapter 7 brings together the insights from bounded rationality research from multiple disciplines and formal modeling and evaluation in IR and discusses the open problems and new directions under our behavioral economics research agenda. Specifically, based on the research gaps identified in Chap. 6, we take a step forward and discuss more specific problems that need to be addressed in bias-aware IR under three broad sub-areas: Characterizing bounded rationality in IR, developing bias-aware interactive search systems, and bias-aware evaluation. We introduce different ways in which researchers could incorporate the knowledge of bounded rationality into formal user models and different modalities of search systems (especially conversational information seeking and search). Also, we connect our research on bias-aware IR to a broader definition of FATE and present our vision of BITS system, which considers and addresses the negative effects of both algorithmic biases and human biases in human-information interaction and critical decision-making under uncertainty. We hope that the ideas and questions presented in this chapter could encourage future students and researchers to further explore the specific problems and methodological challenges in bias-aware user modeling, system design, and FATE-based system evaluation and include boundedly rational users in the studies of IR and human-AI interaction in general.

References

Agarwal, A., Wang, X., Li, C., Bendersky, M., & Najork, M. (2019). Addressing trust bias for unbiased learning-to-rank. In *The world wide web conference* (pp. 4–14). ACM. https://doi.org/10.1145/3308558.3313697

Ai, Q., Bi, K., Luo, C., Guo, J., & Croft, W. B. (2018). Unbiased learning to rank with unbiased propensity estimation. In *The 41st international ACM SIGIR conference on research & development in information retrieval* (pp. 385–394). ACM. https://doi.org/10.1145/3209978.3209986

Ai, Q., Yang, T., Wang, H., & Mao, J. (2021). Unbiased learning to rank: Online or offline? *ACM Transactions on Information Systems (TOIS), 39*(2), 1–29. https://doi.org/10.1145/3439861

Azzopardi, L. (2021). Cognitive biases in search: A review and reflection of cognitive biases in information retrieval. In *Proceedings of the 2021 ACM SIGIR conference on human information interaction and retrieval* (pp. 27–37). ACM. https://doi.org/10.1145/3406522.3446023

Büschel, W., Mitschick, A., & Dachselt, R. (2018). Here and now: Reality-based information retrieval: Perspective paper. In *Proceedings of the 2018 ACM SIGIR conference on human information interaction & retrieval* (pp. 171–180). https://doi.org/10.1145/3176349.3176384

Chen, R. C., Ai, Q., Jayasinghe, G., & Croft, W. B. (2019). Correcting for recency bias in job recommendation. In *Proceedings of the 28th ACM international conference on information and knowledge management* (pp. 2185–2188). ACM. https://doi.org/10.1145/3357384.3358131

Chen, N., Zhang, F., & Sakai, T. (2022). Constructing better evaluation metrics by incorporating the anchoring effect into the user model. In *Proceedings of the 45th international ACM SIGIR conference on research and development in information retrieval* (pp. 2709–2714). ACM. https://doi.org/10.1145/3477495.3531953

Craswell, N., Zoeter, O., Taylor, M., & Ramsey, B. (2008). An experimental comparison of click position-bias models. In *Proceedings of the 2008 international conference on web search and data mining* (pp. 87–94). ACM. https://doi.org/10.1145/1341531.1341545

Culpepper, J. S., Diaz, F., & Smucker, M. D. (2018). Research frontiers in information retrieval: Report from the third strategic workshop on information retrieval in Lorne (SWIRL 2018). In *ACM SIGIR forum* (Vol. 52, pp. 34–90). ACM. https://doi.org/10.1145/3274784.3274788

Deldjoo, Y., Trippas, J. R., & Zamani, H. (2021). Towards multi-modal conversational information seeking. In *Proceedings of the 44th international ACM SIGIR conference on research and development in information retrieval* (pp. 1577–1587). ACM. https://doi.org/10.1145/3404835.3462806

Dungs, S., & Fuhr, N. (2017). Advanced hidden Markov models for recognizing search phases. In *Proceedings of the ACM SIGIR international conference on theory of information retrieval* (pp. 257–260). ACM. https://doi.org/10.1145/3121050.3121090

Eickhoff, C. (2018). Cognitive biases in crowdsourcing. In *Proceedings of the eleventh ACM international conference on web search and data mining* (pp. 162–170). ACM. https://doi.org/10.1145/3159652.3159654

Ge, Y., Zhao, S., Zhou, H., Pei, C., Sun, F., Ou, W., & Zhang, Y. (2020). Understanding echo chambers in e-commerce recommender systems. In *Proceedings of the 43rd international ACM SIGIR conference on research and development in information retrieval* (pp. 2261–2270). https://doi.org/10.1145/3397271.3401431

Gershman, S. J., Horvitz, E. J., & Tenenbaum, J. B. (2015). Computational rationality: A converging paradigm for intelligence in brains, minds, and machines. *Science, 349*(6245), 273–278. https://doi.org/10.1126/science.aac6076

Gilboa, I., & Schmeidler, D. (1995). Case-based decision theory. *The Quarterly Journal of Economics, 110*(3), 605–639. https://doi.org/10.2307/2946694

Hardt, M., Price, E., & Srebro, N. (2016). Equality of opportunity in supervised learning. *Advances in Neural Information Processing Systems, 29*.

Hendahewa, C., & Shah, C. (2013). Segmental analysis and evaluation of user focused search process. In *Proceedings of the 2013 12th international conference on machine learning and applications* (Vol. 1, pp. 291–294). IEEE. https://doi.org/10.1109/ICMLA.2013.59

Jansen, M., Bos, W., Van Der Vet, P., Huibers, T., & Hiemstra, D. (2010). TeddIR: Tangible information retrieval for children. In *Proceedings of the 9th international conference on interaction design and children* (pp. 282–285). https://doi.org/10.1145/1810543.1810592

Joachims, T. (2002). Optimizing search engines using clickthrough data. In *Proceedings of the eighth ACM SIGKDD international conference on knowledge discovery and data mining* (pp. 133–142). ACM. https://doi.org/10.1145/775047.775067

Joachims, T., Swaminathan, A., & Schnabel, T. (2017). Unbiased learning-to-rank with biased feedback. In *Proceedings of the tenth ACM international conference on web search and data mining* (pp. 781–789). ACM. https://doi.org/10.1145/3018661.3018699

Johnson, D. G. (2021). Algorithmic accountability in the making. *Social Philosophy and Policy, 38*(2), 111–127. https://doi.org/10.1017/S0265052522000073

Jones, E. E., Rock, L., Shaver, K. G., Goethals, G. R., & Ward, L. M. (1968). Pattern of performance and ability attribution: An unexpected primacy effect. *Journal of Personality and Social Psychology, 10*(4), 317–340. https://doi.org/10.1037/h0026818

Kahneman, D. (2003). Maps of bounded rationality: Psychology for behavioral economics. *American Economic Review, 93*(5), 1449–1475. https://doi.org/10.1257/000282803322655392

Kahneman, D. (2011). *Thinking, fast and slow*. Farrar, Straus and Giroux.

König, P. D. (2020). Dissecting the algorithmic leviathan: On the socio-political anatomy of algorithmic governance. *Philosophy & Technology, 33*(3), 467–485. https://doi.org/10.1007/s13347-019-00363-w

Lagun, D., Hsieh, C. H., Webster, D., & Navalpakkam, V. (2014). Towards better measurement of attention and satisfaction in mobile search. In *Proceedings of the 37th international ACM SIGIR conference on research & development in information retrieval* (pp. 113–122). ACM. https://doi.org/10.1145/2600428.2609631

Lankton, N. K., & McKnight, H. D. (2012). Examining two expectation disconfirmation theory models: Assimilation and asymmetry effects. *Journal of the Association for Information Systems, 13*(2), 88–115. https://doi.org/10.17705/1jais.00285

Law, E., Yin, M., Goh, J., Chen, K., Terry, M. A., & Gajos, K. Z. (2016). Curiosity killed the cat, but makes crowdwork better. In *Proceedings of the 2016 ACM SIGCHI conference on human factors in computing systems* (pp. 4098–4110). ACM. https://doi.org/10.1145/2858036.2858144

Leon, K., Walker, W., Lim, Y., Penman, S., Colombo, S., & Casalegno, F. (2019). Tangible map: Designing and assessing spatial information retrieval through a tactile interface. In *International conference on human-computer interaction* (pp. 329–340). Springer. https://doi.org/10.1007/978-3-030-22636-7_24

Li, H. (2011). A short introduction to learning to rank. *IEICE Transactions on Information and Systems, 94*(10), 1854–1862. https://doi.org/10.1587/transinf.E94.D.1854

Li, Y., & Belkin, N. J. (2008). A faceted approach to conceptualizing tasks in information seeking. *Information Processing & Management, 44*(6), 1822–1837. https://doi.org/10.1016/j.ipm.2008.07.005

Lin, J., Liu, W., Dai, X., Zhang, W., Li, S., Tang, R., He, X., Hao, J., & Yu, Y. (2021). A graph-enhanced click model for web search. In *Proceedings of the 44th international ACM SIGIR conference on research and development in information retrieval* (pp. 1259–1268). ACM. https://doi.org/10.1145/3404835.3462895

Liu, J. (2021). Deconstructing search tasks in interactive information retrieval: A systematic review of task dimensions and predictors. *Information Processing & Management, 58*(3), 102522.

Liu, J. (2022). Toward Cranfield-inspired reusability assessment in interactive information retrieval evaluation. *Information Processing & Management, 59*(5), 103007. https://doi.org/10.1016/j.ipm.2022.103007

Liu, J., & Han, F. (2020). Investigating reference dependence effects on user search interaction and satisfaction: A behavioral economics perspective. In *Proceedings of the 43rd international ACM SIGIR conference on research and development in information retrieval* (pp. 1141–1150). ACM. https://doi.org/10.1145/3397271.3401085

Liu, J., & Shah, C. (2019). Investigating the impacts of expectation disconfirmation on web search. In *Proceedings of the 2019 ACM SIGIR conference on human information interaction and retrieval* (pp. 319–323). ACM. https://doi.org/10.1145/3295750.3298959

Liu, J., & Shah, C. (2022). Leveraging user interaction signals and task state information in adaptively optimizing usefulness-oriented search sessions. In *Proceedings of the 22nd ACM/IEEE joint conference on digital libraries* (pp. 1–11). ACM. https://doi.org/10.1145/3529372.3530926

Liu, J., & Yu, R. (2021). State-aware meta-evaluation of evaluation metrics in interactive information retrieval. In *Proceedings of the 30th ACM international conference on information & knowledge management* (pp. 3258–3262). ACM. https://doi.org/10.1145/3459637.3482190

Liu, M., Mao, J., Liu, Y., Zhang, M., & Ma, S. (2019). Investigating cognitive effects in session-level search user satisfaction. In *Proceedings of the 25th ACM SIGKDD international conference on knowledge discovery & data mining* (pp. 923–931). ACM. https://doi.org/10.1145/3292500.3330981

Liu, J., Sarkar, S., & Shah, C. (2020). Identifying and predicting the states of complex search tasks. In *Proceedings of the 2020 ACM SIGIR conference on human information interaction and retrieval* (pp. 193–202). ACM. https://doi.org/10.1145/3343413.3377976

Luo, J., Zhang, S., & Yang, H. (2014). Win-win search: Dual-agent stochastic game in session search. In *Proceedings of the 37th international ACM SIGIR conference on research & development in information retrieval* (pp. 587–596). ACM. https://doi.org/10.1145/2600428.2609629

Maddalena, E., Basaldella, M., De Nart, D., Degl'Innocenti, D., Mizzaro, S., & Demartini, G. (2016). Crowdsourcing relevance assessments: The unexpected benefits of limiting the time to judge. In *Proceedings of the AAAI conference on human computation and crowdsourcing* (Vol. 4, pp. 129–138) https://ojs.aaai.org/index.php/HCOMP/article/view/13284

Ma-Kellams, C. (2020). Cultural variation and similarities in cognitive thinking styles versus judgment biases: A review of environmental factors and evolutionary forces. *Review of General Psychology, 24*(3), 238–253. https://doi.org/10.1177/1089268019901270

Mao, J., Luo, C., Zhang, M., & Ma, S. (2018). Constructing click models for mobile search. In *The 41st international ACM SIGIR conference on research & development in information retrieval* (pp. 775–784). ACM. https://doi.org/10.1145/3209978.3210060

Nickerson, R. S. (1998). Confirmation bias: A ubiquitous phenomenon in many guises. *Review of General Psychology, 2*(2), 175–220. https://doi.org/10.1037/1089-2680.2.2.175

Ong, K., Järvelin, K., Sanderson, M., & Scholer, F. (2017). Using information scent to understand mobile and desktop web search behavior. In *Proceedings of the 40th international ACM SIGIR conference on research and development in information retrieval* (pp. 295–304). ACM. https://doi.org/10.1145/3077136.3080817

Posch, L., Bleier, A., Lechner, C. M., Danner, D., Flöck, F., & Strohmaier, M. (2019). Measuring motivations of crowdworkers: The multidimensional crowdworker motivation scale. *ACM Transactions on Social Computing, 2*(2), 1–34. https://doi.org/10.1145/3335081

Rogstadius, J., Kostakos, V., Kittur, A., Smus, B., Laredo, J., & Vukovic, M. (2011). An assessment of intrinsic and extrinsic motivation on task performance in crowdsourcing markets. In *Proceedings of the international AAAI conference on web and social media* (Vol. 5, pp. 321–328) https://ojs.aaai.org/index.php/ICWSM/article/view/14105

Roitero, K., Checco, A., Mizzaro, S., & Demartini, G. (2022). Preferences on a budget: Prioritizing document pairs when crowdsourcing relevance judgments. In *Proceedings of the ACM web conference* (pp. 319–327). ACM. https://doi.org/10.1145/3485447.3511960

Rosenthal, R. (1976). *Experimenter effects in behavioral research*. Irvington Publishers.

Scholer, F., Kelly, D., Wu, W. C., Lee, H. S., & Webber, W. (2013). The effect of threshold priming and need for cognition on relevance calibration and assessment. In *Proceedings of the 36th international ACM SIGIR conference on research and development in information retrieval* (pp. 623–632). ACM. https://doi.org/10.1145/2484028.2484090

Schwartz, R., Vassilev, A., Greene, K., Perine, L., Burt, A., & Hall, P. (2022). *Towards a standard for identifying and managing bias in artificial intelligence*. NIST special publication, 1270.

Sekulić, I., Aliannejadi, M., & Crestani, F. (2021). Towards facet-driven generation of clarifying questions for conversational search. In *Proceedings of the 2021 ACM SIGIR international conference on theory of information retrieval* (pp. 167–175). ACM. https://doi.org/10.1145/3471158.3472257

Shen, S., Hu, B., Chen, W., & Yang, Q. (2012). Personalized click model through collaborative filtering. In *Proceedings of the fifth ACM international conference on web search and data mining* (pp. 323–332). ACM. https://doi.org/10.1145/2124295.2124336

Simon, H. A. (1955). A behavioral model of rational choice. *The Quarterly Journal of Economics, 69*(1), 99–118. https://doi.org/10.2307/1884852

Speicher, M., Both, A., & Gaedke, M. (2015). SOS: Does your search engine results page (SERP) need help? In *Proceedings of the 33rd annual ACM conference on human factors in computing systems* (pp. 1005–1014). ACM. https://doi.org/10.1145/2702123.2702568

Thaler, R. H. (2016). Behavioral economics: Past, present, and future. *American Economic Review, 106*(7), 1577–1600. https://doi.org/10.1257/aer.106.7.1577

Thomas, P., Czerwinksi, M., McDuff, D., & Craswell, N. (2021). Theories of conversation for conversational IR. *ACM Transactions on Information Systems (TOIS), 39*(4), 1–23. https://doi.org/10.1145/3439869

Thomas, P., Kazai, G., White, R., & Craswell, N. (2022). The crowd is made of people: Observations from large-scale crowd labelling. In *Proceedings of the international ACM SIGIR conference on human information interaction and retrieval* (pp. 25–35). ACM. https://doi.org/10.1145/3498366.3505815

Trippas, J. R., Spina, D., Cavedon, L., Joho, H., & Sanderson, M. (2018). Informing the design of spoken conversational search: Perspective paper. In *Proceedings of the 2018 ACM SIGIR conference on human information interaction & retrieval* (pp. 32–41). ACM. https://doi.org/10.1145/3176349.3176387

Tversky, A., & Kahneman, D. (1991). Loss aversion in riskless choice: A reference-dependent model. *The Quarterly Journal of Economics, 106*(4), 1039–1061. https://doi.org/10.2307/2937956

Vardasbi, A., de Rijke, M., & Markov, I. (2021). Mixture-based correction for position and trust bias in counterfactual learning to rank. In *Proceedings of the 30th ACM international conference on information & knowledge management* (pp. 1869–1878). ACM. https://doi.org/10.1145/3459637.3482275

Venkatesh, V., & Goyal, S. (2010). Expectation disconfirmation and technology adoption: Polynomial modeling and response surface analysis. *MIS Quarterly, 34*(2), 281–303. https://doi.org/10.2307/20721428

Weber, R. A., & Camerer, C. F. (2006). "Behavioral experiments" in economics. *Experimental Economics, 9*(3), 187–192. https://doi.org/10.1007/s10683-006-9121-5

White, R. (2013). Beliefs and biases in web search. In *Proceedings of the 36th international ACM SIGIR conference on research and development in information retrieval* (pp. 3–12). ACM. https://doi.org/10.1145/2484028.2484053

Yamamoto, Y., & Yamamoto, T. (2018). Query priming for promoting critical thinking in web search. In *Proceedings of the 2018 international ACM SIGIR conference on human information interaction & retrieval* (pp. 12–21). ACM. https://doi.org/10.1145/3176349.3176377

Yan, R., Li, J., & Yu, Z. (2022). Deep learning for dialogue systems: Chit-chat and beyond. *Foundations and Trends in Information Retrieval, 15*(5), 417–589. https://doi.org/10.1561/1500000083

Zhai, C. (2016). Towards a game-theoretic framework for text data retrieval. *IEEE Data Engineering Bulletin, 39*(3), 51–62.

Zhang, Y., & Zhai, C. (2016). A sequential decision formulation of the interface card model for interactive IR. In *Proceedings of the 39th international ACM SIGIR conference on research and development in information retrieval* (pp. 85–94). ACM. https://doi.org/10.1145/2911451.2911543

Zhang, Y., Chen, X., Ai, Q., Yang, L., & Croft, W. B. (2018). Towards conversational search and recommendation: System ask, user respond. In *Proceedings of the 27th ACM international conference on information and knowledge management* (pp. 177–186). ACM. https://doi.org/10.1145/3269206.3271776

Chapter 8
Conclusion

Abstract Our book brings together the multidisciplinary insights, methods, and empirical findings related to bounded rationality and human biases in decision-making and presents a behavioral economics research agenda under which a series of specific research questions, new directions, and methodological challenges can be further investigated by students and researchers in future IR studies. In this final chapter, we summarize the contents of previous chapters and discuss the contributions, practical implications, and related new directions under our behavioral economics research approach to IR problems. We hope that this book can serve as a useful starting point for studying bias-aware IR and motivate students and researchers from diverse backgrounds to further explore and advance the science and technology on supporting boundedly rational people interacting with information.

Understanding how people behave and why they behave in such ways is a central topic to information seeking and retrieval research. The knowledge learned about users' search behavioral patterns, strategies of search result judgments, and evaluation of system performances is essential for not only predicting users' in situ search actions and feedback but also developing built-in formal user models for retrieval and ranking algorithms, search recommendation techniques, as well as scalable evaluation metrics. In contrast to the rational assumptions of existing formal models, people tend to be boundedly rational and are affected by a series of human biases and heuristics when making decisions under uncertainty (Kahneman, 2003; Simon, 1955). Behavioral economics researchers have explored and empirically tested a broad range of human biases and factors that contribute to bounded rationality in a variety of real-life and simulated simple decision-making scenarios (Kahneman, 2003; Thaler, 2016; Weber & Camerer, 2006). Although the operation of System 1 and the adoption of mental shortcuts enable individuals to simply the decision-making process and make quick judgments without processing a large amount of new information (Gigerenzer & Brighton, 2009), the decisions and associated outcomes tend to be affected by higher error rates and deviate from the optimal results predicted by rational models. Many of these systematic deviations have been ignored or abstracted out from formal user models and simulation-based experiments, which

J. Liu, *A Behavioral Economics Approach to Interactive Information Retrieval*, The Information Retrieval Series 48, https://doi.org/10.1007/978-3-031-23229-9_8

largely restricts the actual contributions from the advances in IR algorithms and systems to understanding and supporting real-world users engaging in information search interactions.

To address the above research gap, our book brings together the multidisciplinary insights, methods, and empirical findings related to bounded rationality and human biases in decision-making and presents a behavioral economics research agenda under which a series of specific research questions, new directions, and methodological challenges can be further investigated by students and researchers in future IR studies. Specifically, Chap. 1 offers an overview of the theoretical basis and involved disciplines related to the problem of bias-aware IR and clarifies the structure of this book. Chapter 2 thoroughly reviews the basic structures and recent advances in a series of mainstream formal user models applied in various sub-areas of IR (e.g., click modeling, simulation of search sessions, offline evaluation experiments) and highlights their contributions in modeling search behaviors and limitations with respect to accommodating biased human decisions. Based on this review on formal models, Chap. 3 briefly introduces the gaps between simulated rational agents or assumptions and empirically confirmed human biases that frequently appear in real-world decision-making activities.

To further enrich our discussions on the identified gaps and bring in the relevant insights from behavioral economics, Chap. 4 goes beyond rational agents and presents a comprehensive overview of behavioral experiments and findings on the human biases and heuristics emphasized in Chap. 3. Built upon the identified gaps and knowledge regarding both formal modeling and human bounded rationality, Chap. 5 revisits the rational assumptions underpinning user models and evaluation metrics and proposes reasonable approaches to revising and extending the rational oversimplified assumptions and offering the assumptions a more solid behavioral and psychological basis.

Built upon the knowledge synthesized in previous chapters, Chap. 6 moves forward by introducing the progress we as a research community have made on understanding human biases and bounded rationality in IR and related fields (e.g., Azzopardi, 2021; Liu & Han, 2020), including information seeking and recommendations (e.g., Agosto, 2002; Ge et al., 2020; Xu et al., 2020). Based on the identified research gaps and existing findings, Chap. 7 presents a full behavioral economics research agenda that addresses three different aspects of bias-aware IR, including characterizing bounded rationality, building search systems, and developing bias-aware search evaluation. In particular, we highlight the importance of going beyond traditional evaluation metrics focusing on relevance-based search effectiveness and discuss a new vision named BITS system, which can proactively address the negative impacts from both algorithmic biases and human biases and offer unbiased support for users engaging in complex tasks. With respect to developing reliable, ethical, and trustworthy IR and AI in general (cf. Schwartz et al., 2022), we also discuss how the studies on human bounded rationality could further extend current conceptualization and research on FATE in IR and redefine the assessment and regulation of AI-assisted interactive search systems and retrieval algorithms.

Compared to mature standardized IR evaluation experiments (e.g., TREC[1]) and recent fast-growing research on algorithmic bias and fairness,[2] the research on human bounded rationality and its applications in IR problems is still at a very early stage. However, with the increasing interests on human perceptions and cognitive biases in multiple fields of computing research (e.g., Barbosa & Chen, 2019; Dingler et al., 2020; Draws et al., 2021; Lee & Rich, 2021; Taniguchi et al., 2018; Saab et al., 2019), it is an appropriate timing to draw attention to and further investigate the intersection between bounded rationality research and IR experiments. Our book contributes to this line of research mainly by clarifying the related theoretical roots and technical basis, synthesizing the insights and empirical findings from multiple disciplines that may be useful for IR modeling and evaluation, and developing a bias-aware research approach with specific open problems and new directions. To address the identified research problems (see Chap. 7), future studies will need to make further progresses on four aspects:

1. Further studying the search behavioral patterns, cognitive activities, and decision-making models of boundedly rational users through user studies conducted in naturalistic settings
2. Designing, testing, and fine-tuning different forms of bias-aware formal user models and assessing their performances in predicting user behaviors (e.g., examination, clicking, query reformulation, and search stopping) and facilitating in situ adaptive ranking and recommendations
3. Developing and implementing experimental search systems of varying modalities (e.g., desktop search, mobile search, conversational search) that can detect potential human and algorithmic biases in real-time search sessions
4. Designing and meta-evaluating bias-aware search evaluation metrics that measure the actual contributions of search systems and retrieval algorithms to improving search effectiveness and addressing both human and algorithmic biases in decision-making activities.

In addition, to achieve these four goals, researchers also need to go beyond existing user study design and tools (e.g., Kelly, 2009; Liu & Shah, 2019) and overcome a series of new methodological obstacles, such as collecting users' in situ feedback on the role of biases in searching at different moments of sessions, designing realistic search tasks that could trigger the adoption of mental shortcuts in decision-making, and disambiguating the divergent effects that come from different cognitive biases.

Current methods for predicting and resolving the potential harmful impacts of algorithmic biases in IR mainly focus on computational components from ML pipelines (Mehrabi et al., 2021). However, human biases and societal factors are significant sources of AI biases in intelligent information systems of varying types

[1] Text Retrieval Conference (TREC): https://trec.nist.gov

[2] A new research community emerged and is growing rapidly around the ACM Conference on Fairness, Accountability, and Transparency (ACM FAccT): https://facctconference.org/

and are usually overlooked (Schwartz et al., 2022). Therefore, to address the challenges in developing unbiased, reliable search systems, IR researchers need to take all forms of biases into consideration. We hope that this book can serve as a useful starting point for the above research journey and motivate students and researchers from diverse backgrounds to further explore and advance the science and technology on supporting boundedly rational people interacting with information.

References

Agosto, D. E. (2002). Bounded rationality and satisficing in young people's web-based decision making. *Journal of the American Society for Information Science and Technology, 53*(1), 16–27. https://doi.org/10.1002/asi.10024

Azzopardi, L. (2021). Cognitive biases in search: A review and reflection of cognitive biases in information retrieval. In *Proceedings of the 2021 ACM SIGIR conference on human information interaction and retrieval* (pp. 27–37). ACM. https://doi.org/10.1145/3406522.3446023

Barbosa, N. M., & Chen, M. (2019). Rehumanized crowdsourcing: A labeling framework addressing bias and ethics in machine learning. In *Proceedings of the 2019 ACM SIGCHI conference on human factors in computing systems* (pp. 1–12). ACM. https://doi.org/10.1145/3290605.3300773

Dingler, T., Tag, B., Karapanos, E., Kise, K., & Dengel, A. (2020). Workshop on detection and design for cognitive biases in people and computing systems. In *Extended abstracts of the 2020 ACM SIGCHI conference on human factors in computing systems* (pp. 1–6). ACM. https://doi.org/10.1145/3334480.3375159

Draws, T., Rieger, A., Inel, O., Gadiraju, U., & Tintarev, N. (2021). A checklist to combat cognitive biases in crowdsourcing. In *Proceedings of the AAAI conference on human computation and crowdsourcing* (Vol. 9, pp. 48–59) https://ojs.aaai.org/index.php/HCOMP/article/view/18939

Ge, Y., Zhao, S., Zhou, H., Pei, C., Sun, F., Ou, W., & Zhang, Y. (2020). Understanding echo chambers in e-commerce recommender systems. In *Proceedings of the 43rd international ACM SIGIR conference on research and development in information retrieval* (pp. 2261–2270). https://doi.org/10.1145/3397271.3401431

Gigerenzer, G., & Brighton, H. (2009). Homo heuristicus: Why biased minds make better inferences. *Topics in Cognitive Science, 1*(1), 107–143. https://doi.org/10.1111/j.1756-8765.2008.01006.x

Kahneman, D. (2003). Maps of bounded rationality: Psychology for behavioral economics. *American Economic Review, 93*(5), 1449–1475. https://doi.org/10.1257/000282803322655392

Kelly, D. (2009). Methods for evaluating interactive information retrieval systems with users. *Foundations and Trends in Information Retrieval, 3*(1–2), 1–224. https://doi.org/10.1561/1500000012

Lee, M. K., & Rich, K. (2021). Who is included in human perceptions of AI? Trust and perceived fairness around healthcare AI and cultural mistrust. In *Proceedings of the 2021 ACM SIGCHI conference on human factors in computing systems* (pp. 1–14). ACM. https://doi.org/10.1145/3411764.3445570

Liu, J., & Han, F. (2020). Investigating reference dependence effects on user search interaction and satisfaction: A behavioral economics perspective. In *Proceedings of the 43rd international ACM SIGIR conference on research and development in information retrieval* (pp. 1141–1150). ACM. https://doi.org/10.1145/3397271.3401085

Liu, J., & Shah, C. (2019). Interactive IR user study design, evaluation, and reporting. *Synthesis Lectures on Information Concepts, Retrieval, and Services, 11*(2), i–93. https://doi.org/10.2200/S00923ED1V01Y201905ICR067

Mehrabi, N., Morstatter, F., Saxena, N., Lerman, K., & Galstyan, A. (2021). A survey on bias and fairness in machine learning. *ACM Computing Surveys (CSUR), 54*(6), 1–35. https://doi.org/10.1145/3457607

Saab, F., Elhajj, I. H., Kayssi, A., & Chehab, A. (2019). Modelling cognitive bias in crowdsourcing systems. *Cognitive Systems Research, 58*, 1–18. https://doi.org/10.1016/j.cogsys.2019.04.004

Schwartz, R., Vassilev, A., Greene, K., Perine, L., Burt, A., & Hall, P. (2022). *Towards a standard for identifying and managing bias in artificial intelligence*. NIST special publication, 1270.

Simon, H. A. (1955). A behavioral model of rational choice. *The Quarterly Journal of Economics, 69*(1), 99–118. https://doi.org/10.2307/1884852

Taniguchi, H., Sato, H., & Shirakawa, T. (2018). A machine learning model with human cognitive biases capable of learning from small and biased datasets. *Scientific Reports, 8*(1), 1–13. https://doi.org/10.1038/s41598-018-25679-z

Thaler, R. H. (2016). Behavioral economics: Past, present, and future. *American Economic Review, 106*(7), 1577–1600. https://doi.org/10.1257/aer.106.7.1577

Weber, R. A., & Camerer, C. F. (2006). "Behavioral experiments" in economics. *Experimental Economics, 9*(3), 187–192. https://doi.org/10.1007/s10683-006-9121-5

Xu, Z., Han, Y., Zhang, Y., & Ai, Q. (2020). E-commerce recommendation with weighted expected utility. In *Proceedings of the 29th ACM international conference on information & knowledge management* (pp. 1695–1704). ACM. https://doi.org/10.1145/3340531.3411993

Glossary

Algorithmic fairness Refers to the absence of any favoritism or prejudice toward an individual or group based on their inherent or acquired characteristics in the predictions and decisions of algorithms.

Ambiguity effect Refers to the phenomenon that people prefer options and outcomes with low uncertainty or ambiguity to the ones with high uncertainty, even if the latter has higher expected utility value.

Anchoring bias Refers to the phenomenon that people are more likely to accept the information that is consistent with the information they initially encountered.

Asymmetric dominance effect/decoy effect Refers to the phenomenon that people change their preferences between two choices when presented with a third option (i.e., the decoy) that is asymmetrically dominated.

Bandwagon effect Refers to the phenomenon that people tend to choose an option or make certain decisions simply because other people do so.

Behavioral economics The area of study that focuses on the impacts of psychological, cognitive, emotional, cultural, and social factors on the decisions of individuals and groups and how those decisions deviate from the predictions from classical economic theory.

Bias-aware intelligent task support (BITS) system Intelligent systems that can predict and proactively address the negative impacts of both system biases and human biases in real-time information interactions and offer scalable, unbiased informational support for people engaging in complex search tasks.

Bounded rationality A human decision-making process where people attempt to satisfice or find "good enough" options, rather than pursuing optimal outcomes predicted by formal models built upon perfectly rational assumptions.

Click models Mathematical models that characterize a typical user's decision-making activities as the user interacts with the search engine result page and infer users' judgments on document relevance from user actions (e.g., browsing, skipping, examination, and clicking).

J. Liu, *A Behavioral Economics Approach to Interactive Information Retrieval*, The Information Retrieval Series 48, https://doi.org/10.1007/978-3-031-23229-9

Confirmation bias Refers to the phenomenon that people tend to accept the information and option that are consistent with their prior beliefs and expectations.

Contextual triggers In this work, contextual triggers refer to the search contextual factors that trigger the cognitive, perceptual, and behavioral impacts of human biases and heuristics.

Evaluation metrics Refers to the measures employed to assess how well the retrieved search results satisfy the user's intent associated with the submitted query.

Expectation confirmation Refers to the phenomenon that an individual's decision to continue using or purchasing a system is affected significantly by the individual's expectation and previous experience with the system.

Framing effect Refers to the phenomenon that people's reactions or decisions on options depend on whether the options are framed as a loss or a gain.

Human-computer interaction (HCI) A multidisciplinary field of study focusing on the design, implementation, and evaluation of interaction interfaces between human and computing systems.

Human-side fairness In this work, human-side fairness refers to the goal or evaluation requirement that users with different backgrounds, experiences, and knowledge levels should have equal opportunities to obtain desired or optimal outcomes through search interactions and decision-making, regardless of their vulnerabilities to potential cognitive and perceptual biases.

Information behavior (IB) The study of the interactions between people and information objects in situations and tasks where the interactions occur.

Interactive information retrieval (IIR) The area of study focusing on users' interactions with search systems and their judgments and satisfaction on retrieved information.

Information retrieval (IR) The area of study concerned with searching for documents (relevant to an information need), information within documents, and related metadata, as well as searching structured storage, relational databases, multimedia resources, and the World Wide Web.

Information seeking (IS) The process or activity of purposively seeking for relevant and useful information through human and technological sources.

Learning to rank (LTR) The area of research that applies machine learning techniques in the construction and enhancement of ranking models and interactive IR systems.

Loss aversion Refers to the phenomenon that people prefer avoiding losses to acquiring equivalent amount of gains in decision-making activities.

Machine learning (ML) The area of study focusing on the design, use, and evaluation of algorithms and computer systems that are able to learn and draw inferences from patterns in data, without following explicit instructions or predefined rules.

Nudging Design features and components that encourage users to follow the designer's preferred paths and behavioral patterns in users' interactions with systems without explicitly intervene or disrupt the interaction process.

Peak-end rule Refers to the phenomenon that an individual's evaluation of a session or sequence of options, decisions, and/or interactions is often significantly affected by several key reference points within the session, such as the initial points, peak points, and end points.

Position bias Refers to the tendency of users to interact with top ranked information items with higher probability than with the items ranked at lower position of the result list.

Priming effect Refers to the phenomenon that an individual's exposure to a stimulus subconsciously affects their response to a subsequent stimulus.

Recommender system (RS) A subclass of information systems that suggests relevant items to users based on predicted ratings and preferences of users.

Reference dependence Refers to the phenomenon that people evaluate outcomes associated with each option based on the perceived gains and losses with respect to a reference point.

Relevance Refers to the extent to which a retrieved document or set of documents satisfies the information need of a user.

Salience bias Refers to the phenomenon that when reviewing different options or reviewing multiple information objects, people are more likely to interact with the items that are especially remarkable or prominent and pay less attention to those that lack prominence.

Satisfaction Fulfillment of a specified goal or desire.

Search intention A local or subgoal that a user seeks to accomplish under a query in a search session or a sequence of queries motivated by an overarching task.

Theory of satisficing Satisficing is a cognitive heuristic that entails exploring the available options until an acceptable or "good enough" option.

Users Refer to the people who are using a system.

User model A data structure that is used to characterize the features of individual users' profiles and predict their actions and experiences in interactions with systems.

Printed in the United States
by Baker & Taylor Publisher Services